□ HOW I □
ACCIDENTALLY
JOINED THE
VAST
RIGHT-WING
CONSPIRACY
(AND FOUND INNER PEACE)

· HOW I ·

ACCIDENTALLY

JOINED THE

VAST

RIGHT-WING

CONSPIRACY

(AND FOUND INNER PEACE)

Harry Stein

DELACORTE PRESS

Published by Delacorte Press
a division of Random House, Inc.
1540 Broadway
New York, New York 10036

Grateful acknowledgment is made to the *New York Post*
for permission to quote from an editorial by Eric Breindel.

Letter from Tennessee Williams to *Esquire*
quoted by permission of The University of the South,
Sewanee, Tennessee.

LIBRARY OF CONGRESS CATALOGING-IN-PUBLICATION DATA
Stein, Harry
How I accidentally joined the vast right-wing conspiracy (and found inner peace) /
Harry Stein.
p.   cm.
ISBN 0-385-33396-X
1. Stein, Harry, 1948–.   2. Stein, Harry, 1948—Political and social views.
3. Authors, American—20th century—Biography.   4. Journalists—United States—
Biography.   5. Right and left (Political science)   6. Conservatism—United States.
I. Title.
PS3569.T366 Z465 2000
818'.5409—dc21
[B]   00-026311
CIP

Designed by Kathryn Parise

Manufactured in the United States of America

Published simultaneously in Canada

June 2000

10   9   8   7   6   5   4
BVG

To those celebrities who, against all odds,
have selflessly kept their political views to themselves.

Acknowledgments

❏

This business of thanking people who've helped in the formulation or preparation of a book is always rough: invariably someone feels slighted by having been left out. The task this time is doubly difficult—because there'll be some who'll surely be offended by being included.

So let's start with a disclaimer: I am indebted to all of the following, but not enough that anyone but me can be blamed for anything on these pages.

Over the years I have been blessed with wonderful friends, many of whom (to one degree or another, some more intentionally than others) were helpful in this endeavor: Cary Schneider, Denis Boyles, Ken Rotner, Sybil Adelman, Martin Sage, Stefan Kanfer, Jenny Tripp, Gerry Garibaldi, Mark Smith, Lary Greiner, Kate Buford, Garry Apgar, Bernie Goldberg, Ron Mitchell, Chris Evans, David Black, John Leo, Peter Bloch, David List, Steve Hanks, Laura Berman, Roger Rosenblatt, Neal Gabler, Cy Stein, Jack Kammer, Peter Cross, Christina Sommers, Carl Waynberg, Kevin Dawkins, Myron Magnet, Barry Golson, Dana Motley.

Generally, the mention of agents and editorial people in these sections is pretty pro forma: they've done nothing more than their job, after all. But given the character of the book, this time my appreciation is deep and heartfelt. The truth is, all of the following disagree with a good deal of what I have to say; yet—in the spirit of *true* liberalism—they did their damndest to make sure it got to be said. Joy Harris is an agent of ferocious loyalty and tenacity, admirably supported by Leslie Daniels and Kassandra Duane. My original editor (and great friend) Leslie Schnur stuck her neck out to get this book going; Irwyn Applebaum made sure it survived her departure; and, his own strong reservations notwithstanding, Tom Spain, who took over the editing of the project, helped make the manuscript immeasurably stronger. Thanks, too, to his assistant, Andrea Nicolay. It is too early to tell, but I sincerely hope that in years to come I will also have many kind things to say about Vicky Flick, who has been charged with the unenviable task of generating publicity for a book attacking the mainstream media.

A quick word about a couple of individuals no longer with us. As noted further on, Eric Breindel was a journalist of enormous integrity, fighting the good fight at great personal and professional cost. Dr. Lawrence Spiegel, exonerated in a New Jersey courtroom after a false charge of child sexual abuse, spent the rest of his life trying to see to it that that nightmare was not visited on others. Both are a continuing inspiration.

Finally, there's my family, whose love and support are everything to me. In fact, my greatest apprehension just now is that there are those who might take out their feelings about me on my children. So a reminder to my kids' teachers, future employers, etc.: they don't necessarily agree with everything in here, either. If nothing else, we've succeeded in teaching them to think for themselves.

▫ **HOW I** ▫

ACCIDENTALLY

JOINED THE

V A S T

RIGHT-WING

CONSPIRACY

(AND FOUND INNER PEACE)

Introduction

◻

My first-ever appearance on a network television program did not go
nearly as smoothly as I'd hoped. It was on the *Today* show back in the
early eighties, and the subject was ethics, about which I'd recently
started writing a column in *Esquire* magazine.

Sitting on the set with me beforehand, waiting for the commercial before my spot to end, Jane Pauley put me at ease with her small talk. Then
the little red light came on and Pauley read a brief intro from the
TelePrompTer. She turned, smiled and hit me with her opening question.
"An *ethics* column in *Esquire*? Come onnnn . . ."

I was stunned speechless, then started making like Ralph Kramden
in extremis: Hmmmma, hmmmma, hmmmma.

"Well," I eventually managed halfheartedly, "you're probably
not proud of everything on NBC, either," a response that resulted in a furious call from *Esquire*'s editor-in-chief within minutes of my return
home.

For a while I was pretty annoyed with Pauley, but of course she was
right. What right did a publication largely devoted to promoting self-
indulgence as the key to the "good life" have mouthing off about moral
behavior? More to the point, what the hell right did *I* have to do the
mouthing? I'd never even read an ethics book. My degree is in journalism, which is not, but should be, called a B.S.

But no matter. TV being TV, six months after Pauley dissed my column, I was invited back on the same show, this time as a bona fide ethical expert. Vanessa Williams had been forced out as Miss America after appearing in *Penthouse* with her nose in places it didn't belong, and someone was needed to make ethical sense of it. Already starting to enjoy the adrenaline rush of having the whole world seem to stop while the camera sucks you in, I dutifully complied, and indeed, over the next few years I was identified on all sorts of shows, from *Donahue* and *Oprah* to *Nightline*—sometimes literally, in words under my name—as a moral authority.

I realized at the time this was insane. In a self-respecting world, the competence of anyone claiming expertise on *anything* would be prudently assessed; those who spoke to matters utterly central to human health and happiness would be greeted with particular skepticism.

But, hey, I wasn't complaining. I always left the studio feeling great about myself, the well-known hosts having been friendly, even deferential. And why not? We were all basically of the same tribe—status hunters and gatherers—and the same generation, which meant we shared a common set of important life experiences and guiding assumptions: not only on hot-button topics like abortion, but on things like what was funny (*SNL*—this was the eighties, remember), what was scary (the Moral Majority) and how to make the world a better place (larger doses of compassion).

But then something odd began to happen—mainly to the country, and incidentally to people like me. As feminism and multiculturalism more and more sought to remake society, attacking much that had served humanity well as narrow or even antique, we concluded we could no longer in good conscience remain on that side. There was both too little respect for the accumulated wisdom of the ages and too much playing havoc with truth and common sense. Indeed, many of us were soon startled to find ourselves tagged conservatives (and often worse) for holding firm to the values of old-fashioned *liberalism*: a bedrock commitment to fairness and individual liberty.

Along the way, I lost a couple of good friends. But I also made remarkable new ones, some of whom had arrived at the same destination by the same route, some who had been there all along. The startling thing, for one raised in America's most progressive precincts, was that this was a world less of yahoos than of humane and principled souls, fighting against the junk values that pervade the culture and, perhaps even more so, against the dumbed-down thinking that allows them to flourish.

Since being dumb—or at least oblivious to history, subtlety, sophistication and nuance—is often what it takes these days to pass as a correct thinker, lots of people who should know better now act that way as second nature. Just the other day, a writer friend was telling me how much trouble he'd had getting a project on Al Jolson off the ground because of "the blackface thing."

"But that doesn't mean Jolson was racist," added the guy quickly, immediately off into his standard Jolson defense, pointing out that Jolson was just a creature of his time and place and that you had to put it in *historical context.*

I mean, has it really come to this? Does my friend really think he has to go around talking this way to avoid being branded racist himself?

Indeed, from this distance, it strikes me as nearly lunatic that anyone would choose to live that way, constantly monitoring oneself for rogue thoughts. There's so much less stress following one's gut instead of the crowd. And in recent years—the Clintons, anyone?—there's been so remarkably less to have to justify.

It was during the impeachment saga, watching people I like and respect laboring to defend Clinton—in some cases, outraged he was even under assault—that I had a realization as terrifying as anything confronted by a whimpering Scrooge as the ghosts dragged him through the wreckage of his existence. That used to be me! If not for a few happy twists of fortune, it still could be me!

"Must it be, Spirit?! Am I doomed to forever look upon perjury and gross amorality and yet see nothing? Am I so besotted with my own goodness that indecency need only be on my side and it will be defended?"

Ah, but no—I wake up to find myself at peace.

Right is still right and wrong still wrong.

This book is the story of that journey.

How to Tell if You've Joined the Vast Right-Wing Conspiracy

- You hear someone talking about morality and you no longer instantly assume he must be a sexually repressed religious nut.

- You're actually relieved that your daughter plays with dolls and your son plays with guns.

- You sit all the way through *Dead Man Walking* and at the end *still* want the guy to be executed.

- You understand that the homeless guy who mumbles to himself and stinks of urine is not "disadvantaged" but a lunatic.

- Watching network news, you notice that the person opposing affirmative action is identified as a "conservative spokesman," while the one supporting it is just a "Harvard professor."

- Christmas season rolls around and it hits you there may be a religious connection.

- Black history month seems to last from February to July.

- At your kids' back-to-school night, you are shocked to discover the only dead white male on your tenth grader's reading list is Oscar Wilde.

- And by the end of the night you realize the only teacher who shares your values teaches phys. ed.

- Someone's going on about how fantastic San Francisco is, and it suddenly hits you that's the one place on earth you *never* want to live.

- Try as you might, you just can't get yourself to believe screwing around on your mate qualifies as an addiction.

It's all my wife's fault.

I realize this may sound petty and, even worse, smacks of that cardinal sin of the age, a refusal to take personal responsibility.

But—what can I tell you?—she's the one who introduced me to the universe of kids.

And for me, as for so many others, that was the beginning of the end.

The beginning of the beginning was almost two years before: the spring evening in 1979 I first spotted her outside a movie screening—heart-stoppingly beautiful in a blue dress, head tilted back in laughter. At that moment, I was utterly at peace with my world. Impeccable liberal credentials in order. The old certitudes unquestioned. Lots of people who mattered in my business thought of me as a good guy, and my career was booming.

A mere couple of Super Bowls later, under her influence, I was writing stuff that was not only eliciting hate mail from strangers but alienating old friends.

How'd she do it? How'd she turn me into someone destined to be reviled in *The Village Voice* as "a well-known asshole"—and, even more pathetic, actually reduced to finding solace in the words "well-known"?

As a couple, we started out conventionally enough. When Priscilla arrived at an Indian restaurant on New York's Upper West Side for our first date, minus makeup and in sweater and jeans, she looked so different from the evening we'd met I was momentarily disappointed. But by the time the tandoori chicken was on the table, I was already impressed by her quirky humor and fierce critical intelligence. We were both grizzled veterans of the dating wars and before the evening's end confessed how sick we were of having to produce an entertaining version of our checkered past for each new romantic prospect, agreeing that, for all our supposed liberation, love had surely been much more blessedly simple, and probably more thrilling, in our grandparents' day.

Yet it was a moment on our second date that left an even more enduring impression. I remember I was following Priscilla up the stairs to her apartment, and while studying the view I was telling her how many of my closest friends were women, going on about how I'd always found them easier to talk to than men because they're so much more open with their feelings, when she suddenly wheeled, flashing bemused incredulity. "That old line? Come *on*!"

I hesitated, momentarily defensive, then cracked up.

It's not precisely that what I was saying was untrue—I did have close women friends, and did find them easy to talk to—just that it also *was* a line, though I'd never thought of it in precisely those terms; one I'd slipped into conversations with new women lots of times before, always with satisfactory results.

But here was this woman ready to *argue* the point.

I probably should have ended it right there. This kind of contrarianism wasn't going to do me a damn bit of good—not in my circle.

Not that any of this is meant to suggest that she, any more than I, was ready yet to step off the deep end politically. A Berkeley grad, she'd done her fair share of protesting during the glory years. When we met, she had a gay male roommate, and so was much involved in the particulars of *that* revolution, getting regular firsthand, blow-by-blow reports from the front. ("Actually," she notes, stopping in my office, "usually it was 'blow job by blow job.'")

And, yes, much as she was even then given to mocking feminism's more ludicrous claims and intense self-seriousness—I recall her laughing over the sisterhood's veneration of Ruffian, "the gallant little filly" who had to be destroyed after injuring herself in a match race against the despised colt Foolish Pleasure—she very much saw herself as a feminist. She was, after all, a career woman, having moved from a consulting firm to a prestigious-sounding position in the movie business—East Coast story editor for Columbia Pictures, charged with scouting out new books and plays as potential films. Far more, she was a veteran of the sexual revolution, with all the battle scars to prove it.

As, God knows, was I.

In fact, before we go any further, let's pause for what the weasels in the press like to call "full disclosure."

My wife says I include this chapter—dwelling as it does on my sexual past—only as a means of bragging. As such, she says, it registers as "pathetic."

I have considered this carefully. There is some merit in her view. I include it anyway because, as I've informed her, there is a larger point to be made, even if at my own expense: that this notion that those of us who've moved right are prudes is malicious bunk.

We loved sex in the sixties and seventies, we love it now. In fact—listening, Priscilla?—sometimes we love it even more *because* it's been with the same person for so long.

In any case, what follows are excerpts from the transcript of my testimony had I ever been called to appear before an independent prosecutor's grand jury.

QUESTION: Mr. Stein, we'll begin by turning to something that has come to our attention relating to certain events that occurred in 1969.

ANSWER: Nineteen sixty-nine?! I was in college!

QUESTION: Exactly. And would it be accurate to say you had a girl-friend at that time? A Ms. Jane Mallory?

ANSWER: I'm sorry, you would have to define the term "girl-friend."

QUESTION: For our purposes, we will accept the definition as set forth and enumerated during your deposition. That is, one of the opposite sex whom you saw on an average of at least once weekly with the intent to arouse or gratify.

(Mr. Stein consults briefly with his attorney.)

ANSWER: Would kissing be covered by this? And, if so, how would you define it?

QUESTION: Mr. Stein, was it not your understanding with Ms. Mallory that yours was to be an exclusive relationship?

ANSWER: I have no specific recollection of that.

QUESTION: And do you not recall meeting a certain Ms. Barbara Schoenfeld on the New York subway during Christmas break, and do you not recall accompanying her to her parents' apartment where you could be alone? Do you doubt that your girlfriend would have regarded what you did there as "cheating"?

ANSWER: What is your definition of "alone"?

QUESTION: I'd like to move on if we might to the time you spent in Paris. Do you recall that period?

ANSWER: Paris, Texas?

QUESTION: France, covering most of 1976 through 1978. According to testimony and documentary evidence, you were working on an En-glish-language newspaper there.

ANSWER: That could be, I have no specific recollection.

QUESTION: Do you acknowledge that on your return to the United States you more than once boasted to colleagues that during your time abroad you had "sowed enough wild oats to fill a barn"? Do you stand by that statement?

ANSWER: It depends what one means by . . .

QUESTION: The terms "sowed," "oats" and "barn" being defined as previously set forth in the glossary of relevant terms. And during your stay in Paris, do you recall meeting—once again on the subway—a cer-tain Ms. Anabelle Browning, whom you befriended? Do you recall Ms.

Browning subsequently confiding in you that she sometimes worked as an "escort service girl" to pick up extra cash?

ANSWER: So what, nothing illegal in that.

QUESTION: There is, actually, even in France. But do you recall that far from being repulsed, you found the fact that other men paid for her services extremely intriguing?

ANSWER: I might have found her stories intriguing, not the fact of the "work" itself.

QUESTION: And do you recall some time afterward securing a job for Ms. Browning at your place of employment as a temporary receptionist?

ANSWER: It seems to me that's just something a friend does for a friend.

QUESTION: Did you not confide to an associate that you had secured this job for Ms. Browning in the hopes of "finally getting in her pants"? And subsequent to that conversation did you not, in fact, succeed in getting in her pants?

ANSWER: I would deny that. By "pants" do you mean underpants—because there is a vital distinction there.

QUESTION: Do you recall the occasion of your thirtieth birthday?

ANSWER: Not specifically, sir, a person in my position has a lot of birthdays.

QUESTION: I'm referring to the arrival at your home of a Ms. Barbara Slater, a photographer friend from Paris, who informed you she had a very special surprise. Were you not delighted when her surprise proved to be a visit that evening to Plato's Retreat, New York's notorious "swap" club of that era?

ANSWER: At the time I was a reporter, it was my business to observe the human condition in all its variety.

QUESTION: So you are denying that you participated in the activities at the club?

ANSWER: I recall I may have walked around, which is an activity, and drank a soft drink, which is another activity.

QUESTION: I am referring to participating in sexual relations.

(Mr. Stein consults with his attorney.)

ANSWER: I would like it noted for the record that I am married, and that all of the alleged activities, none of which occurred, took place well before that wondrous and life-changing event, which left me a changed man.

QUESTION: So you say. I must tell you, Mr. Stein, we've only just begun . . .

When Priscilla and I married, Ronald Reagan had been elected President two weeks earlier and Priscilla was pregnant. It is an embarrassing reminder of who I was that I saw those two facts as being tragically linked; for a time I actually turned into one of those fools brooding on the pointlessness of bringing children into a world such madmen were sure to send spiraling into nuclear winter. Though Priscilla now likes to tell people she laughed at my doomsday monologue, trust me, at the time it could get her pretty rattled. Shortly after the election, she joined some friends in a group they called—no kidding—Women Against Right-Wing Scum.

Not that, for all the dramatics, impending fatherhood had much reality to me. I'd never had much interest in babies or small children—not, at any rate, since my own dimly remembered boyhood, and then the small child I'd been most interested in was myself.

In fact, I was so disinterested in babies that it struck me as nearly inconceivable (as it was inconceivable to the public feminists) that any reasonably bright person could feel otherwise. One evening over dinner seven or eight years before, while I was working as an editor at a magazine called *New Times,* a French woman journalist friend, a recent mother herself, suggested a piece on what she said was the hot new birth method in Paris. An obstetrician named Leboyer had written a book called *Birth Without Violence,* which, so said my friend, marked a stupendous new advance over traditional childbirth: dim lights, soothing sounds and extreme gentleness all but eliminating the wrenching trauma of entering the world. Yet as my friend rattled enthusiastically on, all I was thinking was: (a) how am I gonna do this nice person a favor and get this idiotic notion past my editor? and (b) if I do, given her abominable written English, guess who'll get stuck with putting the damn thing in shape?!

But, hey, a friend's a friend, so I persuaded my reluctant editor to go for it (though at a mere eight hundred words), and I spent half a morning reworking my friend's garbled text. And that, I figured, was that.

But then the piece appeared in print and the mail started coming—lots of it, *tons,* as passionate as any we'd ever received, almost all of it from women. It's hard to say who was more startled: the editor, who wondered why we hadn't done a longer piece; or me, pretending I'd known it was a wonderful idea all along.

In fact, that episode probably constituted the sum total of all the thought I gave to birthing babies through my twenties. Like so many guys of my generation, I assumed kids were probably an inevitability, but only in the vague, vast, indeterminable future.

Now, with that time at hand, I basically let myself figure things would go on nearly as before. There would naturally be some small adjustments and a few inconveniences—I'd already arranged for an office outside our small apartment—but, within a few months, our kid would be in day care and weekdays, at least, would again be our own.

After all, this was how most everyone in our circle was approaching the kid thing. More to the point, it was what the fashionable magazines were recommending as the *better* choice: better not only for high-powered moms, who could fly back to the office scarcely missing a beat, but also for the kids, who would blossom among trained caregivers and contented peers as they never could in the less stimulating environment at home.

Made sense to me.

So I was flabbergasted when, two days after Sadie was born, Priscilla announced that she'd be quitting her job to stay with the baby.

I remember that I didn't argue—not then. After all, her brain was flooded with hormones; surely she'd come to her senses in a few days.

And even if she didn't, even if it took five or six months, I was doing well enough just then that the financial issue could be finessed, at least in the short term.

Thus it was that I took the first baby steps down the road to a happy home life and an uncertain ideological future.

‭❏

It frankly took me a while to grasp that Priscilla didn't care all that much about her career anyway—at least not the way I cared about mine. I mean, sure, she had enjoyed flashing the studio credentials and she would definitely miss the leisurely expense account lunches. But since no one in Hollywood ever took the suggestions of anyone in New York seriously anyway, it's not as if she'd deluded herself that Columbia's whole East Coast operation was basically anything other than window dressing.

In fact, the only career possibilities I'd heard her talk about with real enthusiasm were ones that might have occurred to Walter Mitty. Before I met her, she and her roommate had actually traveled down to Washington and taken a test to join the CIA. Both were disqualified; the roommate because, as an extremely obvious gay person, he was deemed a potential target for blackmail; Priscilla because, thinking they would respect her honesty, she had idiotically volunteered on the form that she'd taken all kinds of drugs back in college.

In brief, as ambition is defined on the world's terms, Priscilla was pretty much ambitionless. Talk about culture shock: here was a person who could actually get as much enjoyment out of something profound or witty written by a stranger as something she wrote herself! Which from my own hard-driving, Jewish, outer-directed perspective was even more alien than her *Mayflower* ancestors and the amazing nicknames that ran in her family: Sis, Beany, Munnie and Topsy.

A fervent advocate of feminist principles, especially those that served my own interests, I'd always presumed that my eventual life partner would be the Evolved Guy's ideal, caring as much about getting ahead in the world as I did; we would happily pool our incomes and, as we breezed through life, I'd get almost as much ego gratification from her success as my own.

Instead, it was soon clear she was getting more satisfaction in an hour with our child in our tiny Upper West Side apartment than she had in all her time over at Columbia's imposing office on Fifth Avenue.

But here's the thing: now she began doing a job on me.

Basically, she did this by badgering me into spending a lot more time with this tiny new presence in our cramped apartment than I ever would have spent on my own, knowing, *knowing* I'd get hooked.

How could I help it? Having assumed babies were basically slightly more animate shrubs, I couldn't believe how *interesting* this tiny being was—how complex her reactions to her surroundings, how each day brought out a new facet of her personality, how she seemed literally to blossom in the warmth of our love.

Which is to say, in record time I turned into one of those insufferable new dads who believed that he had invented the role, even while pretending to make light of the fact.

"I can't believe it," as one journalist pal nastily put it to me, his own wife back at her magazine editor's job within a few months of their daughter's birth. "You guys are like an *old-fashioned* family."

It was like a rabbit punch to the heart. But who could blame him? If positions had been reversed, I'd surely have said the same thing to him.

Besides, he was right. Completely inadvertently, we were doing the baby thing differently from everyone else we knew; depending on your point of view, it was either a revolutionary act or a reactionary one. In a remarkably short time, my wife began feeling isolated—then defensive. On the streets of our West Side neighborhood, arguably the single most liberal few square miles in the entire nation, most every other stroller was pushed by a baby-sitter or nanny; and on the rare occasions we went to dinner parties, Priscilla was invariably the only mom at home with her child, ending up with little to say as the chatter about office politics proceeded apace.

Then there were the meetings of her Scum Group, whose other members were journalists or publishing types. Though surely not intended to be, their question always came off as condescending: "Don't you get *bored?*"

"No, dammit," she'd rant on her return, "I'm *not* bored! But if you tell them that, they think you're a moron!"

But, then, the defensiveness was definitely cutting both ways. As we now know from so many books since written on the subject, a great many of these women were themselves torn between the imperatives of work and motherhood. Indeed, the choice to stick with their careers was for many probably even more personally wrenching than my wife's, since they felt every waking moment that someone or something was getting shortchanged.

The difference back then was that Priscilla had only me to gripe to; they got to make their case to the whole world. For at the time almost every women's magazine regularly ran pieces extolling the virtues of parenting by proxy. In *Glamour* and *Parents* and even *Ladies' Home Journal,* the drumbeat was relentless and alternative views were absent—although somehow it was never mentioned that those articles were written and edited by women who had already made the choice they were determined to justify.

Since we were regulars at the supermarket checkout line, these articles were unavoidable, and the sight of them rarely cheered up my wife. Her position began to take on a razor-sharp edge: very young kids need parents. The notion that day care produced better-adjusted kids was self-serving palaver. Sure, it was one thing when a woman was driven to put her kids in day care by stark economic necessity—but it was quite another when she made a choice based principally on her own desires, and then justified it on the highly suspect theory that a-contented-mom-makes-for-a-happy-child.

A child was as well off in an institutional setting as with a parent? It sure didn't *sound* right.

Smart and fiercely passionate on the subject, my wife got to be really impressive making this case. Plus we had the happy example of our own child, whose own stay-at-home way of life was also under assault.

And there was I—like new fathers through time immemorial, taking my cues on all baby-related questions from my wife. No question, if she had been one of those driven, Hillaryesque women who made business calls from her hospital bed an hour after labor, I would have been sure that *that* was the way to go, making fun of stay-at-home, cookie-baking moms with the best of 'em.

But no such luck.

Thus it was that, overcoming my own doubts to follow her, I found myself dragooned into what would soon come to be known as "The Mommy Wars."

❏

One of the reasons we were feeling reasonably secure financially at the time was that the "Ethics" column I'd started in *Esquire* had proved unexpectedly popular. The column had not been my idea; appalled at the holier-than-thou sound of the thing, I'd first begged the editor who'd approached me with it to let me take a shot at a humor column instead. In fact, it was his wiseass response—"Fine, make it funny and throw in an ethical point at the end, we'll call you Shecky Spinoza"—that helped me determine its voice.

Yet for all its lightness of tone, the column was before long about genuine dilemmas in my own life and the lives of my friends, the contradictions that come with simultaneously looking to see oneself as decent and moral and behaving in various ways that were anything but. Most months I found myself having to work through layers of self-justification to arrive at what felt like the truth, reexamining attitudes and assumptions that had become second nature.

A philosophy major in college, Priscilla had at first tried to help out by presenting me with a stack of Plato, Kant and Spinoza, which I dismissed out of hand—who the hell needed *those* guys? But soon she got with the program and became a sort of auxiliary conscience. And, subtly, though even I was unaware of it at the time, a theme began to run through those pieces: that some of the moral precepts people like me had

19

so casually jettisoned in the sixties as woefully antique—like, oh, the more demanding of the Ten Commandments—have served humanity pretty well, after all.

So when my friend the *Esquire* editor happened to call again wondering if I wanted to contribute to an upcoming special issue on women, Priscilla had the idea that I do a piece on day care.

Nah, that's not true, I can't blame her for everything. Actually, I suggested it myself. On the other hand, it was probably her idea to tell the editor—an unmarried heterosexual—the only words sure to provoke keen interest in such a squishy-sounding idea: it'll generate real heat.

This is probably the place to note that I'd never been one of those journalists who courted controversy, at least not within my circle; I had thus far always publicly identified myself as on the side of the angels, which is to say left-of-center, a view certainly reinforced by the "Ethics" pieces. I was gratified so many readers seemed to feel the column spoke to them. But why wouldn't it? Most had more or less traveled the same road, and it was easy to assume a common view of ourselves as good people who basically had our values in order and, though admittedly sometimes selfish or childish, cared mightily about becoming the best versions of ourselves.

So, call it naive, but I truly believed a thoughtful, probing piece on day care would elicit a positive response, even among readers not necessarily happy with its message.

That is not to say I approached the subject with an entirely closed mind. I tried to keep it open at least a crack, which was a helluva lot more than you can say for most of those writing for the women's mags. For one thing, at the urging of my journalist friend I agreed to spend a couple of days at the fancy-schmancy day care center where his eight-month-old daughter was a "student," reputedly one of the best facilities in the city. In addition, I sought out a range of prominent child care types on both sides of the issue.

Looking at the piece again after all this time, I'm actually surprised by its mildness. Basically it did nothing more than pose the essential unasked questions: Was day care indeed all that its proponents claimed? And might there be, at least for some children, emotional costs?

Obviously, I was aware it included some highly provocative stuff. For one thing, after my couple of days at the pricey day care place, I noted that the pair of young Hispanic women charged with caring for the very youngest kids were clearly overwhelmed; yet, in interactions with the kids' mothers, both sides tended to adopt a policy of don't-ask, don't-tell. I watched one four-month-old new arrival at the facility cry bloody murder for most of an afternoon; yet when his power-suited young executive mom breezed into the place a little past six, he was asleep. Beaming, she exclaimed he'd never looked so happy—and no one told her the truth.

Then, too, one of the experts I quoted was the renowned child psychologist Lee Salk, who had this to say: "I love dogs, but I'd never keep one in a New York apartment because it's not fair to the dog. I think parents who are unwilling to give their children the attention they need should consider not having any."

It turned out he'd had problems with day care all along, but no reporter had ever before questioned him about it.

Still, most of the other experts, even those with serious reservations, were pretty mealymouthed. In fact, the most eminent of them all—Dr. Spock—forbade me to quote him at all, saying off the record that, though he did have serious doubts about day care, he wasn't ready to publicly air them.

That should have been a tip-off right there: I mean, c'mon, the guy was eighty years old, it's not like *his* reputation was in jeopardy.

The avalanche of denunciations that greeted the piece was unique in my experience before or . . . no, that's not quite right, there have been a couple of others since. Let's put it this way: some of the letters from enraged women were little more than a string of epithets. There was much made of my sexism and misogyny and general backwardness. Several people I knew, a couple not all that well, called to bawl me out on the phone. Another casual acquaintance stopped me on the street to say that when she read it she felt like boxing my ears.

The editor wife of my journalist friend was so enraged she forthwith assigned a day care article for her own magazine, and it was reliably reported that she gave at least one prospective writer my article as a test; when the writer failed to detest it with sufficient vigor, she assigned the piece to someone else.

As an indication of how quickly elite opinion on the day care question would turn, when the magazine editor had a second child several years later, she left work to stay home.

But that didn't do me any good then. Indeed, for a while after the day care debacle I was frankly shell-shocked. It didn't compute. As liberals, weren't we supposed to care about the well-being of children above all else? When it came to a subject with social implications as far-reaching as day care, shouldn't we welcome a debate?

In this regard, I was well behind my wife—her evenings with the Women Against Right-Wing Scum had long since taught her otherwise.

From the start her reports of the meetings had been a source of fascination to me. The group included some of the most powerful women in media, so what they said and thought *mattered.* Yet, as my wife told it, the group's original purpose—to generate fund-raising and other political action—had long since been forgotten, and the meetings had turned into extended gripe sessions.

As these things go, what they mainly griped about was men. "The amazing thing to me was that nothing was ever their fault," she recalls now. "One of the magazine editors used to go on and on every session about her ex-husband, this guy she'd met and married and had kids with, and stayed with for years, as if all this had just *happened* to her. And all the other women just sat around and nodded sympathetically. Of course, most had also had assorted schlubs, losers and jerks inflicted on them. All of these women presented themselves to the outside world as strong and capable and successful—they gave advice to other women on the pages of their magazines—and yet they were so determined to see themselves as powerless!"

Since Priscilla has a pretty good eye for detail, at first her accounts were pretty amusing. But in time they grew increasingly desultory. The problem, as she told it, was that there was never a real exchange of ideas—no back and forth, no impulse to challenge, only to affirm.

One night she came back looking particularly stricken. They'd spent the evening discussing Lisa Steinberg, the six-year-old who had recently been murdered by her father, Joel Steinberg, as her mother, Hedda Nussbaum, looked on. What most upset them was the possibility that Nussbaum might be prosecuted along with Steinberg, their feeling being that any of *them* might under other circumstances have ended up in Hedda's shoes. "They were just so invested in seeing women as victims," recalls my wife, "even highly successful women like themselves, that it trumped common decency. To them Hedda merited our understanding and sympathy. But the dead child was an afterthought."

All these years later, Priscilla still gets agitated discussing it. She concedes that she didn't speak up as much as she should have—although she spoke up enough to get a reputation as "unsupportive."

In any case, shortly afterward she stopped going altogether.

"It's funny," she says now, "when the group formed, I saw myself as a fighter against right-wing scum. By the time I left—at least by their definition—I was well on my way to *being* right-wing scum."

Priscilla exaggerates, of course—that's her way. The fact is, it was years before either of us would look in the mirror and see anything but a liberal staring back.

But, no question, the process was already subtly under way; and unbeknownst to us, it was the same one a surprising number of our contemporaries were going through. As one of the friends I've made since—wiser than most of those I left behind—puts it, "It's having children which gave almost all of us our first push to the right."

Call it growing up—all right, if you want call it something else—but as we looked around at the world being remade, it seemed to us that something fundamental was out of whack. For amid all the upbeat talk about the wonders of parenthood, kids' actual needs weren't getting taken all that seriously.

We've heard a lot more about this lately, of course—especially since the horrendous events at Columbine High. Within days, the murders were being described as a cultural watershed, one of those moments—akin to our recognition of the high school science gap after Sputnik or of the breadth of the racial divide after the riots that followed the murder of Dr. King—when the obvious became so glaringly evident we could no longer turn away. By the millions, American parents have been neglecting their children—if not materially, then in ways that arguably matter even more, involving emotional safety, security and the legacy of a world worth inheriting. As William Damon, director of the Stanford University Center on Adolescence put it to the *New York Times,* "There has never in the history of the civilized world been a cohort of kids that is so little affected by adult guidance and so attuned to a peer world."

There is of course no satisfaction in noting that millions of us have long been aware of this disaster in the making. The question is what to do now; for the fact is engineered by the shift toward a focus on self our generation has become so ingrained in that it's probably beyond altering.

Obviously, that's a stark and awfully sweeping indictment, and it has been much sneered at over the years. *How the hell do you generalize about a whole generation that way? We're talking fifty million case histories, each distinct.*

But then, that's the nature of social transformation—the sum total of innumerable personal choices—and you don't know it till you see it.

Personally, it hit me full force one afternoon in the early eighties when I read the opening line of a piece in *The New York Review of Books* by Christopher Lasch, the acclaimed author of *The Culture of Narcissism:* "This is a profoundly anti-child culture."

Of course. That was it! We could babble on about children all we wanted, and come out with all the stylish new parenting manuals and magazines in the world, but the dispiriting reality was staring us in the face. Even in well-off families—indeed, often even more so—the kids had a rough time of it, because suddenly, by consensus and with the enthusiastic backing of the trendsetters, it was okay if they came second, or third or fourth.

Nor were nearly so many of us as in prior generations prepared to take on the really hard part of the job: the day-to-day character-building by example. Desperate not to be loathed as authority figures, eager to be our kids' pals, we failed to offer them the structure and the emotional shelter of certainty and durable standards; or even protection from a coarsening popular culture that places zero value on what was once so treasured—the wondrous innocence of unspoiled childhood.

This had at first seemed to me a human question, and not necessarily a political one. But of course by now I knew that was naive. As I'd seen by the reaction to the day care piece, and as Priscilla had found each week at her Scum sessions, the cataclysmic changes afoot reflected the triumph of an ideology—several related ideologies, really—that made a positive virtue of attention to self.

This is why an assault on the supposedly empty pieties and manifold hypocrisies of prior generations very quickly became part of the package. Already the notion was taking hold that the fifties had been a kind of Dark Age, not just inhospitable to spontaneity and innovation, but spiritually repressive. Who with a functioning brain and conscience could doubt that this new era, with its emphasis on individual expression, was an infinitely better time to be alive? Indeed, if one did doubt, even a little—if anyone stopped to ask what we'd lost as well as gained, or questioned the new contempt for old values—this was *prima facie* evidence of backwardness. After all, as the feminist sloganeers had been saying all along, "the personal is political."

If there seemed a contradiction between the vaunted reverence for free expression and the ready contempt directed at actual diversity of thought, no one in progressive circles made much of an issue of it. But it clearly was not yet playing all that well in the rest of the country, the despised Reagan winning reelection over Walter Mondale—Eleanor's dad, for you Clinton *aficionados*—by an even greater margin than Richard Nixon's over George McGovern.

Though chastened by my own experience, I still very much saw myself as a liberal, and a year or so after the election I wrangled a *New York Times Magazine* assignment aimed at looking into what had gone wrong. The working premise of the piece was that the electoral debacle had occurred in large part because we liberal Democrats had handed the so-called "values issues" to the other side by default. Utterly sure of ourselves, ideologically rigid, we had imposed litmus tests on so many issues—from abortion and affirmative action to bilingualism and, yes, day care—that we'd made pariahs of millions who might have been our allies, but who had broken with prevailing progressive wisdom, as a matter of deeply felt principle, on one or another such question.

My approach was to explore each issue in some depth, letting a number of said pariahs have their say. For instance, on day care I focused on James and Debbie Fallows—he a former Carter speechwriter and future editor of *U.S. News & World Report,* she a policy analyst who had quit her high-powered job to be with their kids and then had the temerity to write a book urging others to consider doing likewise. "Why," as Jim Fallows asked, "should you have to be a conservative Republican to want to watch your children grow up?"

On abortion, I sought out the obvious candidate: Nat Hentoff, the respected civil libertarian and columnist for the leftist *The Village Voice* who's also a passionate and outspoken pro-lifer—a matter, in his view, of moral consistency.

Yes, he confirmed, such a belief had left him isolated both at the *Voice*—"by last count, three women editors won't talk to me"—and in the progressive community in general. "There's just a real disinclination on the part of liberals to listen to those who disagree with them, or even to give them a hearing at all. Group-think tends to promote fierce objection to heretics."

Since this was precisely the thesis of the piece, I was taken aback when my editor informed me that the entire Nat Hentoff section would have to be dropped. It seemed that among those the columnist had rubbed the wrong way over the years were certain higher-ups at the *New York Times.*

Speaking of irony, one of the others I spoke to for the piece was Tipper Gore, under assault at the time as a tight-assed would-be censor for her part in the campaign against obscene rock lyrics. Sitting with her in the Gores' comfy Virginia parlor—a Norman Rockwell setting, down to the half-finished, homemade Halloween costumes visible on the dining room table—I found myself agreeing with almost everything she said about the impact of the most degrading elements of pop culture on kids' lives, and couldn't help but be impressed by the intelligence and passion this former child psychology major brought to the subject. "All we're saying," she concluded, "is let's look at what we're doing to our children; for heaven's sake, let's look at what we're doing to *ourselves.* Is that really so unreasonable?"

Of course, to her opponents it really was. "Mrs. Gore is trying to impose her own blacklist," a bristling Danny Goldberg of Gold Mountain Records told me. "As far as I'm concerned, she's another McCarthy, an agent for the far right." For good measure, by way of exposing her concern for kids as the sham he knew it to be, Goldberg pointed to her real motive: "She's married to a Southern Democrat who thinks it's a good way to appeal to Southern bigots."

Who could have guessed back then that Tipper and her husband would one day make a pilgrimage to Hollywood seeking their fair share of show biz loot, and beg forgiveness for the anti-obscenity crusade, calling it "a mistake" that "sent the wrong message"? Or that Goldberg himself, now a full-fledged mogul as CEO of Mercury Records, as well as chairman of the American Civil Liberties Foundation of Southern California, would emerge as a key Clinton-Gore Hollywood supporter?

Yet, in reporting the story I actually ended up learning at least as much about those on the other side: those altogether alien creatures known as cultural conservatives. For where most in the liberal universe were made deeply uncomfortable by talk of values, or even standards of behavior, these cared about those things passionately. And, on the evidence, so did their man in the White House. "One of the great mistakes the liberals keep making," as Ed Rollins, who'd run the Reagan campaign, put it, "is in refusing to recognize that Reagan's appeal isn't just that he's a charming guy. He also deeply feels things—about right and wrong, about fairness—that an awful lot of other Americans also feel."

A few short years before, hearing this, I'd have had to resist laughing out loud. Everyone I knew took Reagan to be a clueless boob, wholly a creature of his handlers, his vaunted moral beliefs a load of cynical drivel.

But, no, the message was belatedly sinking in: that wasn't it at all.

Maybe the problem was with us and a perspective as pitifully narrow and provincial as that of any of the small-town Baptists about whom we always assumed the worst; without, of course, having ever met one.

❏

Which is to say, when Bill Clinton appeared out of L'il Abner country, oozing charm and full of talk about "brain-dead" liberalism and how the Dems had to recapture the center, I was among those more than ready to listen. These were just the sorts of things some of my friends and I had been saying for years.

Within a few days of first catching the guy on TV, I wrote his headquarters in Little Rock asking where to volunteer for his New York campaign.

Then the trouble started.

I personally first heard whispers about Clinton's recklessness even before I got a response to my letter to Little Rock. A reporter I knew claimed he'd been at a campaign rally in Michigan where the candidate showed up with *two* women who were not his wife. Word was, said my friend, he was absolutely out of control.

I remember being both disappointed and deeply annoyed. What was *wrong* with the guy?! If someone as totally out of the loop as I was hearing about this, it would definitely soon get out, and Clinton, like Gary Hart four years before, would be dead meat.

Of course, in short order there were a couple of other explosions from the minefield of the candidate's past: the controversies over whether Clinton inhaled and, far more important, his behavior when faced with the draft. Suddenly, in his person, it was as if the mores of an entire generation—*our* generation—were on trial.

Still hopeful about Clinton, it seemed to me the crisis might also be an opportunity. I believed at the time, and am even more convinced now, that had he come clean—acknowledging that, yes, he'd sought to avoid fighting in a war he detested (and even belatedly conceding how insulting that surely seems to those who served)—he would have been elected anyway, helping to heal divisions of twenty years' standing by that display of forthrightness in the process. Indeed, for lots of us such a stance would have signaled genuine political courage (a term not often associated with Clinton since), thus being of a piece with his candor on the failures of liberalism—another principled, gutsy move essential to clearing the air and moving on.

Then, again, for that the man would have needed a character transplant.

Instead, we found ourselves with a warmer, fuzzier New Age Nixon: fudging, obfuscating, doling out tiny morsels of truth as changing circumstances dictated.

At the same time, we were getting to know Hillary, who proved a different kind of revelation. Articulate and reportedly razor smart, she was starting to seem the better half of the "Buy one, get one free" deal. Until, that is, she was caught on videotape belittling stay-at-home moms, snapping about how miserable she would have been had she "stayed home and baked cookies and had teas."

This was an advocate for children?

Next came the Gennifer Flowers brouhaha—his pious *60 Minutes* nondenial, her head-bobbing supportive act—a transparently self-serving display if ever there was one. "If he had an Italian last name," as John Gotti was heard on wiretaps critiquing Clinton's performance, "they would've electrocuted him." But, boy, were they smooth; not a flicker of self-doubt in either.

Then again, as we learned back as kids, you can tell a lot about people from how they lie—and often even more from how they react when they're caught.

I recognized these people; I'd known others like them. Invariably, they were the most successful of the go-getters at prestigious magazines and in Hollywood, souls whose every relationship is useful, their bottomless narcissism masked by surface charm. Ultimately that is what made them so scary: it was all gloss. When push came to shove, nothing was real but the ruthlessness and amorality.

The final straw for me with Clinton was the Rickey Ray Rector episode.

Who?

Conveniently, the name has been all but forgotten. But for a few days there, early in the '92 campaign, it generated headlines: the young Arkansas black man on death row for killing a cop. Formerly a foe of capital punishment, candidate Clinton refused to stay the execution; in fact, he flew home from the campaign trail in New Hampshire to appear before the cameras and deny the stay in person.

Now, no one says Clinton didn't have the right to change his mind on the issue. I did myself. With the ethic of personal responsibility in headlong retreat, it seems to me an eye for an eye is a pretty fair way for society to let the bad guys know where we stand.

Still, one makes allowances for circumstances. And, as widely noted at the time, Rickey Ray Rector was not remotely capable of such understanding, a failed suicide attempt after the crime having left him severely brain damaged. In the reports the day after his execution, a single detail said it all: when he was taken from his cell to the death chamber, he left behind a slice of pecan pie, planning to enjoy it later.

There was a small outcry over this at the time, but generally it was shrugged off as just politics.

In fact, it was a certain kind of politics, the sort as time passed we'd come to know as vintage Clinton: the act of a man whose ambition was unchecked by any of the nobler impulses. Rickey Ray Rector had to die because Clinton, his every action dictated by focus group data, needed to show he was tough.

As a class, our politicians are unarguably cynical, but it is rare that one is able to rise quite so high being *that* cynical. I remember my shock at learning that Joe McCarthy was privately not even particularly anti-Communist, the one revelation that could have driven him even lower in my estimation.

But where McCarthy was finally done in by TV, which revealed him as the sleaze he was, the camera loved Clinton. It loved him for his amazing ability to project empathy and warmth, loved him even when he was lying through his teeth.

I was working part of that summer of '92 with a friend involved in the Clinton campaign—in fact, the guy who engineered the candidate's famous appearance on Imus's radio show, when he got to showcase his hip, self-effacing side—and the two of us spent weeks of lunches arguing, he trying to persuade me Clinton wasn't nearly so bad as I supposed, me trying to persuade him he was far, far worse.

I ended up casting a protest vote that fall for Ross Perot, the first time in my adult life I'd failed to support the Democrat.

Not that I make any claim for my own prescience—again, I *did* vote for Perot. And, anyway, by then plenty of people had the same gut sense about the depth of Clinton's shamelessness. Nor were all of them ideological adversaries. It was Jesse Jackson who noted famously during the campaign, "There is nothing this man won't do. He is immune to shame. Move past all the nice posturing and get really down there in him, you find absolutely nothing . . . nothing but an appetite." And it was Nebraska Senator Bob Kerrey, as a rival for the nomination a particularly close-hand Clinton observer that primary season, who commented, "Clinton's an unusually good liar, unusually good."

Then there was the Arkansas *Democrat-Gazette*'s legendary Paul Greenberg—a Pulitzer Prize winner and one-time liberal hero for his crusading journalism on behalf of civil rights, who had been on to the guy back when the rest of us were focused on Jimmy Carter and the gas crisis, dubbing him "Slick Willie" in the first place. Years later, Greenberg would wistfully recall Robert Bolt's observation in *A Man for All Seasons*, that "there is a special kind of shrug for a perjurer; we feel that the man has no self to commit . . ."

Eventually, the only surprise was in the capacity of others to forgive, excuse, overlook. We've always known that human beings are infinitely adaptable, and that's not always a bad thing, but who could have predicted so many would set aside what once seemed guiding principles?

But part of the Clinton genius would prove to be his ability to play on his supporters' better impulses, encouraging their sense of rectitude even as he stripped his own actions of moral meaning. Even in the midst of a crisis that was entirely of his own making, he persuaded supporters that he represented not merely himself but larger principle, so that in the end, it was not just he but *they* who were being deeply wronged.

He was able to do this because of something fundamental to the progressive mind-set: the idea that politics is holy war, that one's adversaries are not merely mistaken but evil, that they must be shown no understanding and allowed no quarter. Thus the primacy of the soul-surrendering doctrine "The enemy of my enemy is my friend," which no public figure ever wielded to greater effect than Bill Clinton.

It could not have been more symbolically appropriate that Jesse Jackson would emerge as one of Clinton's most ardent defenders after six years of being proved right. Or that so many decent, thoughtful people who had long ago recognized that Nixon's lack of either scruple or restraint made him not just personally repellent but dangerous found themselves, with Clinton, ready to shrug off perjury, obstruction of justice and more.

The all-purpose explanation became that these things were complicated, not to be reduced to banal simplicities about right or wrong, that we have to live in the real world, even that lying under oath is not necessarily perjury. Were we not all human? Ought we not to be capable of charity and, more than that, perspective?

We simply demand too much today, as Dick Gephardt explained congressional Democrats' enthusiastic show of support for the beleaguered Clinton, we seek after "unattainable goals of morality."

Is that really so? Only in the fog of cynicism fostered by this President must we remind ourselves that virtue cannot be redefined according to circumstances or need; and that we put at risk not just the country's long-term well-being but our own when we imagine that it can.

Indeed, Gephardt's observation, coming as it did from a national leader, ought to have been taken as shocking. Hasn't that always been the point, to aim high? Isn't that what we learned as children? What we try to teach our own? No, we're not saints, but every serious soul understands that one must measure oneself by exacting standards, and that there is immense reward in the effort. If we're truly interested in living in the real world, and living meaningfully and well, that's a fundamental truth worth learning: those who regard moral goals as "unattainable" are in big trouble before they start.

For me, as it happens, Clinton's single most despicable act had nothing to do with illegality. It involved a lie he told at a press conference a few days after JFK Jr.'s death: his misty-eyed revelation that "John Kennedy had actually not been back to the White House since his father was killed until I had become President."

"In fact, however," as the *New York Times* blandly observed (though it buried the story in a single, late edition; and the network newscasts, which had given Clinton's claim wide play, failed to note it at all), "the President's son had visited the White House on at least two previous occasions, once in 1971 when Richard M. Nixon was President and again in 1985 when Ronald Reagan was President."

But then there was the topper—the part which, in a better time, would have left the entire nation cringing: "Mr. Clinton, informed by aides later that Mr. Kennedy had been to the White House before, said he had based his statements on what Mr. Kennedy had told him."

Which probably makes this as good a time as any to bring up a concept that's taken an especially tough beating in the national street fight of recent years.

Honor.

For many, the very concept registers as archaic, as meaningless in this modern age as the calling card. As the contemporary formulation has it, honor—like morality—means different things to different people according to their varying life experiences, and nothing wrong with that. Who are *we* to impose *our* standards on anyone else?

Let's face it, that's the heart of the problem right there.

For honor is not meaningless. Nor is it changeable. It is the sum total of those traits—integrity, courage, perseverance, fidelity—by which, throughout recorded history, individuals of worth have measured themselves and one another. And lately we've been paying a woeful price for failing to give it its due.

I'm thinking just now of a kid I know, a friend of my daughter Sadie's, who's been going through some of the same things as did Chelsea Clinton, for a couple of the same reasons. He is just eighteen, a terrific kid, smart and funny with limitless possibilities. But his dad—a guy with a serious case of sixties' nostalgia and the ponytail to prove it—started screwing around with a much younger woman, and moved out of the house "to find himself."

One more unembarrassed values-challenged asshole messing up his kids' life and not giving a damn. A man completely without honor.

The startling thing is that no one calls him on it. Everyone is far too sophisticated to hold him to account.

Everyone except his son. Always a sunny kid and terrific student, in this crucial year that he's applying to college, he has predictably become withdrawn, his grades sharply off. Yet, reports a sympathetic parent, he responded to a suggestion that he transfer from advanced calculus to a less demanding math course with a slow shake of his head. "I'm not my dad," he said. "I'm not a quitter."

"Well," as the parent put it afterward, "I guess he's earned the right to be judgmental."

Maybe—except that not so long ago that was something that didn't have to be earned, but came with membership in the larger community. One could act miserably, all right—in a free society, the liberty to misbehave is indeed a kind of right—but there was invariably a price to be paid in embarrassment and shame.

As the essayist and academic David Gelernter observes, it is only since the late sixties that "judgmental" has been a pejorative at all. In his brilliant, autobiographical *Drawing Life*, Gelernter (who, having been maimed by the Unabomber, has presumably also earned the right to make such judgments) notes that more than anything else it is intellectuals' abandonment of the concept of evil that has led us to our current sorry state. By way of chilling example, he quotes the president of Northwestern University on a Holocaust-denier on his faculty: "I believe his views are monstrous. But I don't want to set myself up as a censor of his views. Who decides what is distasteful?"

Of course, observes Gelernter, such a purportedly generous-spirited but in fact utterly craven attitude has by now come to touch every corner of American life. He points to a display of nonjudgment that touched him and his family personally, one spectacular even by contemporary non-standards: the anointing by *People* magazine of the Unabomber (along with the likes of Brooke Shields and George Clooney) as one of its most "Intriguing" people for the year 1996.

Would that make Benedict Arnold one of the most intriguing people of 1780? If not—for though he had a sexy young wife, Arnold also had an unsightly gimpy leg—surely matinee-idol-turned-assassin John Wilkes Booth would've made the cut for 1865. And how about the brilliant and mischievous George Metesky—remember him, the "Mad Bomber," who signed his notes F.P. for Fair Play?—for 1958?

But, no, we know our past better than that; know enough, at least, to sense that even as some labor to drag the history book heroes of the past down to the level of the soap opera present, it just wasn't so. Sure, those men and women were human and, absolutely, some were vile. But almost never publicly so, and not without grasping the consequences. For honor was part of the fabric of the age; to risk one's good name was to risk all.

From this distance, the ways that played out can seem quaint, even idiotic—and, in fact, they sometimes seemed so even then. In 1819, the great naval hero Stephen Decatur denounced the widely held practice of dueling as "a barbarous practice which ought to be exploded from civilization"; yet, less than a year later, feeling his honor impugned, he accepted a challenge and paid for it with his life. After the Civil War, former Union General Fitz-John Porter, his good name tarnished by a military court's finding that he had behaved badly during the Second Battle of Bull Run, fought the ruling for twenty-three years, through seven presidencies, before it was reversed.

The concept was alive and well right up to the near-present. Though the fifties are routinely derided today by media heavies as socially and morally backward, at the time it seemed absolutely appropriate that cult sensation Charles Van Doren, his wrongdoing exposed, should retreat from the spotlight into lifelong obscurity. And for what? The sin of having lied on a TV quiz show, misrepresenting himself as smarter than he was. Do we doubt that in similar circumstances today he'd be almost instantly rehabilitated via a teary *mea culpa* to Barbara Walters or, at worst, plead "substance abuse" and spend a month or so in rehab?

Wonder of wonders, sometimes there was honor even in politics back then.

I witnessed a little of that firsthand. In the mid-sixties, as Vietnam picked up steam, my great hero became Oregon's flinty old senior senator, Wayne Morse. Morse had started out as a Republican, quitting the party during the 1952 presidential race after an adviser to GOP nominee Dwight Eisenhower privately assured the pro-union senator that Ike would not be nearly so hard on unions after he won as he was suggesting on the campaign trail. Morse immediately went public, calling Eisenhower a hypocrite who would readily betray principle to get elected, later adding for good measure that he "was undoubtedly the most stupid president we've ever had in the White House."

As a Democrat, Morse was by far the sharpest thorn in a Democratic administration's side, one of only two in Congress to vote against 1964's Tonkin Gulf Resolution granting Lyndon Johnson extraordinary warmaking powers, and a brutal critic of the still-popular LBJ and his minions in the months that followed. "You're a liar, Rusk!" he growled, his thick white eyebrows high in indignation, when the amiable Secretary of State showed up to explain Vietnam policy to the Senate Foreign Relations Committee. "A brazen *liar!*" A century earlier, it might well have provoked a duel.

In 1968, his stand on Vietnam ended up costing him the seat he'd held since the Roosevelt years, narrowly lost to a young Republican named Bob Packwood.

Six years later, when Morse was trying to win it back, I nabbed an assignment to cover the campaign and was at his side for three days. In fact, up close he wasn't what many would regard as a particularly nice man. Crusty and brutally frank, lousy at small talk, he would come alive only when discussing public policy. Even his belated vindication on Vietnam seemed to give him little satisfaction; he had known it all along. "Right from the beginning, we had a majority on the war in private," he told me about his Senate colleagues. "They just didn't have the guts to vote against it . . . At least I don't have blood on my hands." This was the season of Watergate, and he'd also been right all along on Nixon, whom he'd met back in 1948. "In the Senate, the only legal tender you have is your integrity," he snarled. "Nixon wasn't there ninety days before many of us knew he was bankrupt."

That was the thing: for Morse, integrity was everything. This campaign for the Senate was costing a grand total of sixteen thousand dollars; he was staying in Portland at a ten-dollar-a-night hotel, the campaign car was his own Hornet. I was with him before a radio interview when he stooped to pick up a penny from the studio floor. "Look," he said, "a lucky penny." He turned to a guy in headphones. "But I gotta give it to your station."

"Why don't you keep it, Senator?" said the guy.

Morse actually looked stricken. "No, no, no, it's not mine. By law it's the station's."

I don't mean to suggest a man like this couldn't be elected today. To the contrary, in this feelings-oriented and morally aimless time, the hunger for such individuals can almost be felt. We saw it in the willingness of voters to elect a Jesse Ventura, both for what he was—utterly straightforward (even if sometimes stupidly so)—and what he was not: a Democrat or a Republican.

We see it even more so in the endless stories the mass media churns up about ordinary people doing extraordinarily selfless things. A typical story in *The National Enquirer* has an American business executive in Colombia exchanging himself for one of his employees held hostage by heavily armed guerrillas. "The hardest part is explaining to the daughters he loves so much why their daddy isn't coming home. It breaks my heart every time they ask about him," the executive's devoted wife told *The Enquirer*. "He is a good man. He is a man of honor and deserves to come home alive and well."

The same week, the *New York Times* ran an amazing front-page story about a man serving twelve years in a California state prison who, in an attempt to save the sixteen-year-old girl he had deserted as a child, had already donated one kidney and was now trying to give her the other. Though the *Times* had predictably dressed up this whizbang human interest story as sociology—"GIRL AWAITS FATHER'S 2D KIDNEY, AND DECISION BY MEDICAL ETHICISTS"—no one's fooling anyone; at heart, this was an astonishing tale of redemption and parental sacrifice, and God only knew what *The Enquirer* would've paid for it. "We want the world to know that this man is giving himself to his daughter," the paper quoted the girl's mother. "We're demanding that the State of California honor this man."

Indeed, self-sacrifice, putting one's very life at risk for something precious beyond oneself, is the very essence of honor. A well-lived life is a succession of difficult choices made for the right reasons; even in an era when self-justification is so easy to come by, most of us instinctively understand this. It is why no abstraction in our communal vocabulary so readily stirs the blood or moves the spirit; why we love Rick in *Casablanca* when he chooses the world's good over his own, and stand in astonished admiration watching Sir Thomas More go to his death in *A*

Man for All Seasons rather than swear to what he does not believe; and why, after *Saving Private Ryan,* even a lot of kids who too often seem to think the world began the year they were born suddenly looked with respect on the old men who are their grandfathers, listening to stories of courage and hardship that seem almost impossible to believe.

And yet, they're very nearly the same stories old men have been passing on to children since ancient times.

Kids need it. Instruction by example in honorable behavior is a vital part of the training for inheriting the world; both as preparation for crises, when self-sacrifice might be called for, and in placid times, as practice in thinking beyond themselves.

It's been hard to stop thinking about that poor kid: "I'm not my dad. I'm not a quitter."

Good for him. Still, that doesn't make it any easier.

By now we have more than enough research pinpointing the precise damage such a life-altering experience often leaves in its wake, from an inability to trust to a terrible coldness where there should be compassion.

Which makes all the more amazing the willingness of people like this kid's father to behave as they do anyway. I don't begrudge him his regrets; we all have some. But you don't do what he did to the people you love. You just don't.

Once, before it became the rage to live life to the fullest and never stop thinking young, that was simply understood. You had obligations in life, and you met them. This gave daily existence both its rhythm and its larger meaning. In fact, it was presumed your primary purpose on earth was biological, seeing to it that your kids grew up prepared to be responsible adults in turn. What you did to earn a living—or whether you were *fulfilled*—didn't matter a damn.

Yet here's the irony: by such a process (though the fact was probably never remarked upon), chances are you *were* fulfilled, likely far more deeply than most today who so aggressively inhabit the present.

Obviously, for many it is still that way, we just don't hear much about it. When the grandfather of Yankee superstar Derek Jeter died not long ago, it made the *New York Times* only because of his proximity to celebrity. A modest man who awoke mornings at four-thirty to supervise maintenance at both an elementary school and his church, he never missed a day of work in thirty-six years. Moreover, according to his grandson, he passed on that work ethic to his children and theirs.

"It will be a long time before we see the likes of Sonny again," said the monsignor who presided at his funeral. "I've seen the way Derek carries himself, and in the long run, hopefully, he'll be the man his grandfather was. If he is, he'll really be accomplishing something in his life."

Cynics will of course say that there's a lot of sentimentalizing in this sort of thing, and surely there is some. For most people life has always been a struggle and the world has certainly never lacked for angry, vicious and troubled souls.

But it is not myth, it was once the creed that most lived by; indeed, it is a measure of how jaded we've become that we are so readily persuaded otherwise.

One need only recall the letter so memorably reproduced in Ken Burns' *Civil War*, penned by an ordinary soldier named Sullivan Ballou to his wife days before his death in battle. At the time of the broadcast, it had a terrific impact, and has since been reproduced on innumerable Web sites.

Still, strikingly poetic though it is, it is most remarkable for the fact that, as evidenced in numberless similar letters by other soldiers, the sentiments it expressed were then so ordinary.

I know it's old news. Forgive me. But frankly, if I could, I'd see it printed on place mats, book covers and milk cartons.

July the 14th, 1861
Washington D.C.

My very dear Sarah:

The indications are very strong that we shall move in a few days—perhaps tomorrow. Lest I should not be able to write you again, I feel impelled to write lines that may fall under your eye when I shall be no more.

Our movement may be one of a few days duration and full of pleasure—and it may be one of severe conflict and death to me. Not my will, but thine O God, be done. If it is necessary that I should fall on the battlefield for my country, I am ready. I have no misgivings about, or lack of confidence in, the cause in which I am engaged, and my courage does not halt or falter. I know how strongly American Civilization now leans upon the triumph of the Government, and how great a debt we owe to those who went before us through the blood and suffering of the Revolution. And I am willing—perfectly willing—to lay down all my joys in this life, to help maintain this Government, and to pay that debt.

Sarah, my love for you is deathless, it seems to bind me to you with mighty cables that nothing but Omnipotence could break; and yet my love of Country comes over me like a strong wind and bears me irresistibly on with all these chains to the battlefield.

The memories of the blissful moments I have spent with you come creeping over me, and I feel most gratified to God and to you that I have enjoyed them so long. And hard it is for me to give them up and burn to ashes the hopes of future years, when God willing, we might still have lived and loved together and seen our sons grow up to honorable manhood around us. I have, I know, but few and small claims upon Divine Providence, but something whispers to me— perhaps it is the wafted prayer of my little Edgar—that I shall return to my loved ones unharmed. If I do not, my dear Sarah, never forget how much I love you, and when my last breath escapes me on the battlefield, it will whisper your name.

Forgive my many faults, and the many pains I have caused you. How thoughtless and foolish I have oftentimes been! How gladly would I wash out with my tears every little spot upon your happiness, and struggle with all the misfortune of this world, to shield you and my children from harm.

But, O Sarah! If the dead can come back to this earth and flit unseen around those they loved, I shall always be near you; in the garish day and in the darkest night—amidst your happiest scenes and gloomiest hours—always, always; and if there be a soft breeze upon your cheek, it shall be my breath; or the cool air fans your throbbing temple, it shall be my spirit passing by.

Sarah, do not mourn me dead; think I am gone and wait for thee, for we shall meet again.

Sullivan

❏

THE TITANIC TEST

It was still that way when the *Titanic* went down in 1912. The press reports over the days that followed are full of accounts of heroism and honor. Financier Benjamin Guggenheim, who had been heading home for his nine-year-old daughter's birthday party, spent the ship's last two desperate hours comforting other children, during which he was heard to remark, "We're dressed up in our best, and are prepared to go down like gentlemen." Another man, struggling in the icy water after the sinking, managed to make his way to a packed lifeboat, only to see there was no room. "That's all right, boys," he quickly reassured the survivors, moving off into the frigid dark to die. "Keep cool. God bless you."

The following verse appeared that week in newspapers in London and New York, summing up the feelings of the day:

> *Women and children first,*
> *That is the law of the sea.*
> *The law that holds unwritten,*
> *Should ever the need arise.*
>
> *The laborer's wife in the steerage,*
> *The lady of high degree*

Go down to the boats together
Wherever the old flag flies.

That is the privilege granted
To man that he stand aside
For thus he may prove his manhood
By looking death in the face.

Now, we know there's plenty of hyperbole here: not everyone on the doomed ship acted as selflessly as Leonardo DiCaprio, accepting his fate without hesitation or complaint. In many ways it was a heartless age and those in steerage, women as well as men, were largely abandoned in that moment of mortal danger. And of course we also know there were some men who pushed their way onto lifeboats, or died trying, and who otherwise behaved miserably.

Still, it is safe to say, not nearly as many as would be the case now: responding to a *Pittsburgh Post-Gazette* survey taken on the eightieth anniversary of the sinking, only one of three men said he would surrender his seat on a lifeboat to a woman to whom he was not related.

Which gives rise to some legitimate speculation: How would various well-known individuals today behave in such a situation? Considering what we know about each of those listed on the next page, hazard a guess on what he or she might have done in those final terrible moments aboard the *Titanic*.

	Gone Down with Ship	Cried, Then Gone Down with Ship	Tried Arguing Way onto Lifeboat	Disguised Self as Woman
Bill Gates				
Elton John				
Mark McGwire				
Ted Kennedy				
Donald Trump				
Bill Bradley				
Colin Powell				
Jerry Springer				
Woody Allen				
Gloria Allred				
Dennis Rodman				
George Bush				
George W. Bush				
Geraldo Rivera				
Leonardo DiCaprio				
Jesse Ventura				
Jimmy Carter				
Ken Starr				
Bill Clinton				

□

From the first, of course, there was lots of talk about Bill Clinton's affinity for Hollywood, truly a match made in—let's give them both the benefit of the doubt—purgatory. "Clinton is a set of contradictions," as Marshall Herskovitz, co-creator of *thirtysomething*, *My So-Called Life* and *Once and Again*, delicately observed shortly after the world learned of Monica Lewinsky, "and many of those contradictions work quite well within the moral structure of Hollywood."

The moral structure of Hollywood: now there's a subject well worth exploring.

In fact, here's an idea. Since cultural studies are so big at colleges these days, comprising classes in everything from advertising slogans to the meaning of *Mr. Ed,* how about one that might truly help them understand our ever-more value-free world? . . .

Sociology 69: Deconstructing the Celebrity Bio (credit awarded also in the departments of Psychology, Anthropology and Film Studies).

When closely examined, such volumes offer a far clearer sense of where we are as a society and how we got there than all but the most searching works of traditional scholarship.

There are of course zillions of books that fall into this category—Roseanne's alone presents a bonanza for the judicious researcher. Marilyn Manson's *The Long Hard Road Out of Hell* should have been

4 8

required reading for all those commentators spouting off post-Columbine on nihilistic teens. "As a bipedal animal," reflects Manson, explaining why he chose a conscienceless mass murderer to name himself after, "man by nature (whether you call it instinct or original sin) gravitates toward his evil side . . ."

But for those of us mainly interested in the degrading of mainstream, middle-class culture—the amazingly fast journey, if you will, from *American Graffiti* to *American Pie*—it is the most seemingly banal works that often offer the greatest riches. Take, for instance, Eddie Fisher's *Been There, Done That,* in which Eddie marvels at the astonishing gullibility of the public back in the fifties, utterly oblivious to the distance between stars' images and who they really were. Far better to know his sweetheart Debbie Reynolds was conniving, manipulative and sexless; and that even in her glory years Elizabeth Taylor—still the great love of his life— was a drugged-up floozy who enjoyed getting beaten up. "Divorces were still relatively rare," he observes mournfully of the scandal brought on by his split from Debbie and its effect on his career. "Unhappily married people stayed together for their children. So the unexpected breakup of our seemingly loving marriage shook that bedrock. People believed in Debbie and me. I think they saw us as representative of the young couples who were beginning to shape America's future.

"And it turned out that's exactly what we were."

Indeed, that's a theme running through an amazing number of such books: that we may be deeply flawed, but so be it. We should celebrate who we are, warts and all—that's what makes us human. There's nothing, *nothing,* we do or feel or believe that merits embarrassment or self-reproach.

In my own search for enlightenment on the shifting cultural tides, I find it especially useful to delve back into celebrity bios of the recent past—Shelley Winters's, Cheryl Crane's—for here, amid the dross (and in the authors' need to remain relevant), one is apt to run across nuggets of surprising unvarnished truth.

My all-time favorite passage in a celebrity bio may well be a philosophical insight in *True Britt,* by dimly remembered Swedish ex-starlet Britt Ekland. Those for whom the name rings a bell will perhaps recall that the fabulously sexy Ms. Ekland was famous not merely for being famous, but for the well-known men who passed through her life. Among these were her husband Peter Sellers, such other actors as Ryan O'Neal and George Hamilton, the rock star Rod Stewart, the erstwhile presidential candidate Warren Beatty and moguls of assorted ages and nationalities.

The passage has to do with her finding herself pregnant for a second time and her reaction to the child's father, rock impresario Lou Adler, telling her (over dinner in their suite at Paris's fabulously magnificent Plaza Athénée Hotel) that he had no intention of marrying her. As she records her anguish on page 152:

"I flew back to London alone. I had to think very deeply about it. My upbringing dictated that if I was to have a child I should be married. I was afraid, not so much for my own sake, but for the stigma that our child might have to face.

"Then I thought of two fellow thespians, Vanessa Redgrave and Catherine Deneuve, both of whom had children out of wedlock. No one had thought badly of them and both were enjoying prominent professional and social lives.

"Besides, we were now into the 'seventies and old taboos had been broken down. . . ."

Well, thank goodness *that* was settled!

For, yes, as it turned out Britt indeed was on the cutting edge. As we now know—from the many reports on the staggering increase in fatherless children—with people like herself, Vanessa and Catherine bravely leading the way, pretty soon only a few sorry old fuddy-duddies were anguishing even that much about the consequences of giving birth without marriage.

Not (it must be said) that marriage meant all that much to start with in the exciting and dynamic circles they inhabited.

Another of the most vivid celebrity observations on the subject of till-death-do-us-part, circa 1972, was Ali MacGraw's wedding-day warning to Paramount honcho Bob Evans, reported in his memoir, *The Kid Stays in the Picture:* "Don't ever leave me alone, Evans, I'm a hot lady."

And, sure enough, when Evans did leave her alone on location with Steve McQueen a short time later, he had to learn his lesson the hard way; she divorced Evans, married McQueen, and Evans, full of regret and self-recrimination, went on to . . . well, a bunch of other deeply meaningful relationships, culminating in a marriage to the lovely Catherine Oxenberg that lasted almost two full weeks.

"Were things really better forty or fifty years ago," my daughter asked recently, "or does it just seem that way?"

"Better how, darling? They sure weren't better for black people in the South or, I don't know, for kids with dyslexia who got labeled stupid."

But of course, as a modern American child fully versed in the rich lore of victimhood, she knew all that. "I mean, were people really less selfish than they are now? Couples especially."

In brief, she was asking as a seventeen-year-old romantic—someone thinking hard about her own future as a wife and mother—growing up during the Clinton presidency in the age of celebrity worship. She was asking about adultery.

As we kicked the subject around, the answer was as simple as it was complicated-sounding: no and yes. No, as the celebs so eagerly assert, people were not innately better; people are flawed, being human's a helluva tough job. But, yes, back then more people behaved better, both because the culture expected them to and because they expected it of themselves; which is to say, when they didn't, they at least knew enough to be ashamed. No one pretended dumping on your loved ones was anything but wrong—to do so marked you as an s.o.b. or, at best, a jerk.

Thus it was that movie studios back then counted on their publicity departments for their very survival. Sure, Eddie and Debbie were a bust from hour one, Joan Crawford was the mother from hell by way of Bloomingdale's and Burt Lancaster's sexual appetites only worsened his second wife's drinking problem; but as far as the public was concerned, all had family lives out of Norman Rockwell.

Today this is known as hypocrisy—but it was hypocrisy in the service of a greater good. Today's publicists are more likely to meet a rumor of a star busting up his family with a bland statement acknowledging that, yes, he had a thing with his costar on location, but he and his wife plan to remain friends for the sake of the kids.

All of which inevitably has an impact on the rest of us.

In fact, even as traditionalists decry the flight from responsibility of so many of the public figures who might once have been embraced as role models, what they project attracts us still. Who doesn't at least sometimes envy their sheer, unembarrassed freedom from restraint? It's not as if such behavior is wholly without appeal, especially—and this part I did not tell my daughter—for guys. If there were no such things as guilt, or consequences, or higher morality, lots more of us would act this way.

Then, again, that's what separates the men from the boys, what makes them better husbands, better fathers, better human beings—what in many places is still known as character. Lusting in our hearts is one thing. The trick is making sure it stays there.

In order to resist temptation, one of my best friends, happily married but always equally happy to reminisce about his premarriage exploits in the seventies, makes a point of hiring only elderly and/or strikingly unattractive women to staff his small office. I, meanwhile, will try almost anything for a legal turn-on. For weeks after reading Bob Evans's book, I begged my wife to repeat the line with a playful malevolence that has nothing to do with her real personality: "Don't ever leave me alone, Stein, I'm a hot lady."

Alas, she wouldn't do it, the same way she almost never puts on that black negligee when I want her to.

Once in a while, it can seem like a rotten bargain. But in the end lots of us stick to it for basically selfish reasons: because it works. Because we love our spouses and don't want to cause them pain. Because the well-being of our kids is immeasurably more meaningful than indulging ourselves. Because somewhere along the way we've learned that having values and sticking to them is the formula for an infinitely more fulfilling life.

The acute narcissism that allows fifty-year-olds to behave like they're eighteen, without a full understanding of consequences or even the merest trace of remorse, is also often the drive behind extraordinary success—and nowhere more than in glamour fields like show biz and politics.

But, in the ways that count, such an approach to life invariably winds up the worst kind of dead end.

That can sometimes seem hard to believe in our celebrity culture. I myself became convinced only through personal experience a while back when I got the notion for a series of pieces called "The Wisdom of Our Elders." The idea was to pick the brains of various celebrated figures—politicians, journalists, show biz types—each at least seventy-five years old, who appeared to have led full and rich lives, and provide them with a forum in which to pass on their insights on the Big Questions: What is truly valuable in life? How does one avoid the most painful mistakes? What constitutes *real* success?

I ended up speaking to maybe a dozen such people, and it truly was an eye-opener—because most were amazingly *un*thoughtful.

It took me a while to see this was more than just coincidence and to discern the pattern: that having spent their entire lives chasing success (and sometimes playing by pretty flexible rules to get it), most were entirely lacking introspection. Indeed, it's no exaggeration to say they had achieved so much largely *because* they'd been unhampered by what the mother of a friend calls "the curse of self-knowledge."

Visiting the law office of gentlemanly former Arkansas Senator William Fulbright—nearly as much a hero to me as Morse, renowned in his day as one of the most astute foreign policy minds going, mentor to the young Bill Clinton—I found a tart-tongued old man still unaccountably nursing grudges with adversaries almost no one else even remembered. A few weeks later I spent a morning on a sun-drenched Hollywood Hills patio with the legendary film producer Hal Roach, nearly a hundred years old at the time but still fully lucid, listening to his experiences with Will Rogers, Laurel and Hardy and the *Our Gang* kids. He said some fascinating things, yet trying to get him to draw any sort of larger lesson from it all proved useless. Totally defined by his work, he told me he didn't think about it, he just *did* it.

And so it was with most of the others, left unnamed because they are still among us.

Finally, reluctantly, I abandoned the project. I'd been poking around celebrity culture nearly six months, but there just didn't seem to be enough genuine wisdom to fill up a book.

But let's be fair. Even on the subject of morality and ethics in Hollywood one can't deal in absolutes. In the course of researching "The Wisdom of Our Elders," I did run across one striking exception to the dispiriting rule—the actress Helen Hayes.

In her early nineties at the time of my visit, with bright white hair, vivid blue eyes, skin pink as a baby's, she offered what I had hoped for all along: meaningful insight earned by hard experience. Despite her acclaim as one of the century's great actresses, what preoccupied her now, near the end, were parts of her private life—notably, the sudden death of her daughter at nineteen of polio; and the alcoholism of her playwright husband, Charles MacArthur, which the tragedy greatly accelerated.

Indeed, sitting with Miss Hayes (somehow, "Ms." just doesn't work) that afternoon on her terrace overlooking the Hudson, listening as she reflected on her life choices with a clarity and a grasp of consequences even more alien in her business than in the world at large, a couple of times I was nearly moved to tears.

In fact, on rereading the interview the other day, I was inspired to get her autobiography. It wasn't easy. *My Life in Three Acts* is long out of print; indeed, its author, too, is well on her way to oblivion.

Then again, this is the way of the world—and, based on the following excerpt from our conversation, can anyone doubt Helen Hayes herself would accept it with equanimity?

My grandmother, Graddy Hayes, was of the last generation of real grandmothers—a woman who made a special grace of age. That sense has only increased with time. It wasn't anything conscious. She simply enjoyed a freedom from anxiety about outward impressions with which so many are burdened; she was past all that. She never put a speck of makeup on her face, it never occurred to her. I think she wasn't aware of herself at all anymore. She was just wholly directed toward her children and grandchildren.

For a child, there was no better person to be around. She was a wonderful lap to sit on, a wonderful bosom to weep on, a pillar of security and strength. And so interesting. I used to sit by her side, separating her silk floss with my less-rough fingers while she embroidered her pillow tops and told stories of her girlhood in Ireland. I feel so sorry for childhoods without such people. No TV show could ever match the excitement of that old woman's stories.

I got a far greater sense of how a life ought to be lived from her than from my mother. My mother was of the new generation—not *very* new, of course, but new enough—and, as they say today, she had her own life to live. More than anything, she wanted a career on the stage. She'd gone to acting schools and appeared in various small productions, and she longed to be backstage among theater folk. So it was classic: since she couldn't do it for herself, I had the career for her.

But I always had that other, longer view—from Graddy Hayes and from my father. My father was a dear, dear man, and it was a source of genuine confusion to him that he had married this wonderful, gay woman, but she never wanted to be at home. He himself was not afflicted with that terrible itch of ambition.

I don't want to convey the wrong impression—I long ago got past thinking of my career as something vicarious for my mother. It was something quite wonderful. By nature, I am a striver after perfection, and it was important to me to be among the top of my time. The work gave me enormous joy and satisfaction.

What I have questioned is having tried to do too much at once. It truly is almost impossible to achieve a balance between my kind of work and the demands of family. Both are strong, urgent and ceaseless occupations. But, looking back, it's not the lost work opportunities that I regret.

It used to hurt me to see what my Charlie [playwright MacArthur] put himself through. There wasn't anything wrong with Charlie. Here he was, a devoted husband of the old school, a devoted father, a great lover. He believed in God and in love, and he fought furiously against fraud and cynicism. On top of it all, he was among the most amusing men in the world. He had a genius for spreading good feeling. I saw it a thousand times: He entered a room and faces would change. Scott Fitzgerald once said, "Other men have to *do,* Helen, Charlie only has to *be.*"

Of course, very few of us are able to look at ourselves that way, through other people's eyes.

We fought furiously about his drinking, and sometimes I felt a sense of despair. I felt deep down that I wasn't doing the right thing: I couldn't have been, or else it wouldn't have gotten as bad as it did.

In a way, of course, I recognize now that's ridiculous. We now know that alcoholism is a disease. But I've always been a strong person—I *know* I could have done more. And I know that, for all the deep satisfaction it gave me, my career was not a good thing for us— or the children.

For the children suffered also. Even as a little girl, my Mary was such a wise old soul. I've never forgotten something she said when she was six or seven and we were walking hand in hand to the front door as I was heading off on another tour: "Mommy, I want to go everywhere with you." It's so easy to shut those things out, to race off and get lost in one's own life. But I knew it was an outcry from that little heart, and it still haunts me.

I don't know—my life is spoken of as a great success. But it's been a long time, and I still feel Charlie's and Mary's absence so acutely. They're both with me all the time. I only wish I'd given it more thought before, when it would have made a difference.

For a good ten years, Priscilla and I had been evolving more or less in tandem. But it was only in the early nineties that we began to slip off what certain friends and family regarded as the deep end.

Since we were both big on current events, she'd always returned from forays to the library with stuff she thought might interest me also, usually articles from dinky magazines I'd never otherwise see like the *Utne Reader* or *The Nation.* But around this time, she also started occasionally coming up with reading from the other side of the political spectrum, stuff like *Insight* and—I couldn't believe it!—*Commentary,* edited by Norman Podhoretz, an individual as despised in my longtime circle as Jesse Helms.

The first time she brought a copy into the house, I sounded like a Fundamentalist minister face-to-face with a copy of *Hustler.* "I don't want this around here," I told her. "I don't want it around the kids!"

We had two now, Charlie having come along in '84.

She actually laughed, then landed on the weasely truth. "You're just embarrassed one of our friends might see it."

"Damn right," I snapped. "What'll it be next, that Moonie paper?"

So that night in bed, it proved a first-class revelation to discover the magazine was as smart and thoughtful—as *challenging*—as anything I'd read in a long time. It was also a lot closer to where I was on all sorts of things than the publications I thought were on my side, including some I wrote for.

All these years later, only our mailman knows our reading habits for sure—and he must be pretty damn confused. For while we continue to get liberal solicitations screaming alarm on the envelopes—"Stop the Christian Right Before It's Too Late! Preserve Every Woman's Right to Choose!!"—we now also get mocking denunciations of the left from the other side, along the lines of "What *else* do liberals and ostriches have in common?—Answer inside."

Then, too, while we keep up with *Time* and *The New Yorker,* we're likely the only ones on his route also getting such outlaw publications as *The Weekly Standard* and *The American Spectator.*

Not long ago, finding myself on jury duty and eager to serve on what looked to be an interesting assault case, I thought this appearance of neutrality actually might work to my advantage; wouldn't someone willing to consider all points of view be an ideal juror? So when the prosecutor asked me to name all the publications I read regularly, I confidently began ticking them off. "Well, the *New York Times* and the *New York Post, Time* and *The Weekly Standard, The New Yorker* and . . . *The American Spectator.*"

Wrong again. I was excused forthwith. And afterward, in the hall, I was approached by another would-be juror who had also been dismissed, in her case evidently for having been too obviously predisposed to believe the defendant. "You really read *The American Spectator?*" she asked, amazed. I mean, I didn't *look* like the devil.

"Yeah, I do, it has some pretty interesting stuff sometimes. You ever read it?"

"I don't have to," she said, and in short order stalked away.

Of course, there is a lot of this going around. Where conservatives can't avoid being exposed to the media they so despise, most liberals loathe conservative publications based almost entirely on assumption and rumor.

They should take a look. The fact is that conservative journals, even if one doesn't agree with them, offer some of today's most provocative thinking precisely *because* they challenge the status quo.

Thus, as a service both to smart liberals—who should at least know what they're arguing *against*—as well as to would-be conservatives, I offer a brief rundown of a handful of notable conservative publications.

The Weekly Standard

Murdoch's entry in the world of weekly political mags is truly, as Martha Stewart might say, "a good thing": a smart, ironic, morally responsible neo-con antidote to the shallowness, amorality and general mediocrity of most Washington-based reporting. Edited by William Kristol, the *Standard* has been especially valuable in the wasteland of spin and obfuscation of the Clinton years. Among its standout writers: David Frum, Andrew Ferguson, Tucker Carlson, Naomi Emoerie and Christopher Caldwell.

The American Spectator

This slick monthly may well be the most despised magazine in America among people who've never read it. That reputation is not entirely unearned—editor Emmet Tyrell can be joyously scurrilous in his mad-dog vitriol toward the Clintons and other political foes. But every one of the *Spectator*'s early investigative pieces about Clinton and his court has held up. Besides, how much can you really hate a publication that identifies its legal counsel on the masthead as: "Solitary, Poor, Nasty, Brutish & Short"?

Commentary

In appearance, it is almost forbiddingly egghead, with type-only covers and unillustrated text-heavy pieces. But if you want a deeply felt and insightful take on the current social and cultural scene—race, education, multiculturalism, the continuing impact of feminism, and the like—there is nothing better. The letters section is a lively give-and-take that can leave one thankful there are still so many interesting, smart people out there uncowed by contemporary dogma.

Heterodoxy

Irreverent is too mild a word. Edited by David Horowitz and Peter Collier, prominent ex-radicals who got their start with the legendary *Ramparts* in the glory years of Vietnam, *Heterodoxy* is a lively romp out there in the tall grasses. Its target is Political Correctness in all its nefarious guises and the war is waged full throttle, on land, sea and air. This is definitely the mag to read to keep up to speed on leftist academic lunacy, a regular staple. *Heterodoxy* also has an entertaining letters section, sometimes featuring screeds along the lines of "Stop sending me your revolting, racist rag" from outraged liberals who've received it unsolicited in the mail. On one memorable occasion, they merrily reproduced a smeared scrawl an enraged uber-feminist had penned with a used tampon.

The National Review

The granddaddy of conservative magazines, Bill Buckley's baby (like Buckley himself) has over the years achieved a measure of respectability in the mainstream—though, again, from people who never read it. In fact, though pretty staid in presentation—something they've been trying to change with a new layout—its politics are not markedly different from the others; often joyously irreverent, a while back, it was also accused of racial insensitivity, due to a perfectly reasonable cover mocking Clinton's Asian connection. Washington editor Kate O'Beirne is no less sharp in print than as a TV talking head, and Florence King, the smart, sassy daughter of the South who writes "The Misanthrope's Corner," is alone worth the price of admission.

The Wall Street Journal

While the *Journal*'s conservative reputation is based on its editorial page, its news section actually runs from mainstream to moderate left; among the reporters who got started there were Jill Abramson and Jane Meyer (who helped eviscerate Clarence Thomas) and feminist icon Susan Faludi, who concocted the appalling *Backlash* and *Stiffed.* Then, again, given the force of the paper's editorials, the reputation makes sense. Edited by Robert Bartley, *Journal* editorials are at once passionate and brilliantly argued, especially in contrast to the flabby thought that consistently marks the ones in the *New York Times*. On any given day, there's also likely to be a jewel among the accompanying op-ed pieces by the likes of Mark Helprin, Dorothy Rabinowitz, Peggy Noonan or Shelby Steele. Moist-eyed columnist Al Hunt is the house dullard.

I guess it was bound to catch up with me. In the world I come from, one false step, one vagrant opinion can be enough!

Even now, I vividly recall the instant I first got called a fascist to my face.

It was Saturday, May 23, 1992, at about 9:30 EST. I know for sure because it was at a dinner party the weekend after Dan Quayle's famous *Murphy Brown* speech.

Now, times have changed a lot since way back then, with most everyone today claiming they more or less agreed with Quayle's basic premise all along; hell, even Candace Bergen, Murphy herself, now says so. And since it's precisely people like these who get to write history, they're on the verge of getting away with it.

So let's just take a second to remember how it really was. In the four days between Quayle's speech and that Saturday evening, it had already become received wisdom in "progressive" circles that the moron veep had established new lows in both hilarity and viciousness, his misbegotten attack on a sitcom character, the thinking went, displayed not just an inability to distinguish real life from fiction but a shocking callousness toward those struggling under the burden of single motherhood, especially in the inner cities. The airwaves and op-ed pages were full of bemused and/or infuriated commentary.

Yet for me, as for millions of others, it immediately seemed pretty clear that Quayle had raised some vital issues. Indeed, since I was doing a weekly column for *TV Guide* at the time, I'd spent that afternoon on a piece taking Sam Donaldson to task for a particularly nasty *Primetime Live* segment on all the terrific new Quayle material various comedians were hurriedly working up.

Still, this was sort of my secret life; in the upwardly mobile commuter community to which we'd moved from the city—a place where few would be caught dead reading *TV Guide*—it was pretty much assumed that everyone adheres to the standard liberal orthodoxies. Walk outside in the early morning, and on almost every lawn sits a slick blue wrapper around the *New York Times*. Suburban social niceties being what they are, I had no interest that evening in making a scene.

So when, inevitably, conversation around the dinner table turned to the subject, I took what seemed a safe middle course. Quayle may have had a point, I noted—but given his personal record of indifference to those at the bottom rung of the social ladder, he was probably not the one who ought to be making it.

It was such a weasely, half-assed observation that I was genuinely surprised by the reaction of the guy across the table. A journalist and writer, not particularly well known but one of those sober faces that turns up on network news shows from time to time commenting on this or that, he could barely get the words out. What the hell was wrong with me, he demanded: What did I want to do, stigmatize all those kids born—here he made quote signs with his fingers—"out of wedlock"!?

"Of course not," I replied, as mildly as I could. "But would it really be such a terrible thing if their parents thought a little harder in advance about consequences? The bottom line is that kids need fathers."

He was red now, literally sputtering, and it took him a moment to get out the coup de grâce. "Jesus Christ, when did you become a fascist?!"

There it was, the F-word. The nuclear bomb in the progressive arsenal, aimed at instantaneously altering the conversational balance of power by branding the other guy a moral cretin. I was abruptly aware of my heart pounding as half a dozen heads turned my way.

Yet, startled as I was, I had no real right to be surprised—not after all the times I'd casually tossed the word around myself.

That is not to say I'd ever really known precisely what it meant: not so that if challenged by someone up on his political science I could've defended myself.

Then, again, I never was challenged. Not once. And had I been, there were plenty of names to throw around. Hitler! Mussolini and his Blackshirts! Brutal, torture-happy junta heads in Latin America! Spain's iron-fisted Generalissimo Franco—long before, lingering for weeks on his deathbed, he got transmogrified by *Saturday Night Live* into one of our generation's running gags!

The point was, we didn't have to be told—we *knew* what a fascist was. A hater. An moral abomination. One opposed to everything good and decent and right. Someone who disagreed with us.

For instance, my friend Freddy Kornberg's mother. Mrs. Kornberg was the first person at whom I recall personally tossing the word, one fall morning in 1964, my sophomore year in high school. A lovely woman and a lifelong Democrat, she'd just informed Freddy and me that she was backing moderate Republican Kenneth Keating in his Senate race against Bobby Kennedy because, as she explained, with LBJ's impending landslide over Goldwater threatening the very future of the two-party system, it was "important to support the 'good' Republicans."

From her reaction—ranting, she threw me out of the house—it was clear I'd touched a nerve. But though I felt a little bad about it for a time, I never for a moment believed I'd done anything wrong. I mean, c'mon, supporting a *Republican* over a Kennedy?! It was worse than asinine, it was close to criminal!

For, of course, already I knew every political choice was an ethical one; and by definition we, unflinchingly antireactionary and pro-underdog, made only the right ones.

It was this mentality I now found myself on the wrong side of at that dinner party; across the table from a face animated by the same outrage French aristocrats surely saw as they mounted the guillotine.

Mea culpa, Mrs. Kornberg, *mea maxima culpa*.

Of course, at the time I only dimly appreciated that for those of my friend's mother's generation, history lent the word an especially venomous sting; it was less than twenty years since relatives of hers, and of mine for that matter, had died in Hitler's camps.

In fact, more than any other factor it was anti-Semitism—rooted in the right in America as in Europe—that had made leftists of our forebears in the first place. My grandparents came to America from a Russia where, under Czar Nicholas II, it was official policy that one third of Jews should accept baptism, one third should emigrate, and the last third should over time be eliminated, if not through terror then by means of starvation. This country was literally their salvation, something they deeply felt the rest of their lives.

Yet even here they knew to be on guard. "The anti-Semitism that prevailed was maniacal," as writer Howard Fast put it in his memoir *Being Red,* explaining his own attraction to the Communist Party back in the thirties, "there is no other way to describe it. And this crazed Christian sickness forced . . . us into a closed, defensive unity." And Fast was talking about New York City!

At least for those of my generation, certainly in the upscale suburb where we lived, that sense of impending menace was long gone by the time I informed Mrs. K. she was a proto-Nazi; I don't think I'd even once experienced anti-Semitism firsthand. Still, among people like us, its legacy—a staunch commitment to the progressive agenda—burned as fiercely as ever. After all, even when complacency was the norm, the left had never failed to stand squarely against the haters.

At that moment the forces of good were even then being put to their greatest and most splendid test yet, as blacks and their liberal white allies mobilized against the real proto-Nazis of the KKK and others violently resisting integration in the Deep South. It was a struggle with which even we indulged suburban kids felt a powerful personal connection. Earlier that year, the nation had been shocked into something like outrage by the murder of the three civil rights workers in Philadelphia, Mississippi. One of the two whites, Michael Schwerner, was the son of close friends of my aunt and uncle. The other, Andrew Goodman, was from my hometown, where a couple of years later I would work under his psychologist mother in a summer program for underprivileged children.

Indeed, as a member of the New Rochelle chapter of the Congress of

Racial Equality, kid division, by then I'd already walked a number of picket lines protesting the appearances of various bad guys, as well as participated in several rollicking civil rights rallies. I vividly recall the moment outside a hotel in White Plains where we were picketing a speech by ex-General Edwin Walker, a then-notorious darling of the hard right, when an infuriated dinner guest told me I should get my sixteen-year-old ass to Russia.

Though mortified at the moment—Russia? my big thing that year was getting my ass out to Shea Stadium to see the Mets!—I was soon proud of it. Besides making a good story, the very telling further established I was on the right side of history.

But all of that was—what?—thirty-five years ago? Don't these people understand times have changed?

Apparently not, for no matter how worn the grooves, the same old record keeps getting played. In his bestselling attack on the right, *Rush Limbaugh Is a Big Fat Idiot*, Al Franken writes of the tales he used to hear as a child from his real estate broker mother about how blacks and Jews were then restricted from buying homes in certain parts of Minneapolis. Franken credits the "strong element of moral indignation" aroused by this and other injustices for the fierce allegiance to liberalism he feels to this day.

Look, Al, you're a smart guy; I'm not about to tell you red-lining doesn't still happen. But when I was a kid, there was a town a few miles away from mine so famous for its anti-Semitism that the name "Bronxville" became almost synonymous with restrictive clauses. Go there today, as I do sometimes to drop off my son at the home of a (Jewish) friend, and you can have a nosh at an absolutely terrific kosher deli.

Besides, you're not the only one with family stories—what counts are the lessons that get drawn. I had an Uncle Sol who, back in the twenties, graduated first in his university class with a degree in chemical engineering. But since at the time that industry was viciously anti-Semitic, he couldn't land even the most menial job; after a year of trying, he was forced to go back to school and he became a pharmacist. By the time Sol died, he was taking real comfort in how astonishingly much things had changed. Then, again, he died back in 1981; if he came back today and saw Jewish kids once again getting screwed out of good jobs and slots at top universities—this time for being white—I *guarantee* you, he'd go howling back to the grave.

Yet it's uncanny how many can't seem to see that—in the same way, for instance, that in their breast-beating about Christian Fundamentalists, they fail to see the magnitude of the threat they themselves pose to those on the other side. Yes, I agree, we have to keep a close eye on those elements in the Religious Right who would ban the teaching of evolution and impose their vision of rectitude on the rest of us. (You think *I* liked hearing Jerry Falwell say the Antichrist is a living adult Jewish male?) But at the same time let's understand that their behavior over the past decade or so has been largely defensive: they were pretty much content in their enclaves until their values and way of life came under assault by the multiculturalists and feminists seeking to impose *their* notions of rectitude, usually with the active cooperation of the news media, government agencies, and Hollywood, all of which somehow get to call their own agenda "inclusive" instead of "narrow."

The fact is, today's progressives often seem unwilling to concede the other side anything at all. In this undemanding era of ours in which it's so much easier to rage and posture, there they are, day after day, on the networks and on the big-time op-ed pages, the self-reverential keepers of conscience, opining the nation's drift from decency and compassion, presenting those who have an alternate worldview as little better than pond scum.

Yet what's amazing, given the extent to which they dominate the public dialogue, is how many of these people see *themselves* as beleaguered—and, thus as models of courage, in addition to all the rest. I know one writer—fairly prominent, you might recognize the name—who likes to make the point in meetings at magazines or publishing houses, that he is among the last of the unapologetic liberals, thus invariably leading (I have observed personally) to great mutual commiseration; which in turn often leads, in the roundabout way these things work, to profitable employment. I managed to remain friends with this guy until it got back to me that he was telling people that *my* political odyssey was a matter of naked self-interest—supposedly a result of vast newfound riches. When I called him on it, pointing out that in fact my revised take on things was surely doing me more professional harm than good, he was the opposite of apologetic. "Everyone knows," he explained, "that selfishness is the reason people move to the right."

At least I can be grateful I'm long gone from the dating market. Let's face it, these days, maybe even more than in the sixties, if you're right of center . . . well, you get off lucky if you're dismissed merely as a nerd. Were I out there looking for love, every day running across personal ads like the following, I truly don't know if I'd be able to resist the impulse to ditch principle entirely: "Attractive, lusty redhead, twenty-six, seeks compassionate, socially aware guy for talks, walks and much more. No Giuliani lovers or smokers, *please!*"

Again, not that I went around spouting off about this stuff at the time of the night in question. Not by nature a troublemaker, I generally watched myself around those I didn't know well, the way gays and Communists used to have to in the old days, letting others do the talking when we strayed from neutral subjects like kids or dogs or baseball.

Then, again, sometimes it's all but unavoidable, as it was that evening.

For a few moments after the jerk's savage onslaught, I was reeling. But then I realized I was far from defenseless, having a lifetime's worth of my own moral superiority to fall back on—which is to say, a nearly inexhaustible supply of slingable bullshit.

Suddenly I was back with one of my first heroes, old Joseph Welch, the wily attorney in the Army-McCarthy hearings who brought the vicious Joe McCarthy to his knees on national TV after McCarthy miscalculated and launched into one of his patented smears of a Welch associate.

Have you no shame, Senator? asked Welch, sad and weary to the very core of his being. *At long last, have you left no sense of shame?*

Later it turned out to have been a trap—Welch had known the attack was coming—but that made the moment no less effective.

Now, I'm no Joe Welch, but I long ago mastered the tone: not so much hurt as deeply, deeply disappointed.

"That's how you argue?" I asked quietly. "By calling me *names?"*

Already a couple of other heads were starting to bob slightly. I shook my own sorrowfully, and moved in for the kill. "My God, is that *really* how you respond to someone else's ideas?"

Old Assumptions vs. New: A Handy Guide

The Media

Old me: Honorable people doing the best they can to keep the public informed. Unjustly accused by right-wingers of bias.

New me: Basically self-congratulatory narcissists looking to promote (a) number one and (b) the sort of society where people like themselves can flourish. So biased they truly don't even know it.

The Religious Right

OM: A bunch of crazed zealots out to impose their repressive, intolerant theocratic values on the rest of us. The greatest threat to our freedom.

NM: A bunch of crazed zealots who pretty much kept to themselves until "progressive" zealots started imposing *their* values on them and theirs via popular culture and the schools. The *second* greatest threat to our freedom.

Feminism

OM: A vitally important movement aimed at full equality of the sexes. Men who oppose it are insecure jerks clinging to the past; women who oppose it are mindless weaklings, brainwashed by patriarchy.

NM: A movement that, since the achievement of legal equality, has poisoned the culture by a relentless war on nature. Those who oppose it know they'll be smeared; women who do so display particular independence and character.

Multiculturalism

OM: An important social and educational movement designed to foster appreciation of the achievements of ethnic and racial minorities previously unacknowledged by a Eurocentric culture. Of special importance in promoting the self-esteem of disenfranchised youth.

NM: A movement that pretends to promote tolerance by rewriting history and otherwise debasing standards. Seeks to deny the inconvenient truth that actual self-respect can come only through rigor and genuine achievement.

Politically Correct

OM: A term used by the right to smear decent people working hard for social change. Tired and out-of-date, it is readily rejected by its targets—who's *not* against ideological overkill?

NM: Term properly describing a "progressive" worldview of litmus tests for right thinking. Hijacked by people like Bill Maher to prove they're not. Seems out-of-date only because it's now so all-pervasive, it has lost the power to shock.

Democrats

OM: The party of FDR, Truman and JFK, pressing the fight for social progress and human dignity. At its worst, the lesser of two evils.

NM: The party of Clinton, Gephardt and Gore. Morally corrupt to the core, preaches hope and decency; practices cynicism, racial and gender extortionism.

Republicans

OM: The party of Nixon and Agnew, composed of boobs, mean-spirited Neanderthals and blow-dried special-interest lackeys; indifferent to the rest of us.

NM: The party of Trent Lott and Tom DeLay, but *also* of John McCain and Ward Connerly. Composed largely of boobs/Neanderthals/lackeys, yet also a few of real character and conviction. Amazingly enough, times being what they are, often the lesser of two evils.

A Perceptive Insight

OM: "Wouldn't it be great if schools got all the funding they needed and the military had to hold bake sales?"—Bumper sticker seen on numerous Volvos.

NM: "A society that exalts virtue has 270 million policemen. A society that scorns virtue cannot have enough."—Ex-lefty Michael Novak.

A Good Person

OM: Someone who's pro-choice, against war (with the exception of WWII) and considers conservatives evil.

NM: Someone who lives his own life thoughtfully and well and refuses to accept pat answers to complex, morally challenging questions.

I came by my affection for old Joe Welch honestly—the same way I came by everything else in my early political consciousness. Via my parents.

By the time I came along, we'd pretty much become your basic fifties liberal Democratic family. Yet behind this lay a past that, throughout my youth and well into adulthood, seemed to me both thrilling and dangerous. Not that it got talked about all that often, not with Red-baiting still very much a fact of life and so many people apt to misunderstand.

Still, in the mysterious way these things happen, I grew up knowing that the American Communist Party had numbered many of the best and brightest of their generation; and that, for all the vile things said about it since, its aim had been to make America live up to its highest aspirations for itself.

I knew this because I knew my parents to be decent and idealistic to the core. If they had been Communist activists, there was nothing wrong with it.

I still feel that way; feel, at any rate, that to them it seemed a compelling and entirely rational choice, given who they were and the world in which they lived. Indeed, I at first had little trouble believing Howard Fast's claim reported in the bizarre quasi-biography *Dutch* (though, as it turned out, offered without substantiation and surely untrue) that Ronald

Reagan himself came close to joining the party back in 1938. Why not? Reagan was then a liberal Democrat, and in his way would always remain an idealist.

That is why it took me so long to fully come to grips with the sobering truth that the version of the story I grew up with was woefully incomplete; that nobly intentioned as were those drawn to communism, most were also painfully naive. For the doctrine they embraced was as evil as its vilest opponents had always claimed.

Obviously, such an observation will hardly register as big news to most. But in the circles where I ran—including, by then, mainstream journalistic ones—equating leftist doctrine with human misery was still pretty much unheard of, not because there was no truth to it (everyone knew there was) but because it gave aid and comfort to the right. As such, it was a kind of treason. "Scholarship with an agenda," as University of Virginia history professor Nelson N. Lichtenstein denounced the recent findings that document the extent to which Moscow used the American Communist movement to recruit Soviet agents; its aim is to discredit "the whole anti-racist, anti-capitalist impulse in American life."

Nonsense, replies Ronald Radosh, among the most prominent researchers and himself the child of a Communist family. "I deal with issues of historical truth. The left's inability to accept this truth is what discredits the left."

Which is to say, to leave one group and migrate toward the other, even in the privacy of my own head and heart, was as fundamental a break with my past as any yet. More than simply looking at history through different eyes, it meant rethinking the present: no longer reflexively assuming that the Sandinistas were good guys, for instance, or that in labor disputes the unions are always right.

Even more, it meant turning my back on the mythology that gives the left its emotional power—the unshakable sense of its own virtue.

Those only glancingly familiar with that mythology—peopled as it is with figures as diverse as Paul Robeson and Salvador Allende, the Hollywood Ten and Bella Abzug, Che Guevara and journalist I. F. Stone— have trouble grasping its enduring presence in people's lives. Better to cast it in religious terms. For, truly, as much as the most demanding faith, progressivism requires unquestioning acceptance of its guiding assumptions—which, to take the analogy a crucial step farther, look increasingly hollow once one begins to doubt.

The faith is passed down much like any other, moral myths at its core. Growing up on a street of large, well-tended homes in New Rochelle, my brothers and I were keenly aware of the epic battles of the thirties and forties—the union fights, the Scottsboro Boys, the desperate campaign for Republican Spain—and were inevitably fired by our own suburban passion for justice and right. We loved Stevenson because he cared about the dispossessed, and hated the Republicans because they cared only about the rich. We were Brooklyn Dodgers fans because of Jackie Robinson and hated the Yankees because they were racist and, as people used to say, rooting for them was like rooting for General Motors.

To be sure, there were occasional contradictions within our family that were tough to ignore. I remember my older brother and I getting an enormous kick out of chiding our parents for having a black maid, with whom there was no pretense of equality. Why was Mom "Mrs. Stein" while she was "Del"? Why didn't Del eat at the table with us?

A good and decent woman, my mother didn't quite know how to respond, except to say that the world wasn't perfect and that this was a very good job for a poor girl with limited education. And, anyway, Del wouldn't be comfortable eating with us.

Years later a writer friend named David Black remarked of our generation how uncannily many of the truest of the true believers of the sixties were children of either lapsed Catholics or lapsed Communists. Himself the son of a committed Trotskyite father in Springfield, Massachusetts, David (as he described it in his terrific novel *Like Father)* once used the toy printing press he got for his twelfth birthday to distribute leaflets up and down his street reading "Workers of the World Unite, You've Got Nothing to Lose but Your Chains," thus eliciting a visit from the local cops.

At college in the relative wilds of Southern California, Richard Nixon country, I used to like shocking people with the revelation that my parents were once Commies. Far from being a stigma, in the anti-Vietnam era this gave me real cachet; after all, mine was an antiestablishment lineage that ran all the way back to the *thirties*!

In fact, I was more and more interested in the particulars of that earlier time myself. I did my senior history thesis on Earl Browder, the aged former CP leader, over Christmas break, and again over Easter, lugging a heavy reel-to-reel tape recorder to the pretty little home in Princeton, New Jersey, where Browder lived with the family of one of his sons, the chairman of Princeton's math department. A year later, while at journalism school, I used that material to write a magazine profile of Browder, which one of my professors gave to his wife, an editor at *American Heritage,* and the tapes, in straight interview format, ended up being the first piece I ever got into a legitimate publication.

A few years after that, looking to launch a career as a professional writer, I came up with a book proposal for an oral history of the Communist Party of the United States of America. Its title will suggest its spirit: *Saving the World Together.*

In fact, reading it over after all these years leaves me a bit wistful, recalling as it does the thrilling sense of nobility and purpose I once felt writing of that heady time. "During its heyday in the Thirties and early Forties," ran my proposed introduction, "the Communist Party of the U.S.A. sheltered many thousands of individuals who, compared with their contemporaries, must be regarded as visionaries. They were young, most of them, but they were out to make a world in which social justice would be the norm. Many of the causes for which they worked—antifascism, trade unionism, social security, civil rights—considered radical when they espoused them, were subsequently embraced by respectable politicians and the American mainstream."

To augment the introduction, I did several brief sample chapters, interviews with former party members. One was with my mother, who at the time had recently been diagnosed with the cancer that would kill her less than a year later. I remember how she came alive during our talk, both her self-mocking humor and passionate idealism intact as she explained how to a young, poor girl of the Depression, with the headlines full of Hoovervilles and hunger strikes, "it seemed obvious the Communists were the only ones who cared about helping poor people. At the time, I wasn't old enough to join the party, so I decided to join the International Labor Defense, which defended political prisoners and which I'd been assured was a Communist front. When I got to the I.L.D. office there was a very officious man sitting at the front desk. I asked him if the I.L.D.

was a Communist organization. He looked at me and shook his head violently. 'No, no, no, of course not—whatever gave you that idea?' I told him in that case I didn't want to join, so he had to reconvince me. His attitude was, 'Well, we aren't, but we are.' That was good enough; I joined.

"The political work kept us terribly busy—much more so than school, about which we couldn't have cared less. It's a funny thing, a few years ago, when I was in Paris, I ran into someone who had been in that group. I was on vacation but he, because he was still in the movement, was there to attend a conference organized by the North Vietnamese. I asked him what he was doing for a living, this sweet man who looked so old and shabby, and he said, 'What I do during the day is unimportant, it's what I do at night that's vital.' It was so strange to hear this after so many years, but at that time, that's how we all felt.

"The people I met during that period of my life were, unquestionably, the finest, most committed people I've ever known."

I also did a chapter on a family friend who had served in Spain with the Lincoln Brigade, a sweet, modest man who'd gone on to make quite a success of himself in advertising. His story was riveting—about how at nineteen he and a small group of friends, committed Communists appalled at the totalitarian terror aimed at civilian populations, made their way to France and over the Pyrenees into the savage meat grinder that was the Spanish Civil War. How they trained with tree limbs for rifles and, armed with their ideology, were sent to a front already woefully undermanned: "In battle after battle—at Belchite, at Huesca, at Teruel— we just couldn't break through. The reason was simple; they had the weapons, not us. They had the artillery, the tanks, the trench mortars. But most important, they had the planes. Fifty, one hundred planes would appear day after day and bomb the shit out of us. The Republic had only a few Russian fighters, which we first saw infrequently and then never saw at all. This was the story of Spain. They had the planes. We had nothing to hold them off. Sometimes we lay on our backs and shot at them with our rifles, just to keep occupied, to feel we were doing something . . .

"The war dragged on. We knew we were losing. There were few highly dramatic moments, few great battles. There were just less and less and less people around you as time went by."

Such individuals were principled and courageous in ways beyond the understanding of most today; and, yes, in key respects they were right—about social justice and the monstrousness of the threat posed by Hitler. The point to be made certainly has nothing to do with innate decency or depth of conviction.

Yet, too, in the most basic sense they were so appallingly wrong that it must inevitably color all the rest.

I concluded my introduction to the proposal for the Communist book—which thankfully never saw print—with the following: "The vast majority of Americans continue to believe that the American Communist Party was nothing more than a fifth column for a sinister international conspiracy. That notion, born of ignorance and nurtured during the Cold War, is provably false."

In fact, in the end it is provably *true*. We now know, by body count alone, that Stalinism was on a murderous par with Hitlerism, as we also know the entire seventy-year Soviet experiment was a debacle, as inefficient as it was brutal. Had they succeeded, the world would have experienced a terrible siege of cruelty and darkness.

Moreover, from the Venona decryptions, five thousand pages of secret intercepts of Soviet cable traffic back in the forties, we've learned the depth of the Communist penetration into American government agencies, discovering along the way that Alger Hiss and Julius Rosenberg, far from innocent martyrs to hysterical anticommunism, were guilty, as charged, of espionage. The evidence on Ethel Rosenberg is far less conclusive.

Browder, too, was an active agent. In our interview sessions, I'd asked him about the espionage charges routinely leveled at the party; he blithely shrugged them off, and I moved on, accepting his denial as all that needed to be said on the subject.

If I should have known better, so should the true believers of the prior generation. The evidence was there, too readily dismissed as propaganda from the enemies of social justice. The Moscow show trials in the late thirties that led to the purging of hundreds of thousands were widely reported in the Western press. George Orwell, himself a disillusioned volunteer for the Republic, established the actual nature of the Soviets' role in Spain with chilling clarity in *Homage to Catalonia*.

One might expect there would now be some humility from those who got it so wrong. One would think there'd at least be a little hesitation about coming off as quite so certain the next time.

No chance. For while Joe McCarthy and the other witch hunters have rightly been creamed by history, most of those on the other side and their heirs to this day invariably fail to acknowledge the character of their mistake; indeed, into the eighties many were incensed that Ronald Reagan had the gall to refer to the Soviets as "evil."

There's a good reason for that: they don't think there's anything to explain. Even recognizing they might have sometimes been mistaken in the particulars, in their guts they still don't believe they were *wrong*. Or, more precisely, that even if they were, that any explanation is called for. After all, isn't it the nobility of intentions that really matters?

It's a great way of looking at things. It makes one right even when wrong.

That's what made the case of Elia Kazan and those protesting his honorary Oscar so revealing.

Shortly after the award was announced, a friend told me of a heated discussion the news had prompted with a fellow liberal.

Her feeling—think of it as Progressive Stance #1 (or the Warren Beatty position)—was that, odious as Kazan's "naming names" during the blacklist period had been, he was being honored not for his personal behavior but for his body of work. Moreover, adding an interesting wrinkle, to deny him such recognition would set a dangerous precedent, for it would mean that others—gays, socialists, *anyone*—could be similarly blackballed on that basis.

Her friend—PS #2, the Nick Nolte position—flatly decreed that forgiveness was out of the question, for an artist cannot be assessed independent of his public life. And, anyway, Kazan's was a special case, of particular enduring moral meaning to the film community: for not only had he devastated people's lives, he'd *never apologized.*

The odd thing, to people like me, is that they were both so terribly wrong.

My friend was wrong on the wrinkle: in fact, in cases like this, it is entirely appropriate and even necessary to make moral judgments. Would it be okay—if one were to make the leap and imagine O.J. had the skills of a Laurence Olivier—to award *him* an honorary Oscar? Or a Nazi? Should there now be a campaign to give one to Leni Riefenstahl, arguably the greatest of the pioneering documentary filmmakers?

It's not as if the left has ever hesitated to make vital distinctions. As Arthur Schlesinger, Jr., rightly pointed out as the Kazan controversy was heating up, if HUAC had been after Nazis or KKK-ers instead of lefties, the great director would today be lionized for having named names.

Yet her friend was far more wrong.

First on a technicality: the charge that Kazan's act ruined lives is itself somewhat problematic, since the names he named in his infamous appearance before the House Un-American Activities Committee were ones the committee already had. In fact, he could have named many more—including that of actor John Garfield, a fellow alumnus of the Group Theatre then under enormous pressure to admit to Communist affiliations. (Although, too, the claim has also been made that Kazan's selectivity was far from altruistic, and that he named only his enemies.)

Still, that's probably beside the point. The point is, lives *were* ruined—in business and government, in public education, at universities, in law enforcement and, as we know, in show business. By any standard, the blacklist *was* a vicious and horrifying affair, the centerpiece of a period as fundamentally undemocratic as any in our history. And, as blacklisted screenwriter Walter Bernstein put it to the *New York Times* during the Oscar controversy, what the committee was after from Kazan was not so much new information as "his name and his eminence, which was considerable."

Yet there's another, larger point. Over the years Kazan has come to be despised almost as much for what he's refused to do—offer even a Clintonesque veneer of shame or sorrow—as for the betrayal itself. Indeed, he'd repeatedly declared he was *not* sorry. "I was tired of regimentation, being told what to think and say and do," he testified to HUAC of his time in the party, a position he has stood by ever since. "I had enough of their habitual violation of the daily practices of democracy to which I was accustomed."

Kazan's testimony was unquestionably self-serving—saving his professional skin while others far more vulnerable went down on principle—and as such, may fairly be argued as showing a shocking want of character. Kazan knew perfectly well how few Communists ever engaged in anything more subversive than slapping a poster on a wall; as in the sixties, belonging to the movement mainly meant attending interminable meetings and having a lot of overheated conversations about ideology. Read the biography of Lester Cole—one of the Hollywood Ten, the first bunch of screenwriters packed off to jail for contempt of Congress—and you'll find the political act he was proudest of was sneaking into some B-movie a speech in which a character paraphrases the Spanish Republican heroine La Pasionaria to the effect that it's better to die on your feet than live on your knees.

Still, Kazan also knew it was nonsense to claim that in Hollywood the party amounted to little more than "a social club," as blacklisted writer/director Abraham Polonsky termed it during the Oscar controversy. As anyone who bothers to read *Kazan's* autobiography can tell you, his time as a Communist clearly gave him the willies. He describes in particular detail the attempts by Communist functionaries to enforce appropriate thinking in the arts, telling how those whose work failed to reflect the party line were systematically humiliated at meetings and made to recant. It happened to his friend Budd Schulberg—later responsible for the screenplay of Kazan's anti-Communist *On the Waterfront*—for the sin of having written the "bourgeois" novel *What Makes Sammy Run?* And it happened to Kazan himself, when he made the mistake of objecting to the overt politicization of the Group Theatre.

Director Edward Dmytryk—himself jailed as one of the original Hollywood Ten, only to later reverse himself and cooperate with the committee—reported having once told a comrade that he'd just read Arthur Koestler's *Darkness at Noon.* "Good God!" exclaimed the other. "Don't ever mention that to anyone . . . Koestler is corrupt—a liar. He's an ex-Communist and no member of the Party is allowed to read him."

Dmytryk also told of the party's stance on the First Amendment, as propounded by screenwriter and fellow Hollywood Ten member John Howard Lawson, known as an ideological enforcer, at the time the group was working up a common strategy for their HUAC appearances: "You believe in freedom of speech for Communists . . . because what they say is true. You do not believe in freedom of speech for fascists because what they say is a lie."

Given the concern in today's artistic circles about freedom of expression, one would have thought such harrowing accounts might have merited at least passing mention in the debate over Kazan's Oscar.

But no. For the blacklist years are today almost uniformly regarded as having been a struggle between absolute good and absolute evil, with those who fell victim to the witch hunters cast as First Amendment martyrs and those who named names seen as moral monsters. That the far more complex truth is seldom heard is evidence both of the general preference for easy answers and, hardly unrelated, the astonishing degree to which a worldview once deemed radical has migrated into the mainstream. (Indeed, had they been able to look fifty years ahead, postwar liberals would be nothing short of staggered by how many other garden-variety tenets of the Old Left have also taken root in today's progressivism: the assumption that government will cure ills rather than individual initiative; that the police and military are to be viewed with suspicion; that one's individuality matters less than one's identity as a member of a group.)

I used to tell a story about Zero Mostel when he was out of town with *A Funny Thing Happened on the Way to the Forum* prior to its New York opening. The show was in big trouble, and the producers wanted to bring in the gifted director/choreographer Jerome Robbins to put it in shape. But since Robbins had named names, Mostel, who'd been blacklisted, wouldn't hear of it. Until, finally, one afternoon at rehearsal, with the show on the verge of collapse, Mostel held up a hand for silence and strode to the front of the stage. "We of the left do not blacklist," he announced, signaling that Robbins would be permitted to come in and save their collective ass.

I used to love that story—it bespoke such wondrous *principle!*

But, of course, it's as big a crock as so much of the rest. The left blacklists all the time, reflexively and without qualm. Indeed, anyone with views to the right of, say, Richard Dreyfuss, who's looking to get started in the movies, knows damn well to keep his trap shut, lest his career gets aborted before it starts. As the *Times'* Alessandra Stanley noted a few years back, "For every outspoken conservative movie star—Arnold Schwarzenegger, Tom Selleck, Charlton Heston—there are any number of actors, writers and producers who say they dare not deviate from the liberal consensus that symbiotically binds studio executives and celebrity advocates, party-givers and deal makers." The Academy Award–nominated writer Lionel Chetwynd, an active conservative, reports he once lost a job because a producer claimed his politics meant he could not write sympathetic characters. "Nowadays," as Jay Leno smirked during the Kazan brouhaha, "you want to ruin someone's career in Hollywood, you claim they are Republican."

Some joke. I personally know of two instances—the principals will understandably remain nameless—in which writers were eased off projects when it was revealed they were contributors to conservative journals. "It is wrong," as one conservative TV producer told Stanley, explaining her insistence on anonymity, "to 'out' people." Quite simply, for many progressives, the very idea that one can be simultaneously a conservative and of moral worth is beyond comprehension.

This is simply the way it is. It hardly absolves the right of its disgraceful past to point out that disdain for democratic principles has long cut both ways.

As Eric Breindel, the late *New York Post* editorial honcho who regularly went out of his way to call liberals to account for their kinship to the discredited recent past, put it, the mindless, scattershot anti-Communist crusade that was McCarthyism was a disaster, harrowing in its methods and deeply undemocratic in its impulses. But perhaps its most damaging legacy was that it forever skewed the debate. For ever after, "it's been impossible to call a Communist a Communist without inviting charges of 'Red-baiting.' "

Breindel, by the way, was a fascinating and telling case. A product of hip New York and a graduate of Harvard and Harvard Law, he was blessed with abundant charm to go with his steel-trap mind; had he only been less adamant in his politics, he would have surely been welcomed into the fraternity with open arms. But he was also a child of Holocaust survivors and so implacably hostile to totalitarianism in every guise.

When he died in 1998 at forty-two, there was at his funeral much agonized talk from conservatives of how keenly he would be missed, and even some on the opposite end of the ideological spectrum who knew him personally seemed stunned by his passing. His old Harvard roommate, Bobby Kennedy, Jr., concluded his funny, moving eulogy with an improbable observation one sensed he'd used over the years to justify the friendship to others in his circle, and perhaps even to himself: that Breindel's warmth and deep concern for others showed that he was always "a liberal at heart."

But in "respectable" media circles, the overwhelming reaction to Breindel's passing was very different. The vast majority of journalists of my acquaintance frankly loathed the guy—and, like the jerk with whom I tangled at that dinner party, many rarely hesitated to loudly proclaim their feelings in private. Why would they, when they presume—rightly—that everyone in range is likely to agree?

This surely will no longer come as a surprise to very many. Even many fair-minded liberals have come to despise reporters for their amazing self-righteousness and flat-out partisanship. According to a recent survey by the Pew Research Center, fully 38 percent of all those polled characterized the press as "immoral," up from a mere 13 percent in 1985.

Then, again, in a poll of conservatives alone that figure would be far higher; perhaps even approaching 89 percent—the percentage of the Washington press corps, according to that other, infamous poll, that voted for Bill Clinton in 1992.

Like almost everyone else in the press, for years I basically dismissed the charge of media bias as so much right-wing claptrap. The very term "mainstream media" seemed a ludicrous oversimplification; we saw ourselves as a diverse and a highly individualistic lot, and the outlets in which our work appeared as equally distinct.

Only after my own views began to shift did the obvious hit home: forget about agreement, very few people on the networks or big-time publications even have any *respect* for conservative beliefs.

My column on the *Murphy Brown* flap was a sort of personal coming out. *TV Guide*'s editor, a tough-as-nails Murdoch Brit, would later tell me, with a smile even tighter than usual, that when she signed me she thought she'd be getting the liberal take on things—and, boy, was she ever surprised. Actually, I didn't plan to come on so strong, but the coverage of the Quayle speech was so uniformly derisive, so *unfair,* I just couldn't help myself.

Even at that, it was a reported piece, rather than straight commentary. In search of someone to quote on the subject with a maverick point of view, I'd called CBS correspondent Bernard Goldberg. At that point, I'd met the highly opinionated Goldberg just once, over lunch, but now he proved to be equally outspoken on the record. In short, he was an ideal source; i.e., one who says precisely what the reporter wants said, so that the reporter himself can hide behind a veneer of neutrality. Basically, according to Bernie—we've since become good friends—the reaction to Quayle that we saw on network TV was inevitable, since it reflected what most everyone in every newsroom believed. In that sense, he pointed out, it was incorrect to call this a conspiracy; since there was uniformity of opinion, there was no *need* to conspire.

"[W]hat bothers me the most," concluded Goldberg, "is how totally lacking we are in introspection. Why does no one ever ask 'Is it possible our critics are right?' Is it possible we sometimes do slant things?"

Yet for many who came into the business in the sixties and seventies and by now were starting to run things, those were no longer the right questions. The ideal of objectivity was fine, of course; everyone was all for that. Yet on issues of moral consequence, with so much at stake, complete neutrality was impossible. There are good guys and bad guys out there, and surely part of our job was to help people tell which was which.

Until recently, I'd certainly always thought so, with all my heart. And I'm ashamed to admit that only now, all these years later, have I come to fully grasp the consequences.

For me, that belated realization is summed up in a single, extended episode.

On President's Day, 1997, a smallish headline on the *New York Times* obituary page happened to catch my eye: "WILLIAM SCOTT, 81, CONGRESS-MAN SYMBOLIZING G.O.P. RISE IN SOUTH."

I paused, the name registered as familiar.

Midway through the first paragraph it hit me.

Of course—*Bill* Scott.

A figure out of my past life, when I underwent an instantaneous transformation from a sixties activist into—*tah dah!*—mainstream journalist. Indeed, a classic example of the sort of astonishingly easy target upon whom careers continue to be built in newsrooms throughout the land.

The obituary was not a full-scale *Times* send-off but an Associated Press wire story, seven measly column inches below the fold and no photo. One sentence pretty well summed it up: "His upset victory in 1972—over the Democratic incumbent William B. Spong Jr. with 51 percent of the vote—made him the first Republican to win a Senate seat from Virginia since Reconstruction."

I quickly scanned the rest and saw that the detail I was looking for was absent. But then I snatched up the *New York Post*, which also used the AP story but included some other material, and there it was: "In a 1974 poll conducted by *New Times* magazine, Scott was selected 'dumbest congressman' by 200 congressmen, journalists and lobbyists."

Loping downstairs to the living room, I found my then fifteen-year-old daughter, at home for the President's Day holiday, and pointed out the relevant line.

It was a moment before she remembered and placed Scott in the story I'd told at the family dinner table. Then, "They put it right in his obituary?!"

"I know."

But catching my bemused look, she cast me an unexpectedly severe one of her own. "Aren't you ashamed?"

The answer to that is so complicated, it took a while to sort out.

My link with Scott began that fall of 1972 when Scott, hard-right even by Virginia Republican standards, was running his Senate race against moderate Democrat Spong. But, in fact, it goes back to four years before, my sophomore year in college.

The school I attended, Pomona College in Claremont, California, was small and, by standards of the day, socially and politically conservative, and when I arrived in the fall of 1966 the campus was still pretty quiet. But the nightly news reports from Vietnam—not to mention those from places like Berkeley and the University of Wisconsin—quickly changed that. In February, I helped organize the first local protest against the war, a massive candlelight vigil; and by year's end, we'd moved on to open confrontation, a couple of dozen students disrupting a recruiting session in the college placement office by a man from napalm-maker Dow Chemical and escorting him off campus.

There was, to be sure, a large element of seriousness in this: we were convinced the war was horrible and were ready, when called upon, to quote a fair number of reputable sources to that effect. But it was also true that what we liked to call the *struggle* against it was a helluva lot of fun. Take the candlelight vigil. It was actually the brainchild not of any of the handful of campus activists but of a kid across the hall from me in my dorm who, until a week before, had vigorously *supported* the war. But he'd been reading about these vigils at other campuses and liked the sound of it, so he bundled a bunch of us into his car one Saturday morning for the hour trip to L.A. where we invested in a couple of thousand candles. It wasn't until a couple of days before the event, when he and I found ourselves being interviewed by a very attractive young reporter for the local *Claremont Courier,* that he seemed to actually consider what he was doing.

"I think this protest is so wonderful," she prefaced the question, flashing us a heart-stopping, older woman smile. "So when did you guys come out against the war?"

I said something like "Oh, I've had trouble with it from the beginning," and turned to my friend. His panicked look was a plea not to give him away. "Well," he replied, "actually just recently."

No matter, on our campus he was now a certified antiwar leader, and the good times were just starting. Though he, like I, missed the triumphant Dow Chemical action for an art history final, both of us were part of the group that had been granted control of the school's nearly moribund weekly paper, the *Student Life,* and we saw our job as putting it to use in the service of world peace and rollicking times.

In the wake of the Dow Chemical protest, the gentlemanly but appalled school administration issued a policy statement. The Pomona College placement office, it was asserted, is nonpolitical; recruiters for all organizations with jobs available to Pomona students are welcome to use it, and future disruptions will absolutely not be tolerated.

But our paper emphatically *was* political. Fine, we decided with all the can-do zest of Mickey and Judy staging a show, let's test that—and over the summer break, we had someone approach the Communist Party USA. Early in the fall, a letter arrived at the placement office (with a copy to us at *Student Life*) from one Albert J. Lima, identified as Chairman, Communist Party of Northern California. "We would like to interview interested students from Pomona College," wrote Mr. Lima, "for a Summer Project recruiting California Agricultural workers into the Communist Party. . . . As you may know, our organization has fraternal relations with a world movement which, in fifty years, has already been successful in leading Socialist revolutions in nations totaling over one billion people . . ."

Before the administration even had a chance to react, we'd reproduced the letter on our front page beneath the banner headline "COMMUNISTS MAY RECRUIT." Our story, dispatched to prominent alumni that very evening, dutifully noted that it was believed this would be the first time the Communists would be permitted use of placement facilities at any American college or university.

The alumni reaction came with gratifying speed, followed immediately by the statement from the college administration making clear that no way was it about to happen. Presto, we had our issue. If, as was now apparent, the administration *was* making distinctions, why shouldn't the hated military also be banned, or the despoilers of Third World peoples from the Bank of America?

As these things go, there followed weeks of debates and meetings, all aimed at the impending visit of a couple of Air Force recruiters. To disrupt or merely picket outside the building? To seek to stop this misbegotten war in its malformed tracks, even at the risk of one's own neck, or merely whine while the killing went on? For, yes, the administration had announced that any student participating in a coercive demonstration would face severe penalties, up to and including expulsion!

The threat was much on our mind that glorious morning when a couple of hundred of us squeezed into the office with the Air Force guys and the hapless student they were trying to interview—and even more so after the interviewers figuratively threw up their hands and left. From the school's perspective, this was the worst kind of publicity—I still have somewhere a picture published the next day in the *L.A. Times* showing a sullen Air Force guy with my girlfriend and me in the background—and the administration vowed swift retribution.

But it turned out there was no reason for concern. Most of the deans and other senior sorts were also against the war, and the punishment they eventually meted out was—get this—*suspended suspensions.*

I vividly remember the afternoon we got news of the verdict. There was tremendous relief, of course, but mingling with it, at least for some of us, there was also something surprisingly like . . . disappointment, the sort of psychic letdown a child feels when a parent backs down, refusing to follow through on a threatened and justly deserved punishment. In brief, the kind of weeny behavior that by adolescence invariably breeds contempt.

We were adolescents already, and contempt is precisely what we were starting to feel. And not just toward those of our elders who so clearly merited it—LBJ and his minions in Washington—but, almost as much, for those who professed to understand our rage and took us at our own self-dramatizing word. Like the asylum keepers in *The King of Hearts*, a film that millions at the time mistook for profound (and which, not incidentally, Al Gore even now lists as one of his favorite films), the grownups had abdicated responsibility and fled to the woods.

And yet, of course, many continue to recall that time as the best time in their lives, an old bit of news footage or random photograph even now instantly recalling the oversized emotions it generated: the blissful sense that everything was new and anything possible, that each day might bring a fateful encounter, even if it lasted but a single night, and, above all, that our lives had clarity and purpose. (Lynda Obst, one of my fellow antiwarriors at Pomona, would go on to produce *The Sixties,* NBC's valentine to the era.)

In fact, our powerful, enduring sense of being rooted in those years is oddly reminiscent of that of another generation of Americans almost precisely a century before: the Civil War veterans, who forever thereafter, as the Grand Army of the Republic, regularly gathered to reminisce and sing the old songs, and who, by sheer force of numbers, soon came to dominate the political landscape, imposing on society at large the lessons and values learned during those terrifying, idealistic, exhilarating formative years.

The difference is, they fought the war that ended slavery, enduring endless hardships and privations. We opposed a war, smoked a lot of dope, listened to music and got laid.

For those of us who now look back to that time as the moment when things started to go haywire, the collapse of grown-updom—played out in variations of my experience at Pomona on literally hundreds of other campuses—was even then somewhat disorienting. On some level, we knew we'd gone way too far. Furious and arrogant and self-righteous as we were, we *knew* it.

But now we also knew something else: for us there were to be no consequences.

As time went on, what this meant in day-to-day terms was that we were increasingly liberated from the pull of what were taken to be fogeyish rules. Everyone did drugs. Even those who felt uncomfortable about casual sex—mainly women—pretended otherwise. Notwithstanding all the cant about openness and truth, the very definition of honesty became a blur.

I, for example, who prior to the age of eighteen (and to the incredulity of my friends) had never stolen a thing in my life, became a shoplifter. Nothing big time—not like the guy I knew who stole appliances on order—just the occasional candy bar or *Sports Illustrated* from the local Hughes supermarket. I mean, hey, everyone did it: though I never quite figured out how, petty theft was understood to be a blow against multinationals and other agents of the war machine.

Narcissism and self-justification, the twin traits of so many of us who came of age in this period, tend to be a particularly unfortunate combination. So it's probably no wonder that now that we're cast in the role of grown-ups, we have continued to rewrite the rules to suit our tastes, and when the new rules proved inconvenient or too transparently destructive, to rewrite them again.

Thus we roundly condemned greed and materialism—except our own. And, as the statistics on divorce skyrocketed, proclaimed that divorce was often better for kids. And, a quarter century after glorying in Nixon's downfall, readily made moral distinctions and qualifications never before apparent to the naked eye on behalf of a president more to our liking. And if there is a price to be paid, lots of us are determined to go to our graves (if we have to go at all) never paying it.

But it must be said that few in our generation have so fervently embraced the new ethic as those who went into journalism. By definition less thoughtful than aggressively outer directed (our collective motto might be "My byline is out there, therefore I am"), many of us signed on to be close to the action, living vicariously through those we covered. The professed goals of the profession—invisibility and rigorous neutrality—just wasn't *us*. Like previous generations of journalists, we intended, as the much cherished phrase had it, to set down "the first rough draft of history." But we'd do it on our own terms, with ourselves often unapologetically cast as participants.

The way, in fact, we did back in Claremont. Why not? Utterly sure of our moral superiority, knowing at a glance right from wrong, wasn't it our obligation to spread the gospel?

To a greater or lesser degree, almost everyone I knew aiming for the business back then felt that way. My best friend at the time, a kid named Frank Rich I'd met years before at an artsy summer camp, was at Harvard; and, competitive as they come, he seemed deeply unhappy that season that it was the massive student rebellion at Columbia that had seized the nation's attention. When, a year or so later, they at last had riots of their own up in Cambridge, his breathless phone reports made it seem like *Ten Days That Shook the World* all over again, with him and his student journalist pals at the *Crimson* cast as—another Harvard grad!—John Reed.

Alas, it was a Columbia protester who landed a big book deal—James

Kunen, whose quirkily amusing *The Strawberry Statement* made him an object of envy and scorn to us all. In fact, a half dozen years later when I got to know Kunen, he turned out to be a thoroughly decent fellow and, as his prose reflected, far less partisan or demon-driven than most of the rest of us.

Initially, I found the *Crimson* bunch intimidating, until it became clear how deeply intimidated they were by one another: all these really smart people with egos like crystal, ever vigilant to the dictates of prevailing fashion, whether that meant everyone wore pea coats or everyone was hot for those latest darlings of the far left, the Weathermen.

On graduating from Pomona, and then Columbia University's Graduate School of Journalism—where, again, most everyone shared the same politics—I landed my first job, via Frank, in Richmond, Virginia, where he and other veterans of the *Crimson* were launching an alternative weekly.

One of the ideas behind the *Richmond Mercury* was that the six of us serving as writer/editors were to be absolute equals. Though it soon became clear that this didn't work, since some people were inclined to work a lot less hard than others, in the spirit of the day we stuck with it. Another problem that wasn't immediately evident, at least not to us, was that, aside from the couple of editors who were from Richmond and whose family fortunes were subsidizing the thing, we didn't really *fit* in the determinedly backward-looking capital of the Confederacy. God only knows what prospective advertisers made of the photos of us included in the paper's promotional literature. Though I myself made a sincere effort to be presentable, looking at the shot today I can see that my wildly tangled hair, extravagant beard and odd paisley shirt lent me a distinct resemblance to Abbie Hoffman, the amiable Yippie provocateur. Not that had I known I would have changed a thing—not to accommodate the narrow minds of this political and cultural backwater.

Nevertheless, I'd make the best of it as long as I was stuck there. The world had to be changed, and slipping effortlessly, unchallenged into the role of real-life journalists, we were the ones who'd ended up responsible for Richmond.

A piece on Bill Scott was an obvious place to start. This was the season of Nixon-McGovern—an hour and a half north, Woodward and Bernstein were still alone on the Watergate trail—and the Republican Senate nominee, a true-blue hard-right ideological conservative challenging as good a Democrat as a place like this could produce, presented us with an irresistible opportunity to cause a little stir of our own. I can't remember exactly how I landed the job of going after Scott, only that I took up the assignment with relish.

In fact, "researching" the piece proved a snap. Two years before, the *Washingtonian* magazine had run a piece alleging that no congressman in town was more loathed by his own staff—and I had simply to reinterview many of the same sources. Though mostly anonymous, these told tales of amazing penury, mean-spiritedness, bigotry, personal grossness. "His colleagues hate him," as the first unnamed source was quoted right up top. "He's irascible, uncooperative and they avoid him. He's the cheapest man in the world. That story about him making his secretary wash rusty paper clips is absolutely true. He would wash out and dry toilet paper if he could."

Of course, for purposes of deniability, the piece did strive for the requisite gloss of objectivity. Scott's campaign manager and a single ex-staffer were quoted in his defense.

But no one was kidding anyone; the article was ideological to the core. Not only would we never have run such an attack on his opponent, we'd have dismissed anyone who did as a vicious reactionary. I was frankly surprised that the local TV stations played it straight, showing our cover caricature of Scott sweeping immense volumes of dirt under a rug while going on about the story's sensational revelations. Inexperienced as I was, I'd failed to realize they were on our side.

At least one reader seemed to get it, though—the guy with the *Deliverance* twang who kept calling that first night saying I was a Commie sonovabitch and he knew where I lived and he had a gun. Fortunately, he happened to call again just as the Richmond cop I'd summoned showed up at my door and, product of the genteel Old Confederacy that he turned out to be, my stalker gave the cop his name and address and promised to leave me alone.

The intensely satisfying brouhaha the piece provoked lasted but a week, and a month after that Scott was elected.

Cut to a year or so later. By now, both Frank and I had moved on to *New Times,* a fledgling New York-based glossy aimed at the young, progressive mainstream, and one day over lunch we got to talking about the heady experience that had been Bill Scott. Since he was now doing his thing in the Senate, wasn't he ripe for more coverage? Indeed, wasn't he surely the dumbest dumbshit in the whole place?

Done! Our editor-in-chief, recently *Time*'s lead correspondent in Vietnam, quickly okayed the idea and we were off. Obviously I could not do the piece myself, so we turned to our newly hired Washington correspondent, Nina Totenberg.

Reading her effort anew after all these years, I'm reminded it was nothing short of masterful. She named Scott Washington's King of Dumb and selected nine other congressional lightweights to serve (as the accompanying illustration soon had it) as his dimwit court.

Though relying heavily on my *Mercury* piece for her Scott material, she diligently researched the rest—producing both laughs and an overall tone less scathing than sorrowful that such a collection of numskulls blithely strode the corridors of power.

Of course, Nina has gone on to grander things. The doyenne of National Public Radio, she's a regular recipient of awards from schools of journalism. Much of her celebrity is a result of the fact that, nearly two decades after the Scott piece, she played a key role in the near-scuttling of Clarence Thomas's Supreme Court nomination by bringing to the world's attention a former Thomas subordinate named Anita Hill.

In fairness, the splash made by the Scott piece was due, at least in part, to Scott himself. Irate at finding some of the same names on the masthead of *New Times* that he remembered from the *Richmond Mercury*, he called a press conference to adamantly deny the charge in this obscure little publication that he was the dumbest member of Congress.

I mean, yeah, the whole thing *was* funny.

But, in retrospect, it was also something else: stark evidence of what *we* were about—and, indeed, what the profession itself was well on its way to becoming.

All of which is to say that, heavy-handed as he was, poor Bill Scott truly was on to something back then.

My daughter, the kindest soul I know, asked the day we ran across his obit if I thought we'd ruined his life. It's certainly possible. In fact, reading through the stories almost twenty-five years after the fact, I actually found myself hoping Scott really was as thick and oblivious as we claimed, and thus so emotionally disconnected he was able to finish out his undistinguished career, retire and, as they say, move on.

In brief, the old justifications won't wash anymore. What matters is not that I wasn't necessarily all wrong about Scott—I wasn't—but that I didn't give a damn if I got it completely right; and, conscience clear, never even saw the distinction. That was, as it remains, the nature of the corruption—still evident every day on the network news and the big-time front pages; yet, given motives that feel so pure, all but invisible to its practitioners.

No, I told my daughter, *ashamed* is the wrong word. I only hoped that she and her brother would end up more thoughtful than I was back then and, when it counted, a little harder on themselves.

Later, reading the *Washington Post*'s Scott obit on the Internet, I learned a number of details about his life that gave me renewed pause: that he had been a volunteer for a variety of charities, had taught Sunday school for decades, other sympathetic stuff. And then there was this, toward the end of the story, no minor detail in the past of a man who'd ended up in public service: "Scott was born in Williamsburg, Va., one of five children of a locomotive engineer who died while saving passengers at a washed-out trestle in West Virginia. He was 8 years old when his father died."

How was it, I had to wonder, that in all my seeking after useful anecdotes about the man, I'd never heard that?

But then I realized it didn't matter: even if I had, I wouldn't have used it.

Of course, when you get started on what's happened to the press, you very quickly get to what's happened at the *New York Times,* by far the most influential paper in the country.

"News," says Joseph Lelyveld, its executive editor, in the slick little newsletter to us subscribers that showed up one morning between the Sports and Business sections, "has become a little like fast food— not very nourishing. That makes the effort to weigh the news judiciously, if that doesn't sound too pompous, and to make some deliberate judgments about what really matters, more important than ever. Our goal at the *Times*—one we try to reach seven days a week— is to give order and shape to the world and to provide our readers with an overview that's faithful to what's actually going on."

Lelyveld is reportedly an okay guy; no question he was a splendid reporter. But, boy, is that pap!

All right, let's be fair—the *New York Times* in many respects remains a great paper. Its staff numbers some of the most talented reporters and writers in journalism; it is the acknowledged pinnacle of the profession. On an average weekday, its pages contain some two or three hundred pieces, comprising tens of thousands of words on every conceivable aspect of human endeavor. For anyone who hopes to be conversant not just with national and international affairs but social trends or the arts it is an indispensable read.

And, yet, many of us who have read the paper most of our lives, including some who would never call themselves conservative, know that something has happened to the *Times* in recent years that is deeply distressing. For on the most contentious social issues of the day—multiculturalism, feminism, gay rights—today's *Times* is highly unreliable, scarcely even bothering to pretend to neutrality. Indeed, having chosen sides, the paper itself often seems as interested in reshaping society as the most committed activists.

Here's what happens: you're sitting there with your morning coffee and you've just gotten through some unexpectedly interesting piece about the emperor of Thailand or high school soccer, and turning to the next section what do you find? A review of a play headlined HOW A LESBIAN CURSE MADE A GAY BAR SUFFER. "It may take a certain attitude to love 'Burning Habits,' " writes the *Times'* critic jauntily. "A childlike glee in seeing authority figures ridiculed; a thorough distaste for sexual hypocrisy and a strong aversion to organized religion. But if you have those, you will get a major kick out of 'Burning Habits.' "

Needless to say the critic has all three, and goes on to wax ecstatic about the slice of juvenilia in question.

In fact, the *New York Times*—utterly sure of its hip, newfound values, dying to foist them on everyone else—often comes off like a smart-ass teenager, sneering at those who dare think differently as moral cretins.

Back in 1993, there appeared a short signed editorial by Brent Staples, one of the *New York Times'* most highly regarded staffers and someone real tight with management, that actually sought to ban by fiat the term so routinely used to describe the paper itself: "politically correct."

Entitled "Time to Retire a Cliché," the piece argued that "Right-wing ideologues" had succeeded in taking language once owned by the left itself and using it "to describe what they saw as a systematic effort by liberals to crush free and open discourse. But this was an imagined tyranny. . . ." And, worse, "the term is now invoked at every turn: when racial or sexual intolerance is called into question; when a political party chastens an errant member; when someone advocates expanding

the study of Western culture beyond the classics; when people encounter ideas they don't like."

I remember reading the piece and thinking, *"Wow!"* This was au-
dacious even by *Times* standards, reminiscent of nothing so much as
the heavy-handed intellectual discipline imposed back in the thirties
by the American Communist Party Cultural Commissar V. J. Jerome on
those faithful who dared think forbidden thoughts.

What was so telling is that they didn't even have the good sense to
be embarrassed.

Things started to get really bad at the newspaper of record in the early
nineties after the paper's venerable publisher, Arthur "Punch"
Sulzberger, stepped aside for his son, Arthur, Jr., known, not always af-
fectionately, as "Pinch." Under the older man, the *Times* had remained
pretty much what it had been since the turn of the century: the voice
of old-fashioned, respectable, commonsense liberalism, at once patriotic and progressive on issues like civil rights.

But under Pinch the paper was very quickly transformed into something else: a vehicle for the advancement of the kinds of social change
being championed by those, like the young publisher himself, who
imagine themselves the best and brightest of their generation.

In that regard, Pinch had all the credentials; twice, he'd even been
arrested in antiwar protests. Following the second arrest, according to
The Trust, the recent highly sympathetic history of the Sulzberger clan
by ex-*Times* reporter Alex S. Jones and his wife, Susan E. Tifft, Pinch's
father asked what the son calls " 'the dumbest question I've ever heard
in my life': 'If a young American soldier comes upon a young North
Vietnamese soldier, which one do you want to see get shot?' Arthur answered, 'I would want to see the American get shot. It's the other guy's
country.' "

The book went on to offer a shorthand version of his current mission: "He once remarked that if older white males were alienated by
his hipper version of the *Times* then 'we're doing something right.' "

Sulzberger has made good on that promise and then some. Shortly
after his tenure began, he had his top executives attend retreats to hash
out, in nightmarish, sixties-style meetings, various "issues" at the

paper; though in keeping with that spirit, it was understood going in that no meaningful dissent on the important stuff would be tolerated. Everyone already knew full well what the new man expected. "He wants more minority employees in executive positions," as a *New Yorker* profile had it at the time. "He wants more women in executive positions. He wants a less authoritarian newsroom . . . He wants each member of the staff to feel 'empowered' . . ."

He wanted, in other words, to impose a whole new level of authoritarianism while getting to sling the bullshit about opening things up: p.c. with a human face. Indeed, as then-Executive Editor Max Frankel blithely told the *New Yorker*'s Ken Auletta, he had already stopped "the hiring of non-blacks and set up an unofficial little quota system."

Pretty soon even many unalert readers were noticing that approved thinking was to be found not just on the editorial and op-ed pages, or in news analysis pieces, but could turn up *anywhere:* infiltrating the sports and entertainment sections, shaping the tone and content of news stories—indeed, often seeming to determine what was "fit to print" at all. I recall, for instance, waiting to see how the *Times* would cover the controversy touched off during the '96 primary campaign when Bernard Goldberg, angered by the sneering tone of what was supposed to be a neutral CBS report on Steve Forbes' flat-tax proposal, shot off an op-ed piece to *The Wall Street Journal* accusing his own network of over-the-top liberal bias. It was an inflammatory and obviously embarrassing charge that got huge play in every other New York paper, as well as in prestige publications around the country. But in the *New York Times,* which aggressively denies there is such a thing as liberal bias, there appeared not a word. Which of course means, as far as historians of the future are concerned, poring over the files in libraries worldwide, it might as well never have happened; as, indeed, countless other stories inimical to the *Times'* worldview or agenda get similar short shrift.

This is particularly remarkable given the intense seriousness with which the *Times* pretends to go about its news gathering mission. "An article on Aug. 5 about cooking with peaches misstated the era in which cooks in the Topkapi Palace, in what is now Istanbul, created dishes combining peaches and meat," reads a typical entry in the paper's Corrections box. "It was the Ottoman Empire, not the Byzantine."

But where's the correction about the failure to report the charge—from a credible source with nothing to gain, backed by powerful circumstantial evidence and contemporaneous corroboration from others—that the President of the United States raped her, until it was stale news; and, even then, beneath the fold on page sixteen, as a "press" story? (This from the paper that arguably gave more play than any other to Anita Hill's far less substantive charges against Clarence Thomas; and that rushed to print, on the front page, "biographer" Kitty Kelly's specious claim that Nancy Reagan had a White House affair with Frank Sinatra.)

Moreover, since as everyone knows the *Times* sets the agenda for the rest of the press, and especially for the geniuses at the networks, who scan it each morning to discover not just what's important but what to think about it, the paper's view of things tends to quickly leech into that vastly more popular medium. So despite the fact that NBC's gutsy Lisa Meyers had broken the Juanita Broaddrick story on *Dateline*, the *Times'* handling of it enabled the networks, including NBC, to painlessly pass on the rape charge in their flagship newscasts.

Not that the *Times* itself hasn't tried to compete with TV. Even many liberals have been disheartened by the paper's systematic dumbing down, the impulse to limit coverage of complex issues and, never mind the cost to its dignity, fill the paper's news pages with lighter, more accessible features. New advertiser-driven sections for the benefit of the ostentatiously news-indifferent—Food, Shopping, Home—have added physical bulk while daily making the paper more bubble-headed than ever; and not even the very bold will say aloud that, in fact, almost all these are aimed at attracting female readers.

In fact, of course, the consumerist silliness is of a piece with the political silliness, and it is no coincidence that after young Pinch took over, a number of former *Times* luminaries—notably John Corry and Hilton Kramer, both highly decorated veterans of the glory years—went on to author regular columns devoted to critiquing what this once-cherished institution has become. Although their politics had not changed, in the new, *Times*ian universe, both are readily derided as right-wing cranks.

In fact, it's almost too easy to mock today's *Times*, with its high-octane fervor to be Hip and Relevant and Compassionate and

Inclusive, never mind who gets stomped or excluded along the way. When I started on this book, I began clipping *Times* pieces on race, feminism, gay activism, all the obvious stuff, and in short order those files were ballooning.

But in fact, it's in its even less obvious and more incidental ways that the full breadth of the paper's corruption truly shows itself.

For example, there is the work of Natalie Angier, long the paper's most prominent science writer, which a galled scientist I know likened to "a slide of a single lesion that reveals the pathology of the entire organism." With amazing regularity, Angier's stuff manages to be at once gallingly cutesy-poo and politically aggressive; for Angier is one of those feminists who seems able to cast everything in those terms. Her particular forte is canvassing the animal kingdom for examples of female superiority and male inferiority, then drawing sweeping conclusions.

For instance, there was the one, dealing with a little-known ape species, headlined BONOBO SOCIETY: AMICABLE, AMOROUS AND RUN BY FEMALES: ". . . Before bonobos can be fully appreciated, however, two human prejudices must be overcome. The first is, fellows, the female bonobo is the dominant sex, though the dominance is so mild and unobnoxious that some researchers view bonobo society as a matter of 'co-dominance,' or equality between the sexes. Fancy that."

Or the one—WHEN (AND WHY) DAD HAS THE BABIES—about seahorses: "Many working mothers will attest to this: when a woman does the laundry and cooking, she gets clean clothes and food on the table. When a man does the housework, he gets a standing ovation. A good mother is a natural, a good father divine.

"And so it is that the male sea horse has long been viewed with awe, as a kind of submarine saint . . ."

Or this one—THE MALE OF THE SPECIES: WHY IS HE NEEDED?: "Women may not find this surprising, but one of the most persistent and frustrating problems in evolutionary biology is the male. Specifically, where did he come from and why doesn't he just go away?"

Once again, these are *science* reports.

Finally, Angier came out with a whole book of this stuff, excerpted on the pages of the prestigious *New York Times Magazine* (and celebrated by the lunatic feminist fringe), using such research to challenge the very notion of innate differences between males and females.

Quite simply, when it comes to any subject touching even remotely on politics, the *New York Times* just cannot be trusted. Over the years I've often agreed with the paper's longtime film critic, Janet Maslin. But when she raved about Warren Beatty's "controversial" political comedy *Bulworth,* calling it "raucously funny" and full of "both urbanity and chutzpah" and saying "a magically revitalized Warren Beatty . . . has directed his political satire with wit and energy," warning flares went up. I reached right for my *New York Post.* And sure enough, the *Post*'s man spoke of the picture's "dramatic incoherence and infantile limousine leftism" and of a protagonist who "gets misty-eyed and nostalgic for the visionary leadership of Black Panther thug Huey Newton."

Take a look at the film. You decide who had it right.

Of course, the *Times* loathes the *Post,* the feisty, irreverent and often scabrous right-wing tabloid, and especially its publisher, Rupert Murdoch, the *bête noire* of so many liberals. They are constantly going on about the crumminess of Murdoch products, how his Fox network brought a new level of crassness to TV (always conveniently failing to mention such innovative Fox shows as *The Simpsons* and *The X-Files*). So it came as no surprise that the very day the Australian reclaimed ownership of the *Post,* the *Times* hit him with a vicious editorial, saying "his purchase of The Post may save it as a daily journal, but there should be no illusions that he is a healthy influence on American journalism . . . Mr. Murdoch's greatest sins have not been those against taste. His newspaper journalism has often been, at bottom, politically and professionally dishonest. He used his papers to grind the axes of his political buddies, to promote a reflexive conservatism and to make sensationalism rather than accuracy the animating principle of the news pages."

Happily, this was meat for Murdoch's crew—particularly his late brilliant lead editorialist, Eric Breindel. "The New York Times yesterday delivered itself of a remarkably revealing editorial assault on Rupert Murdoch," replied Breindel. "The Times takes The New York Post's new chairman to task for the alleged sin of using his newspaper to advance an ideological agenda. It faults Murdoch-owned papers for indulging in 'sensationalism' and goes on to distinguish between the ostensibly unseemly practice of mass-circulation tabloids and the professional methods of 'quality' newspapers—like the Times itself.

". . . [A]n important message permeates this smug diatribe. Indeed, the Times provides a key clue to the genesis of its animosity when it decries Murdoch 'for using his papers to promote a reflexive conservatism.'

". . . Now, as it happens, Rupert Murdoch isn't 'reflexively' anything. But it is fair to say he doesn't hide his generally right-of-center ideological orientation. And he's allergic by nature to that which is deemed Politically Correct.

"Interestingly—as the Times editorial demonstrates—the liberals and leftists who dominate the American media universe can't face the fact that they themselves are likewise animated by ideological considerations. Those folks actually think that they—and the newspapers they produce—are entirely non-partisan and non-ideological.

"By their lights, conservative journalists are—*ipso facto*—ideologues; liberal editors and writers, on the other hand, believe that they, somehow, manage to check their ideological baggage at the door and carry out their journalistic duties in an entirely apolitical fashion. Unless, of course, they happen to write or edit editorials and columns.

"Americans are expected to accept this fantasy at face value . . ."

Over the years that followed, the *Post* has never missed an opportunity to tweak the *Times*, taking particular relish in the charges of racism leveled at the paper a few years back by some of its own black employees.

Personally, for a time there, I got a little bummed out reading the new *New York Times* and wanted to drop our subscription. But Priscilla objected; she had just started a lighthearted column on the Internet critiquing the media and needed the *Times* to make fun of.

Of course, in the end, she and the *Post* have it right. The most rational response to a typical *Times*ian parody of fairness and clear thought is honest derision. Sometimes they go so over the top, it's impossible not to suspect that on some level even they know it.

Just the other day, there was a classic, jaw-dropping *Times* headline. This one was about a newly released set of Justice Department statistics that over at the paper of record apparently had them totally flummoxed:

PRISON POPULATION GROWING
ALTHOUGH CRIME RATE DROPS

Now, c'mon, guys, think about it, there's a connection there. Think about it *real hard.*

In addition to making life a lot easier for researchers, the Internet tool known as Nexis—which enables the user to isolate key words—has made the claim of objectivity at places like the *New York Times* far harder to defend.

Like the Independent Counsel statute, basically invented by liberals to ensnare those on the right, Nexis has lately been put to what must seem, for journalists claiming neutrality, unsettling uses.

Nexis can reveal even some of the subtler ways the news is slanted. In early 1999, for instance, a guy named Dan Seligman, writing in the *Post,* went back and Nexised the *New York Times* for 1998 and discovered:

- The term "mean-spirited" appeared in the *Times* 102 times—almost always affixed to conservatives and not once to a liberal.
- Twenty stories referred to "right-wing Republicans," just two to "left-wing Democrats."
- The term "advocate" turned up 165 times, invariably to describe highly principled individuals fighting the good fight. There were gay-rights advocates (twenty-nine articles), homeless advocates (thirty-three), privacy advocates (forty-five), etc. There were no "advocates" for race and gender neutral admissions policies, or

"advocates for the unborn" or advocates for any other conservative cause.

Having some time before spotted a remarkable clip on ESPN I decided to run a Nexis search of my own. The clip showed Ted Kennedy making a speech at the height of 1998's home run frenzy, lauding the heroics of *Mike* McGwire and Sammy *Shoosher*. Maybe it wasn't the biggest story in the world, but it was damn revealing. Talk about being out of touch: it was like a pol in 1927 going on about the exploits of Babe *Roth*.

The object: seeing how many papers reported that blunder versus the number that covered Dan Quayle's equally innocuous but now-legendary misspelling of "potato" back in 1992.

Obviously, by definition, such a comparison is somewhat inexact. On the one hand, you have a dimwitted wealthy conservative trying to prove he's a regular guy by falsely claiming to know the spelling of a common vegetable; on the other, you have a dimwitted wealthy liberal icon, the scion of the country's greatest political dynasty, trying to prove he's a regular guy by falsely claiming to know something about baseball.

The results:—1,716 references to Quayle and 37 references to Kennedy—most of those discreetly tucked away in *People* round-ups. The Kennedy gaffe did not appear at all in either the *New York Times* or the *Washington Post*.

□

You should know—if only as a measure of some progressives' grasp on reality—that when I began this book my editor thought it had a shot at getting great reviews.

I was obliged to inform her that was not about to happen.

To be precise, I said if we were extremely, *extremely* lucky, it would not get reviewed at all—at least not in the sorts of places publishers generally wish for.

If it did, this is what an ad for it might look like:

- "A mishmash of bitterness, ideological gibberish and frenzied self-justification."—*New York Times*
- "Stein proves himself at once a bully and an intellectual weakling. His section on the world's greatest newspaper is especially laughable."—*New York Times Book Review*
- "Belongs on Jesse Helms' bedside table, not yours!"—*Washington Post Book World*
- "If the aim of this polemic was to offend, that is the only ground on which it succeeds."—*L.A. Times*
- "One can see what Stein was up to here. But . . . it's hard to come off as likable or witty if your target is the poor and the disadvantaged."—*Publishers Weekly*

- "When St. Martin's shredded the book on George Bush, Delacorte should have taken the hint."—*Kirkus Reviews*
- "One of those books you don't even have to read to know you hate."—*San Francisco Chronicle*
- "On the wrong side of the sixties—the *1860s*."—*Rolling Stone*
- "And he has the gall to call the Clintons corrupt!"—Eleanor Clift, *Newsweek*
- "Original, thought-provoking, a real page-turner! Should be read by every true American."—*New York Post*

━━━━━━━━

❑

Alas, Nexis covers only print—so it's a lot harder to keep tabs on the networks.

Then, again, we already know more than enough about them, don't we? And just in case, there's the Web site of Brent Bozell's "Accuracy in Media"—the right-wing counterpart of the leftist "Fairness and Accuracy in Media"—to do the job for us.

Which happily gives us material for a quick . . .

POP QUIZ: CHOOSE THE MOST BIASED NETWORK ANCHOR

Match the anchor with the words he regrets saying in public.

A) Dan Rather   B) Peter Jennings   C) Tom Brokaw

1. "Some thoughts on those angry voters. Ask parents of any two-year-old and they can tell you about those temper tantrums: the stomping feet, the rolling eyes, the screaming. It's clear that the anger controls the child and not the other way around. It's the job of the parent to teach the child to control the anger and channel it in a positive way. Imagine a nation full of uncontrolled two-year-old rage. The voters had a temper tantrum

last week. . . . Parenting and governing don't have to be dirty words: the nation can't be run by an angry two-year-old."—November 14, 1994, on the massive Republican gains in the recent elections.

2. "Do you think this is a party that is dominated by men and this convention is dominated by men as well . . . ? Do you think before tonight they thought very much about what happens in America with rape?"—August 13, 1996, to a rape victim who's just appeared before the Republican National Convention.

3. "If we could be one hundredth as great as you and Hillary Rodham Clinton have been in the White House, we'd take it right now and walk away winners . . . Thank you very much and tell Mrs. Clinton we respect her and we're pulling for her."—May 27, 1993.

Answers:

1—B

2—C

3—A, speaking via satellite to President Clinton about Rather's new on-air partnership with Connie Chung. Note: Rather wins on (lack of) principle. According to published reports, he went on to savage Chung both in-house and in off-the-record leaks to friends in the press, and she was eventually dropped from the broadcast.

The conscientious *Times* reader, if forced to choose, would probably say that among the subjects that have so galvanized those at the newspaper in recent years, the one to which they bring the greatest passion is gay rights. A quick search of the *Times* via Nexis reveals more than five hundred articles including the words "homophobe," "homophobic" or "homophobia" since 1995. None of these mentions has been positive. In the *Times'* roster of things no self-respecting soul wishes to be called, "homophobic" may well have eclipsed even "racist."

What is remarkable is how quickly such an attitude has taken hold. Less than a decade ago, gay activists regarded the media itself as deeply homophobic, with the *New York Times* considered especially backward; as recently as 1992 the paper of record was still resisting demands that it use the word "gay" in print, clinging to the more unwieldy and unproud "homosexual." Throughout the country, gay reporters— when they risked coming out at all—invariably felt isolated in their newsrooms.

A number of them told me so—most off the record—when I was researching a piece on mainstream coverage of gay-related issues for the *Columbia Journalism Review* in 1991. The story was the result of a long conversation with a gay reporter I met while covering the William

Kennedy Smith trial in Florida. It focused largely on the coverage of an explosion aboard the USS *Iowa*, which the Navy quickly (and erroneously, as it turned out) blamed on a gay sailor named Clayton Hartwig, among the forty-seven who died in the blast. The claim, enthusiastically picked up by a number of news outlets, was that Hartwig had engaged in an act of suicidal sabotage prompted by a romance with a fellow seaman gone bad.

My piece was especially hard on NBC, the network that had trumpeted the bogus report with the greatest fervor. Odd as it sounds now, at the time the possibility of systematic antigay press bias was not something many in the business much thought about—certainly the *Journalism Review* had never run such a piece before—and to my disgust, this one was shelved. As best I could gather, it was deemed insufficiently balanced; i.e., too overtly *pro*-gay.

The fact is, more than twenty years after the Stonewall uprising that launched the modern gay rights movement, many straight reporters did not even know much about homosexuality—and most of those who did sometimes pretended not to. In 1974, for instance, when Morley Safer profiled Rudolf Nureyev on *60 Minutes*, the urbane correspondent actually asked the dancer, "Do you regret that you haven't gotten married and had children and raised small Nureyevs?" Twenty years later, after Nureyev died of AIDS, Safer conceded he knew Nureyev was gay but, "shallow as it is to say," asked the question anyhow.

Which only goes to show how much more sophisticated Safer was than me; when I interviewed Nureyev three years later, while working in Paris, I asked him the very same thing in total innocence.

In fact, my colossal ignorance was surely closer to the norm. It's not that I had never known any gay people before that. There was, for starters, a friend of my parents who wrote for the *Howdy Doody* show; one of the uncle figures in my very young life, he owned a pet monkey and a house in Fire Island and was more full of mischief and fun than any other grown-up I knew. Not that I realized at the time he was gay, any more than I knew it about the couple of friends in college who never seemed to date; or even, after I'd started working as a journalist, about some of my colleagues.

I simply assumed everyone was straight.

Right, I know, from the perspective of here and now that sounds unbelievably naive, *dumb* even. But that's how it was.

And what little I did know from personal experience was, frankly, pretty upsetting. My mother once told me, when we were talking of her own long-ago girlhood, how hard it is for any man to understand what all young girls eventually learn, too often the hard way: that they must always be on guard against predatory men. (And, indeed, a fair number of women have told me since of harrowing episodes they had in their teens or even earlier with conscienceless older men.) What I didn't tell my mother was I understood exactly. My own brush with a creepy character occurred—where else?—in a restaurant men's room. I was just sixteen, and wearing a brand-new suit to go to the theater, when the guy approached me and, pretending to admire the suit, put his hand on my crotch.

"Doesn't that feel good?" he whispered.

"No!" I said, and bolted.

I wouldn't say the experience traumatized me, but I damn well remembered it—and years later still found it too humiliating to tell my mother.

(Not incidentally, this goes directly to why casting the issue of gay scoutmasters solely as a civil rights question strikes me as so amazingly disingenuous. The argument might rage over whether more pedophiles are straight or gay—but in the end, that's almost beside the point. We're talking sexuality here, not skin color. Would we even think of putting a straight man in charge of supervising overnights for a Girl Scout troop?)

But above all, back then, to lots of us, homosexuality was . . . unfathomable. I mean, why would anyone in his right mind want this—yccch!—when they could have *that?*

There's a terrific story in *Easy Riders, Raging Bulls*, Peter Biskind's book on Hollywood in the sixties and seventies, about Warren Beatty reading the first draft of *Bonnie and Clyde* and discovering the character of Clyde Barrow was written as gay. "Let me tell you one thing right now," raged Hollywood's premier liberal, the future creator of *Reds* and *Bulworth*, "*I ain't gonna play no fag!*"

This is not to accuse Beatty of malice or, heaven forbid, bigotry; just of being a typical guy, circa 1968. It's simply how things were.

Until the vast attention accorded the subject in the past decade, that's probably pretty much how most straight people saw homosexuality: as a strange and disquieting and (in the hands of people like Mel Brooks) laughable thing that fortunately had little to do with their lives.

As my plain-spoken, Arkansas-born father-in-law recently put it, "the first seventy years of my life I never heard anything about homosexuals, the last ten it's all I hear about."

□

In early 1988, I was asked by *Playboy,* seeking a prominent and forceful gay man to describe the terrible toll AIDS was taking on the gay world, to interview the playwright Harvey Fierstein.

It is a measure of where we were at the time that Fierstein was still considered on the political fringe. Barely a year earlier, he'd stirred up a sensation at the Tony Awards by—get this—paying tribute to his lover on national TV. Even some in the theater world thought he'd gone too far.

Fierstein turned out to be everything the magazine had hoped, by turns passionate and laughing-out-loud funny, opinionated on every subject, adamant on most. Though between that bizarre foghorn voice and his flair for the dramatic he seemed a largely constructed personality, he made my job a snap. One of the things he was angriest about was what he took to be the hypocrisy of the straight world, very much including those who saw themselves as sympathetic to gays. "They'll shake our hands," he noted at one point, "they'll march with us, they'll go for gay civil rights, they'll talk about housing and employment and all that, but *don't have sex.* Don't put that thing in your mouth. *Please,* don't put that thing in your mouth."

The phrasing aside, it was a cry from the heart. For, of course, he was right: most straight people are intensely uncomfortable with the particulars of gay male sex. And in his view there could never be full acceptance of homosexuals until gay sexuality, in all its manifold variations, was everywhere seen as unremarkable and routine and, indeed, as normal as the straight kind.

And it seemed clear that wasn't about to happen.

Who could have guessed how remarkably AIDS would end up altering the climate?

For even as the horrific disease decimated the gay community, killing tens of thousands in their prime and causing grief beyond measure, it would change the very nature of the discussion.

Overall, that remains a positive thing. For in forcing the straight world to acknowledge the size and diversity of the gay population in its midst, coverage of the plague began humanizing gay people to an unprecedented degree. Cautious at first, television finally took up the story with immense, self-congratulatory passion, in original movies, nonfiction reports and, above all, on talk shows. Hollywood waited longer, but *Philadelphia* ended the taboo and led to a string of sentimental comedies (*In and Out, The Birdcage*) about average Americans faced with the revelation a colleague or loved one is gay and having to look into their souls; and a bunch more (*My Best Friend's Wedding, The Object of My Affection*) in which the gay guy is the wise-cracking yet knowing sidekick of the girl having trouble getting the hunky guy on her own.

Which is to say, generally speaking, American society made the adjustment with remarkable ease. The message ordinary people got was the essential one: gay people are everywhere, and very few of them actually look like Liberace. Mostly they lead quite ordinary lives—some even vote Republican—and their sexual orientation has no more to do with the quality of their hearts than their hair color.

Yet at the same time, as many gays themselves scornfully observe, the movies and TV shows and magazines have presented a carefully sanitized version of gay life. For gay sex remains so problematic for most straights that even the G-rated version is usually verboten in popular media. "The gay issue in our show is a nonissue," sums up Eric McCormack, the actor who plays the gay leading man on *Will & Grace*. "We're trying to show America that gay can be a flavor in people's lives the same way as anything else."

That the flavor is vanilla is inevitable; and perhaps, given the intentions, even honorable.

But it is far less than honest—as even McCormack conceded, as soon he began pressing for, at least, a chaste man-to-man kiss in the show's second season. Yet it is, alas, emblematic of a far more insidious dishonesty that has run through the entire debate on the impact of the gay revolution on day-to-day American life.

"I'm so tired of intolerance," said my friend Laura one recent afternoon over lunch. "I'm just so sick of all the people who hate gays."

Since this was on the heels of Trent Lott's observation that homosexuality is an illness akin to alcoholism or kleptomania, I knew what she meant. Barney Frank may be loathsome in many respects, but his response to Dick Armey's "inadvertently" referring to him as Barney Fag couldn't have been more on the money: "No one has ever accidentally called my mother 'Mrs. Fag.' "

Laura was right. We've seen more than enough mean-spirited ugliness bubbling up from the minds of those who, probably without even knowing any gay people, reduce them to caricature.

But you know what I'm just as sick of? Those on *both* sides of the divide who refuse to deal with difficult truths, trading instead in slogans and mind-numbing simplicities.

Reading back over the Fierstein interview now, I find there was only one point on which I felt obliged to challenge him: his insistence that straights were as much at risk of AIDS as gays. Already there was significant research to the contrary. Among the material I'd brought to our sessions were studies showing that only 2 percent of AIDS cases in this country involved heterosexuals not associated with high-risk groups and that there was little evidence suggesting an imminent breakout of the plague into the non-IV drug-using heterosexual community.

Fierstein adamantly disagreed, claiming the data on straight AIDS had been significantly underreported and that ordinary Middle American high school kids were in every bit as much jeopardy as gay men in San Francisco; indeed, more so, since the ignorance about the disease among straights was so pervasive. "I worry about the girl who gets sent on her sixteenth birthday to a ski lodge and meets a boy and is too embarrassed to ask him to use a condom," he said passionately. "So she gets over the trauma of 'Oh, my God, I had sex,' and goes home and goes to school and all that, graduates from college and gets married, and then she has a baby, and all of a sudden, she's positive and she's dying. She has AIDS."

I don't doubt that Fierstein believed every word of it. After all, having initially been thought of and even called "the gay disease" (indeed, stigmatized by the pitiless right fringe as "God's revenge against gays"), such a view of AIDS had by now become the mainstream one.

Yet, obviously, it also served useful ends. As Randy Shilts, the prescient *San Francisco Chronicle* reporter who would himself succumb to the disease, observed of the early days of the epidemic, "There was profound frustration among AIDS activists and among AIDS researchers that the only time the media seemed to pay any attention to AIDS, the only time the government seemed to do anything about AIDS, was when it appeared that it would affect heterosexuals."

Whether by happenstance or design—or, for some AIDS activists, a harrowing yet fortunate convergence of the two—the old perception was soon gone. Spurred by such hugely publicized cases as Ryan White, the likable hemophiliac teen from Indiana; tennis star Arthur Ashe and Hollywood wife Elizabeth Glazer, who got bad blood during operations; and Alison Gertz, the unfortunate New York teen who contracted the disease during a single heterosexual one-night stand; as well as by the heart-rending shots of stricken newborns in pediatric AIDS wards, the media took up the cry that no one was invulnerable. Indeed, Oprah herself was warning that by 1990 twenty percent of heterosexual Americans would be dead of AIDS.

Nor did the idea strike very many as the least bit implausible. After all, wasn't the epidemic ravaging heterosexual populations in Africa— as in fact, it has continued to nearly unabated ever since—with consequences awful almost beyond comprehension? Nearly 15 million dead before the turn of the millennium, in some countries one in four adults infected.

Yet already some epidemiologists and other neutral observers were concluding nothing of the kind could happen here. These focused on key distinctions between the African situation and that in the developed world: differences in culture, sexual practices and, above all, health and hygiene. In Central Africa, blood supplies were badly tainted and open sores on the genitalia greatly facilitated the spread of heterosexual AIDS; in some areas, female genital mutilation was common. NPR's Laurie Garrett, reporting in 1987 from a Tanzanian village near Lake Victoria, described a local culture where the "level of heterosexual activity . . . may approach those seen among homosexuals in San Francisco before the AIDS epidemic." In his heralded history of the epidemic, *And the Band Played On,* Shilts wrote of Central African clinics that lacked "such basics as sterile rubber gloves and disposable needles. You just used needles over and over again until they wore out; once gloves had worn through, you risked dipping your hands in your patient's blood because that was what needed to be done."

In 1987, an AIDS analyst with the federal government named Michael Fumento published a book, based on the emerging data and the analysis of experts in the field, laying out the case for what he called *The Myth of Heterosexual AIDS.*

Even he did not not claim at that juncture that his case was conclusive, and Harvey Fierstein, among others, certainly had every right to aggressively challenge its conclusions. But the fact is, his arguments never even got a fair hearing. Fumento himself reports that, for all the controversy briefly generated by the publication of his book, it was all but impossible to find. "A group of 30 physicians in the states of Washington and Oregon realized they couldn't find a single store in either state that carried the book," as he writes in *Heterodoxy.* "They reported this to a Seattle, Washington, TV station, KING, which in a televised report noted that it had contacted 80 different stores, also without finding the book. Indeed, only one store had ever carried the book; it sold out quickly and the store didn't reorder until after KING contacted them. One university in Seattle claimed to have over 350,000 titles, including every single AIDS title in print. Except one."

The fact is, Fumento and his book had been vilified by the burgeoning community of AIDS activists. Typical were the comments of *Outweek* editor Michaelangelo Signorile, who publicly dismissed him as a "baboon, racist, homophobe."

For by then to even question the truism that "AIDS does not discriminate" was akin to moral sacrilege.

"Hyping the anxiety of the general population was a calculated policy of the AIDS establishment—a political move necessary to garner support and get people to take the disease seriously," as Willard Gaylin, the respected head of the Hastings Institute, specializing in biomedical ethics, would later observe. "The problem with that position is that you pay a price when you compromise the facts, even for a good end."

In brief, for all its success from a public relations perspective, the universalizing of AIDS also constituted an assault on open and honest debate—and that, too, has had repercussions, both in the gay community and beyond.

What it meant, and to a remarkable extent still means, is that it became virtually forbidden to focus on the link between AIDS and *behavior*. Yet all the while, the evidence only continued to mount that behavior was precisely what cried out to be addressed; and less straight behavior than that of the population groups most grievously affected. "I want to say this again," as Larry Kramer, founder of the radical AIDS activist group ACT UP belatedly observed in 1997, "we have made sex the cornerstone of gay liberation and gay culture and it has killed us . . . We knew we were playing with fire, and we continued to play with fire, and the fire consumed monstrous large numbers of us and singed the rest of us, all of us, whether we notice our burn marks or not. And still we play with fire."

Historically, there are serious ways that serious people have battled such scourges. None of them is pleasant; some, in a democracy, border on the indecent. I remember being struck, reading a biography of Paul Revere to the kids, that when one of the Revere children got smallpox, the entire family was confined at home for the duration, in what was known as a "pest house." And, in fact, that is precisely how the spread of AIDS was effectively controlled in Castro's Cuba, by isolating everyone who was HIV-positive in rural outposts that were, in essence, medical prisons.

It is chilling, unthinkable in a society like ours. But neither ought the concern for human rights and dignity entail the refusal to acknowledge unpalatable facts.

Indeed, in a rational world the willful blindness surrounding the public conversation on AIDS would have been recognized for the lunacy it was. *This was a desperate crisis, finite resources were being squandered feeding people misinformation.* Yet in the world as it was evolving, with all the incessant talk of compassion and caring, it went eerily unchallenged.

By 1992, it was apparent to most serious researchers that the disease was not, in fact, about to break out into the mainstream. In February of that year, the National Research Council, part of the National Academy of Sciences, issued findings that, reported the *New York Times:* "The AIDS epidemic will have little impact on the lives of most Americans or the way society functions . . . In a study made public today, the Council said AIDS was concentrated among homosexuals, drug users, the poor and the undereducated . . ."

But even this had virtually no effect. The media-fed public perception was a speeding freight train. A full year later, newly installed HHS Secretary Donna Shalala was telling Congress that we might not have "any Americans left unless we're prepared to confront the crisis of AIDS." And *Times* op-ed columnist Anna Quindlen, reporting on a memorial of a friend and fellow reporter who'd died of the disease, was ominously warning readers "one day soon you too will find yourself in the shadow of the plague . . . One day soon it will grip someone you know and love. Here is the real domino theory: Gay man to gay man, bisexual man to straight woman, addict mother to newborn baby, they all fall down and someday it will come to you . . ."

That same year, 1993, I was writing a column for *TV Guide* and one afternoon happened to catch a *Donahue* show featuring as a guest a middle-aged woman with AIDS. At one point, a woman in the audience asked her how she got it. Her reply, that that doesn't matter, that it only leads to "blame," brought a hearty round of audience applause.

Come again? When it came right down to it, that was about the only question that *did* matter.

Taking as my hook a forthcoming HBO documentary that followed a gay physician as he wastes away from AIDS, my next column was on TV's handling of the disease. Along the way, I cited the exchange on the *Donahue* show, and closed the piece with the observation of an AIDS researcher I knew: "By and large, people who are responsible will not get AIDS. That's something I wish I could say to women about breast cancer."

I expected plenty of hostile mail and was not disappointed. The reaction to the piece filled an entire week's letters section in the magazine. Much more was forwarded to me at home, a fair percentage of it irate; the phrase "blame the victim" must have shown up twenty times. Still, to my surprise, the majority of the mail turned out to be favorable. Some of this, maybe 10 percent, was from bigots—but most was serious and thoughtful. Many, many people—including a couple of anonymous souls in Hollywood—thanked me for saying what they themselves had been thinking a long time. As someone identifying himself as a medical writer and editor wisely pointed out, "we have the knowledge to stop the spread of HIV infection; what's lacking is the social/political leadership."

Then, weighing in from the blue, came my old buddy Harvey Fierstein. I didn't hear from Fierstein personally—he called my editor, who reported that Harvey shrieked at him for ten minutes, concluding the diatribe with an elitist insult: *Shit, it's only* TV Guide, *no one will see it anyway.* When my friend pointed out the magazine's circulation was close to twenty million, Fierstein soon came back at him with a letter intended for publication refuting the column. According to my friend, if a page of type could froth, this one was doing it. It even included an attack on the photo that had accompanied my column, a still from the HBO documentary that showed the dying doctor with his dog. Fierstein evidently took it to be a shot of me with *my* dog, leading my smug, callous, middle-class, pet-filled, suburban straight life.

The screed was rejected, but Fierstein was allowed instead to do a short piece for the magazine flogging the upcoming HBO AIDS film *And the Band Played On.* Along the way, he got in a few, milder licks but his main point, again, was insisting that "arguably the most harmful lie of our generation is that gay equals AIDS" and to wonder how "myths, lies and disinformation could be accepted as common knowledge."

At least we agreed about something.

By then, of course, I was long past the illusion that there could be rational conversation on such a subject with so committed a partisan. That by 1997 the National Institutes of Health budget was allocating seventy thousand dollars for each AIDS death as compared to five thousand dollars for each cancer death and less than two thousand dollars per death by heart disease was not enough; for AIDS activists, *nothing* could ever be enough. Theirs was the rhetoric of pain and anger, not reason; and what they demanded was attention not only to the horrific disease and the needs of its victims but to the underlying bias against gays, which, so the thinking goes, is itself responsible for the scourge in the first place.

From this unhappy precedent, the character of other public discussions on contentious issues involving gays has followed. Take gay marriage, so routinely reduced by gay rights activists to a simple matter of tolerance versus bigotry. Key questions never even get asked, starting with: What, precisely, is straight society being *asked* to tolerate?

I, for one, am pro any committed, long-term relationship, and some of the gay couples I know are better married than many of the straight. Indeed, as Andrew Sullivan, among today's leading gay intellectuals, observes, such unions take on a whole new level of meaning in the gay world since "love is a firewall" against "the culture of promiscuity," which (something else rarely reported in places like the *New York Times*) continues to run rampant.

Still: will married gay men conform to traditional heterosexual norms—in place largely for the well-being of children—or over the long term must it be straight society that does the adjusting?

Ironically, it is in the gay press far more than the straight that such complexities are acknowledged, with fierce ongoing debates about the desirability and even the feasibility of monogamy. Sullivan himself is among those honest enough to assert that, given the realities of gay life and gay nature, in his view the very character of the institution must be changed.

These are not small matters. We are talking about overturning several millennia of behavior and moral tradition. Serious people ought to be embarrassed to dismiss such concerns with the witch hunt cry "homophobia." The bottom line is, lots of us out here don't want the Harvey Fiersteins of the world imposing *their* version of normalcy on us any more than they want Pat Robertson imposing his on them.

To be sure, there is little reason to believe the angriest gay activists reflect the thinking of the vast majority of gays, plenty of reason to think otherwise. Yet by now that hardly seems to matter. Since the dawn of the AIDS crisis, self-righteous militancy has been the public face of the movement, and it is those views that largely frame the argument in the media.

Incivility and name-calling are so much the norm that they no longer even generate notice, let alone reprimand. As Lott feels free to spout his brand of idiocy, so do activists rarely hesitate to point the bloody finger of accusation. Just recently, there was a story on how some Barnes & Noble outlets in smaller (i.e., more rural and conservative) markets had pulled from their shelves an issue of *POZ*, described as "an AIDS awareness magazine," because its cover featured the promise of a "Free Back to School Condom Inside." In response, *POZ*'s editor felt free to rage about a chain that's carried his obscure little publication since 1994: "They are guilty by their complicity in the spread of AIDS."

The single most startling of such claims I've run across lately may have been the one made by that other notable gay playwright, *Angels in America* author Tony Kushner, who after the brutal killing of Matthew Shepherd by sociopaths in Wyoming wrote in *The Nation* that Pope John Paul "endorses murder" of gays, that the Pope and Orthodox rabbis are "homicidal liars" and that the Republican Party "endorses the ritual slaughter of homosexuals."

Notes the columnist John Leo: "Kushner has a big story here that the media apparently have missed."

But, of course, in the end it's deadly serious. For the way the public discussion of this life-and-death issue has evolved, truth and accountability scarcely register even as afterthoughts. Certain of their claim to the moral high ground, the ideologues dismiss all disagreement, no matter how principled or fair-minded, as bigotry.

I have no doubt that Fierstein, who has lost countless friends and intimates to AIDS, will find it loathsome that I dare discuss any of this on these pages, making the points I do.

But we all speak from our own experience. And these guys should know it better than anyone; it's the very essence of their movement. No one should ever be cowed into silence.

—

In contrast to the surly incivility so common among today's activists—
and still sticking here with gay playwrights—there was Tennessee
Williams.

Indeed, Williams' legendary absence of malice is equally evident in
his work, and has much to do with why it endures. For though in his best
plays he clearly tapped into the profound sense of isolation that came
with being a homosexual in a very different America, they are not rage-
filled; and, for that matter, far from specifically gay. It is likely no playwright in this century, male or female, struck such universal emotional
chords, and surely none invented so many powerful and emotionally persuasive women.

I know about Williams' kindness firsthand. Around twenty years ago,
I was doing a column for *Esquire* called "A Day in the Life." It was exactly what you'd expect; each month I'd interview some notable describing his or her routine, and edit the text into a seamless whole, so it read
as if the notable were addressing the reader directly. That was the
theory, anyway—sometimes it worked a whole lot better than others. The
beauty part for me was that I'd get to meet just about anyone I chose, and
travel to wherever they happened to be.

Tennessee Williams was a natural—America's greatest living

playwright *and* Key West. Once I'd tracked him down via his agent, I was surprised and gratified at how readily he agreed to see me.

I shouldn't have been. He proved to be one of the most gracious people I've ever met. We spent most of the afternoon in his tidy little home on Duncan Street, in an unprepossessing middle-class neighborhood, talking intermittently nearly till dark.

The conversation was only intermittent because Williams by then was not in good shape. Cooperative and obviously eager to please as he was, I quickly began to feel my visit was a strain. I suppose he might have been at least a little drugged; he definitely had a couple of stiff drinks. He kept on his shades throughout, even in the semidarkness of his living room. Sometimes his conversation was vibrant and hugely interesting. "People, I think, enjoy seeing me portrayed as a tragic figure," he wryly noted at one point, referring to the news coverage of his recent "mugging" in downtown Key West. "Well, baby, let me tell you that what happened to me hardly qualifies as a mugging . . . It didn't even accelerate my heartbeat." At another, speaking of old films on TV, he observed, "As a young man, I was a great devotee of the movies, like Tom in *The Glass Managerie,* a leader of that vicarious kind of life. The principal difference between he and I is stamina."

But at other times his answers were little more than monosyllables, and a fair number of his sentences simply trailed off. Still, his patience was infinite; he might have let me stay with him till midnight. But when he turned on Walter Cronkite—"among the most sacred parts of my daily ritual, my lifeline to the outside world"—I watched with him a few minutes, then thanked him and said good-bye.

Unquestionably, it was the most difficult editing job I'd had in the series to date, piecing together the whole sentences and the fragments, putting them in order and looking for transitions so that it read as a coherent whole. But in the end, I thought it worked pretty well.

So I was stunned when, a couple of issues later, the acerbic John Simon, who did a "Language" column for the magazine, seized upon the grammatical error—"the difference between *he and I* is stamina . . ."—that in print had come from Williams' mouth, eviscerating the playwright for a word crime "of unsurpassable grossness." More than that, he used the occasion to go on at vicious length about Williams' loss of talent. "I would like to think, in fact, that the author of *The Glass Managerie* and

A *Streetcar Named Desire* could not have uttered that abomination, but even from the heartbreaking old square who concocted *Vieux Carre* and *A Lovely Sunday for Creve Coeur*, I would have expected better."

Simon, whom I did not know well, claimed in the piece that he'd checked with me and I'd assured him Williams really did use those words. I remembered no such conversation, certainly not one that implied he might write something about it; I suppose it's possible we might have exchanged a passing word about it at an *Esquire* function. But I doubt even that, for the simple reason that I was quite sure Williams did *not* say it—I'd stuck it in to salvage a stray, out-of-context remark he'd made comparing Tom's stamina to his own.

Feeling absolutely dreadful, I shot off a letter to Williams, offering to write something for the *Esquire* letters column accepting responsibility. I never heard from him. But a short time later, he wrote a letter of his own to the magazine.

I am pleased to say, I snagged the original (arguing with the editor into whose hands it had fallen that, hey, I was mentioned by name). It now hangs in my office and occasionally, even now, glancing at it gives me a jolt of inspiration.

July 20, 1979

Dear Esquire:

Will you do me the favor of telling your correspondent John Simon that he is making more of a fool of himself than of me. He very well knows that I am not a scholar of word-usage* but that I certainly am educated in the difference between which forms of the pronoun, first and third, follow a preposition when it seems important to be correct about that, and I usually am when not writing, as sometimes I do, dialogue of illiterates.

I find Mr. Simon interesting only for his remarkable degree of personal malice toward me and most others. Are you sure he does not beat his grandmother with a bull-whip to get her up in the mornings?

Another thing he knows is that I have explained that I do not pretend to be able to produce symphonic drama at my present age and in my present state of health. I can and do write plays more corresponding to "chamber music" by a reputable composer.

I think you would do yourself a considerable service if you took a poll of your readers on his rating as a contributor. I suspect the result would disenchant you with him.

I liked your Mr. Harry Stein and seriously doubt that he shared Mr. Simon's idea that I abuse The King's English except when it helps to clarify what I'm saying.

The moral repair that this country needs even more than new sources of energy is particularly evident in space given to gratuitous viciousness such as Mr. Simon spews forth.

Cordially,

Tennessee Williams

*Would he call it etymology?

❑

Trust me, once you start, the process of seriously rethinking things takes on a life of its own; second thoughts (say, about declining school standards) lead to third ones (the new emphasis on self-esteem over knowledge) and then to fourth (the particulars of the multicultural curriculum).

It's a lot more complicated than that, of course; social beliefs are always an intricate mix of life experience and theory, what one sees and feels, augmented by what one reads and picks up from others. The point is, one by one I found myself ditching assumptions I'd held for a long time simply because they were easy and replacing them with a set of precepts that were constantly challenged and, thus, tested.

I choose to think of this as rigor, an emphasis on logic over unbridled emotion.

Alas, in this Oprahized age, others will readily identify it as coldness and even lack of empathy.

Oh, that's another thing I was starting to realize: according to the contemporary formulation, the depth of feeling you bring to an issue matters a lot more than whether the policy you support actually works.

Since some of the people I love the most in the world are unreconstructed liberals, at family gatherings in recent years a whole range of subjects from A (abortion) to Z (I don't know . . . Zulus) has proven potentially dicey.

I'm not happy about this. The fact is, we still fundamentally believe in most of the same things, and there's a lot more common ground than quicksand. Still, that tends to be forgotten in the frenzy of battle. More than once, things have broken down entirely, with almost everything anyone said getting sneered at, or viciously attacked, or, at best, misinterpreted by someone else. We're talking ugly.

The same way this whole business known as the culture wars has turned ugly. It's like a barroom brawl in an old western that's spilled from the saloon into the streets, the assorted individual fights—over gay rights, abortion, multiculturalism, affirmative action—coalescing into general mayhem, with even little old ladies looking for someone to bop over the head with a bottle.

In this national street fight, the left has the clear strategic advantage. As in the sixties it was easy to be for Peace, Love and Freedom, so it remains easy thirty years later. It's a lot harder trying to make the case for discipline over indulgence, character over glibness, real solutions over feel-good short-term fixes.

I, for one, can respect serious souls who continue to believe that liberalism remains the road to an honorable and humane future. But a lot of contemporary liberal dogma is not so much forward-looking as based on contempt for the past, including what many of us see as our best traditions and most essential values; we are thus deeply affronted by the characterization of both the way things are and how they used to be.

True, both sides are marked by their fair share of intellectual corruption and many on each side have made an art of turning truth on its head.

But it strikes me that the question that needs to get asked and asked and asked again—not glossed over, but seriously thought about—is one which would never even occur to most who see themselves as progressive: Which side is *more* intolerant? Or, perhaps more accurately, which side's brand of intolerance has done more damage lately?

For it is not as if committed cultural liberals refuse to pass judgment. They're endlessly on the lookout for racism, sexism, homophobia, lookism, ageism, ableism, classism, ethnocentrism, you name it, and perceived transgressors can expect no mercy. The only excesses they won't condemn are sexual ones. They're for every kind of diversity going—except diversity of thought.

Obviously, not all who identify with that side are so rigid. The problem, as on the right, is that the most extreme elements have come to dominate the debate, the result being that the rest of us end up fighting the battles of *their* choosing. Difficult as it might be for liberals to believe, for instance, not a single conservative of my acquaintance has the slightest problem with gay people living as they choose; most, indeed, are strongly libertarian. But for that very reason, neither do they want what they see as a radical gay agenda define the terms of "tolerance."

But in this regard as in others, the left has much better PR. Where the strident radicals of the right are readily identifiable as such, the Pat Robertsons and Gary Bauers with their faith-based followings, those on the left get to parade around in mainstream clothing; in fact, often they occupy the most rarefied precincts of academia, popular culture and the media.

But when it comes down to it, progressives are no more willing to give a fair hearing to alternative views on complex social issues than are those on the extreme fringe of the radical right. For them, too, it is essentially a zero-sum game, all or nothing. Their traditionalist foes cannot be accommodated—how can you make peace, after all, with bigots?

As everywhere else, the battles on cultural issues in my life crested during the long agony of Sexgate. The arguments at family gatherings grew so fierce that eventually we tacitly adopted a policy not to speak the name Clinton at all.

There was plenty of irony in this of course. For one thing, in policy terms, Clinton has migrated miles from the liberalism of the eighties; many hard-core liberals will go to the grave condemning him for the initiatives he astutely swiped from the Republicans. For another, even among those progressives with a warm spot for the guy, few were thrilled to have their side in the apocalyptic struggle championed by someone so obviously freighted by lies and rank sleaziness—much as many of us deeply regretted having ours seeming to be represented by Ken Starr, with his creepy fascination with clinical sexual detail.

For a long while there during Sexgate, the *New York Times*—as the primary organ of reputable leftist opinion—actually seemed on the edge of a schizophrenic breakdown. On the one hand, knowing full well how shamelessly corrupt was the man they'd helped put in the White House—and none too pleased, either, with his surrender to the forces of evil on matters ranging from a balanced budget to welfare reform—the paper's news gathering and editorial sides were as much in high dudgeon as any journal on the right. In fact, the *Times'* own reporters, led by the estimable Jeff Gerth, had played a key role ferreting out some of the most damaging information on Whitewater, Filegate, Travelgate, and Chinagate.

Yet on the other, with the Lewinsky affair looming as the Armageddon of the culture wars, such a stance was increasingly untenable. After all, for all the man's "personal shortcomings," wasn't he still one of them, dreaming the same shimmering dream of a multicultural, gender-neutral, nonsexist future?

For months some of us watched with fascination as the dilemma rippled through the culturally left press: how not to throw out the infantile Bill with his fouled bathwater.

Gradually, as the shock of the initial revelations faded, more and more progressives got with the program. The appearance of the Starr Report followed by the release of Clinton's grand jury testimony was a particular turning point; deep-thinking liberal columnists who a few weeks earlier were expressing outrage over having been repeatedly lied to, now decided it really was Just Between Bill and Hillary, or Everybody Does It, or Let's Just Censure the Guy and Move On.

Above all, in enlightened circles everywhere, the same chilling phrase was being endlessly heard: "Sexual McCarthyism."

If it had long been an article of liberal faith that the rest of America is far too uptight about sex (while not being uptight *enough* about, for instance, guns), before the battles had usually been only skirmishes: local fights over sex ed. or some lunatic minister going after *NYPD Blue* for showing a little naked flesh. Here, at long last, this most defining of all issues was joined on a national scale. The enlightened against the repressed! Light versus darkness!

In the *New York Observer*—a bellwether of hip in the hippest town of all—there appeared a piece about a bunch of smart, famous, liberated women getting together and saying how, if given half a chance, they'd all just love to go down on the President themselves. A few weeks later, there was reporter Nina Burleigh, recently of *Time,* revealing in *Mirabella* how delighted she had been to catch Bill admiring her and that, yes, she too would gladly give herself to him, if only in thanks for saving abortion.

Still, the newspaper of record steadfastly remained above the fray for months, running the usual run of letters and op-ed pieces, pro and con, plus a string of how's-it-all-playing-in-the-heartland stories, but otherwise not tipping its institutional hand.

Until, that is, one Sunday six weeks after Bill's famous non–*mea culpa* when there appeared in the *Magazine*—the *Times'* best-read and most influential section—a truly astonishing piece. Entitled "Advice for the Clinton Age," with the subhead "Is the President Kinkier Than His Constituents? The Experts Weigh In," it purported to be a look behind the facade at the reality of contemporary American sexual relations. Right up front, the author, a contributing editor at *Vogue,* claimed that due to epidemic "sexual boredom . . . the outlook for long-term monogamy in any marriage is dim." Indeed, the question ought not be *"How could he?"* but "How could he not?"

It seemed that it was "people who find Clinton's sexual behavior debauched" who have the real problem, "buying into the idea that anything other than missionary-position sex is shameful."

But the real kick was this person's idea of "research." She began with some survey that showed two thirds of married men and a third of married women have cheated, figures that surely hold true, if at all, only in Hollywood and a couple of square miles of New York and Washington. Then she moved on to her version of "experts." Chief among these was a gay sex columnist, who informed the *Times* readership (including lots of people like my ninety-two-year-old aunt Rose, fifteen years later still in mourning for my uncle Dave) that "the sexual model that straight people have created really doesn't work. All it does is force people to lie."

And did he have in mind a *better* sexual model? You bet! "I know gay couples who have been together for 35 years. They have separate bedrooms. Sometimes they sleep together and sometimes they sleep with other people, but they're a great couple."

Along the way the piece managed a couple of sharp swipes at religion—talk about boring, all those absurd Shalt Nots!—as well as at "secular moralists" like Bill Bennett, with all their relentless talk about right and wrong.

Don't they realize there is no such thing? That it's all grays? Don't they understand that the only thing truly wrong is to judge?! As I recently heard the female half of an incestuous couple on *Jerry Springer* yell in response to catcalls from the audience: "Why shouldn't we do it—this is America!"

In our house, the first word on the *Times Magazine* piece came from a good friend of my wife's in suburban New Jersey, who called early that morning trying to figure out whether to be amused or offended. "Who *are* these people?" she wondered. "You're not normal if you *don't* cheat? I mean, I was a sixties person, I lived through the sexual revolution, and I don't know anyone who acts that way. Or wants to! Don't any of these people have children?"

Then my wife read it. "My God," she reported, "it's even worse than I thought. These people are just so pathetic, with their sad, sick need to justify their own total lack of character."

Welcome to our side in the culture wars.

The truth, by the way, if anyone's interested, is that calling the right anti-sex is as gross a slur as calling the left, I don't know, pro-debauchery. If there's any kind of generalization to be made at all on this score, it would be that conservatives see themselves as pro-responsibility. "No conservative I know," as University of Alabama history professor Forrest McDonald puts it, "wants to outlaw any forms of sexual behavior, except to protect children; but every conservative I know recognizes that the consequences of various kinds of sexual behavior can be costly indeed, as witness the widespread incidence of sexually transmitted diseases, illegitimacy and broken homes."

Indeed, adds Michael Novak of the conservative American Enterprise Institute, there's more than a little defensiveness in the frenzied paranoia of the left about "neo-Puritanism." "Not content with the virtually universal tolerance that characterizes present-day America, the left now insists on forcing everyone to vocalize moral approval for its own bizarre agenda."

Speaking of which, amazingly enough, the *New York Times Magazine* was back on the attack the very next week, this time on an even broader front, with a cover story on the very thrust of modern conservatism. Called "The Scolds," its chief target was William Kristol, editor of *The Weekly Standard*, described as the leading theoretician of a "degenerated conservative political and literary culture" that is "not afraid of the state or its power to set a moral tone or coerce a moral order."

Written in apparent white heat by the sometimes-brilliant gay journalist Andrew Sullivan, it rages against the "scolds" on all fronts. After several thousand excoriating words, he concludes by demanding to know what conservatives even have to whine about. They've already won the war and don't even know it! Look at the conservative success at the polls, he fairly shouts, look at welfare reform!

True enough—except such a formulation misrepresents what truly drives most of today's cultural conservatives: the gut-wrenching sense that, when no one was looking, the social norms and shared understandings—the very moral order that for so long gave life a semblance of coherence and sanity—were ripped asunder.

The response to Sullivan's claim is all too apparent: look at the crap that hits our kids every time they snap on the TV. Look at what they're being taught in schools. Look at what passes for serious and ethical thought in the *New York Times*!

Those on the left in the culture war claim to fear for the future if the other side prevails, and given some of their adversaries, that's far from unreasonable. But some of us, seeing the damage they've done, fear an unconditional victory by their side even more. For—need it even be said?—lots of them fervently believe that no one will be truly free till Take Our Daughters to Work Day is highlighted on every calendar and a blushing transsexual graces every third cover of *Modern Bride*.

Inevitably, maybe unfairly, to the extent Clinton lives in the public mind after he's gone it will be as much as symbol as man: for those on his side and their ideological descendants, the victim of a vengeful and narrow-minded neo-Puritanical cabal; but for many on the other, the entire *me* generation in one soft, pink powerful package, from the aversion to self-sacrifice to the mind-boggling ability to justify anything.

For, truly, it is all of a piece: Redefine the language to get around the law? *Hey, if it works for you.* Bankrupt your most loyal followers? *Sorry, but if that's what it takes.* And, too: if minorities are scoring lower on standardized tests, and women are having trouble meeting the physical standards for firefighters? *No problema, change the tests and gut the standards.*

It's not just sex. It never was. It's those who say "So what?" and call it freedom.

□

In our home, as in homes everywhere, the topic of Sexgate was unavoidable. Happily, since our kids were seventeen and fourteen, there were no awkward questions about oral sex or creative uses of fine cigars or alternative meanings of "is"; they knew all that stuff, as they knew our President was a sleaze.

Anyway, one night over dinner, I don't know exactly how, we got into how we'd react if *I* were the President of the United States and got into a similar fix. Would Priscilla stand by me, Hillary-like, and lash out at my political opponents? Would Sadie materialize at my side to show her support? Would Charlie show himself to be as lapdog faithful as, say, Mad Dog Carville? Speaking of which, how would our dog Hank fall on this—still trotting after me onto *Air Force One* like Buddy, or pull a disappearing act like Socks?

A man likes to know these things.

Afterward, I asked each to set down his/her thoughts on the page.

PRISCILLA: Let me put it to you straight, Mr. Fantasy President, if you ever even thought about pulling a Clinton, you could forget about it! If there was any wifely lashing out to be done, it would *not* be at some mythical conspiracy!

And if there happened to be reporters or cameras around, so be it.

True (seeing how things played out for the Clintons), my wronged-wife scorched-earth tactics might backfire. I'd suffer the further indignity of seeing my poll numbers plummet while the antishrew element made yours soar.

I know this is just pretend, but frankly I get furious just thinking about it!

But, Priscilla, I wasn't having sex, she was!

Uh-uh, buster, I don't think so.

The Secret Service would have to start sleeping in the First Bedroom, just to make sure there wasn't a presidential corpse to deal with in the A.M.

SADIE: If you ever behaved like that, Papa, I'd be the first to turn my back—even before Mama. I mean, I guess in your case it'd be different, since you have a whole history of self-righteousness (something I've inherited) to overcome. After all, way back when I was little I asked if you could ever love another woman, and you said no, it was impossible.

So I'd have absolutely no sympathy. It sort of cheapens the whole concept of a family when a parent does something like that, no matter who he is. In fact, for me—to whom something so minor as forgetting a parents' night at school is tantamount to a felony—it would definitely rate a family excommunication. Like what Tevye did to Chava in *Fiddler on the Roof.*

CHARLIE: This is stupid, something like that would never happen (I mean you being President).

No, no, I mean the other thing, too.

But if they both did happen . . . Well, I guess I'd probably be mad for a while. But, then, at least in my mind, I'd think Mama and Sadie were overreacting. If you wanted me to go outside with you to face the microphones on the White House lawn to show my support, I'd probably have to do it.

In fact, I know I would.

But I wouldn't take that the wrong way if I were you, Papa. You know me—I'd take any chance I could to get on TV!

For a lot of people I know, the weirdest (not to mention, most infuriating) aspect of Sexgate was the ease with which Clinton partisans were able to portray those on the other side as a mob of sexually repressed puritans—and so fail to engage on the real issue of presidential contempt for law. But for me personally, perhaps even weirder was how quickly it became a truism that we should be more like the French. The French are *laughing* at us, they'd say. The French can't *believe* what pathetic rubes we are! Why, in France they're so mature and sophisticated that at President Mitterrand's funeral, his wife was joined by his mistress and their—the mistress's and Mitterrand's—daughter.

As it happens, I'm pretty familiar with the French, having lived among them for nearly four years, during much of that time writing a lighthearted column that sought to make sense of their quirky behavior.

So I can tell you with absolute assurance that two thirds of the above is true.

Mitterrand's mistress and their daughter were indeed welcomed at this funeral—there are photos to prove it.

And, yes, beyond question the French were laughing at us. Also sneering. And, around innumerable Parisian dinner tables, and in hundreds of smoky cafés, jabbering on about their own superiority.

But mature and sophisticated?

Try infantile and pompous. And, while we're at it—remember, it's the supposed sworn enemies of cultural stereotyping who started with these wild generalizations—try insecure and morally stunted.

Here's the point: *we* have nothing to be ashamed of. To the contrary, on the basis of centuries of history, tradition and daily practice, it's the French who should be looking to *us* for moral instruction.

And, by the way, not to put too fine a point on it, so should most of the rest of the world.

Actually, I began as a huge admirer of the French. When I arrived for my first extended stay in Paris, twenty-two years old and speaking New Rochelle High School French, I was nothing short of dazzled. God knows they *seemed* to always know what they were doing—the term *savoir faire* didn't come from nowhere. Throw in the fact that I fell in love with some woman gliding down the street every five minutes and I was a goner.

It was only after I'd begun mastering the intricacies of the language and culture, and especially once I'd begun reporting on the place, that I came to know better. Too, the process was helped along by contact with other, more experienced American expatriates. When a friend and I launched an English-language city magazine in the late seventies, I decided to do a piece for the inaugural issue on Jean Seberg, the Iowa-born actress who was *the* prototypical transplanted American in the French capital; indeed, Seberg was a much bigger film star in France than she'd ever managed to become back home, and at the time was working on her third French husband. So I was much surprised by the way in which she discussed the locals, in a tone suggesting bemused contempt. The French were just incredibly "tight-assed," she said. No matter how long you lived among them you could never be fully integrated "because they won't let you." Even the French language itself was "a verbal jungle," designed as much to hinder real communication as to facilitate it.

There was more of the same from Joe Dassin, son of the filmmaker Jules Dassin, who'd settled his family in France after being blacklisted. Joe had gone on to become one of the biggest rock stars in France and, because the name could pass and his command of French was flawless, many of his fans assumed he *was* French. But, in fact, he remained American to the core, down to his easy manner and his self-deprecatory humor. As he himself put it, responding to a question about French musical tastes, "The French attitude is one of more pretension and less so-phistication lyrically. They have no sense of humor, except for enormous slapstick. No tongue-in-cheek. They take lyrics very literally and very seriously . . . Americans will take an old rock lyric and laugh at it, take it to that second level of tongue-in-cheek. The French would say, 'What an idiot this guy is! Look at all the stupid things he's saying!' They have no sense of humor whatever. The French are always worried you might be putting them on. They're extremely sensitive to second-degree humor, 'cause they're always afraid you might be putting something over on them."

Indeed, these were all qualities my American friends and I were al-ready starting to pick up on ourselves: not only the lack of spontaneity and deadly self-seriousness, but the extent to which so many French sought to mask their insecurities behind studied indifference and an ever-ready supply of intellectual bullshit. Finally, a good friend—French herself but having spent a lot of time in the States—offered an explanation that seemed to make a lot of sense. "We French," she said—a paraphrase, but I remember the conversation well—"aren't allowed to have childhoods like Americans do. Here everything is forbidden—making too much noise in the house, making eye contact with strangers on the subway, even playing on the grass in the park. That's why when we get older we get such a kick from ca-ca jokes and car crashes—we're finally able to enjoy things other people laugh at when they're five or six. It also explains our love of Jerry Lewis—though, of course, like every-thing else, it has to be presented in intellectual terms."

At a certain point, I was actually moved to do a piece exploring this thesis, at least the Jerry Lewis part of it. Trying to get to the bottom of the French love affair with *le grand génie comique*, I looked up his number-one booster, a prominent film critic named Robert Benayoun. And, I swear, you should have heard this guy. "I see in Jerry," he rhapsodized as I sat in his elegant sixteenth arrondissement apartment, staring at a life-sized cutout of the comedian, "so many things. I see the Jewish-American inferiority complex, the man smothered by his mother, result-ing in aggressive, anarchic behavior toward society . . . Look at a film like *The Patsy*, which is a true masterpiece. In this film, Jerry proclaims his dilemma."

But there was something else. Like insecure people everywhere, whether kids in a schoolyard or those in the grip of political turmoil, the French tend to be followers. By American standards, independent thinking is amazingly rare. A guy named Roger Cohen, now one of the *New York Times'* top people on the Continent, did a wonderful column for us called "Normalité," its point being that the French categorize almost everything as either *normal*—logical, appropriate, something one does—or *pas normal*—idiotic, foolish, something one definitely does *not* do. "Cigarette smoking, for example, is *normal.* Say what you will about its dangers: show posters of rotting lungs—you won't dent a Frenchman's smile as he lights up . . . He has no qualms, because it's *normal.* Like the fact that the earth goes around the sun, or using suppositories . . ."

On the other hand, for instance, exercising was at the time definitely *pas normal*—more than once I saw French people laughing at Americans out for a morning jog in the park. Though if you go to Paris today, you will note that such behavior has now become *normal,* after all.

The point, as Roger neatly summed it up, is that the French are "a bunch of anesthetized sheep."

Which, back to the morality question, goes a long way toward their behavior during the twentieth century's great test of national character, the Second World War. Forget for a moment the astonishing collapse in 1940 of what was thought to be one of the world's strongest armies; it was what happened afterward that's most revealing. For alone among the conquered nations of Europe, the French were allowed to maintain a quasi-independent government, headed by World War I hero Philippe Pétain and prewar premier Pierre Laval; and, as the Germans themselves acknowledged, this Vichy government, for a time immensely popular, cooperated so willingly with the Gestapo that, in their eagerness to please, the French actually handed over to the Germans *more* Jews than had been requested.

After the war, of course, as the myth of the Resistance took hold, this was rarely acknowledged; in fact, the Resistance movement was proportionally smaller in France than in most other countries, its numbers dwarfed by native Frenchmen actively collaborating with the Nazis. French politicians—even artists and entertainers—spent decades obscuring their behavior during the war years, and almost no one seemed inclined to call anyone to account. For a time, Marcel Ophüls' magnificent documentary about the Occupation, *The Sorrow and the Pity,* was actually banned in France.

The French very much had their own sixties generation—the veterans of May '68 whose street battles with police paralyzed Paris and who, in concert with militant French workers, came close to bringing down President Charles de Gaulle—and, like us, many feel tremendous nostalgia for that earlier time. But, in a sense, their outburst, which occurred in emulation of those in the States, was even more infantile. For it was consciously directed against the very idea of authority. *Défense de défendre* was its overriding slogan—"Forbidden to Forbid." And while in a nation as rigid and hierarchical as this such a rebellion is understandable, ultimately it was only destructive and nihilistic, leaving untouched the real source of the corruption of the French soul: the paralyzing cynicism that foolish Americans today mistake for sophistication.

This cynicism pervades all of French life, evident a dozen times a day in routine conversations and casual asides. But it is especially damaging to the French press, which, to put it mildly, takes its investigative responsibilities considerably less seriously than those of other democratic nations. At one point, our little paper did a case study of the role of the press in a political scandal called "The deBroglie Affair," which, anywhere else, would have been a huge deal; it involved the gangland-style murder, under extremely suspicious circumstances, of an aide and important fund-raiser for then-president Valéry Giscard d'Estaing. But with the French press, after an initial flurry of interest, the story went nowhere. As Charles Gombault, one of the nation's most distinguished journalists—and, more to the point, someone who'd spent the war years in London, watching the English press—told our reporter, "In France, Watergate would have been forgotten in three days . . . Censorship is unnecessary, and so is ordering people around. Everyone just knows what they're supposed to do and so, without even thinking about it, they self-censor."

So, yes, the French press expressed bemused scorn toward the investigations of Clinton. Gombault's old paper, *France-Soir,* called the independent counsel "an ayatollah . . . who doesn't smoke, doesn't drink, and reads the Bible every morning." The prestigious *Le Monde,* their version of the *New York Times* in more ways than one, editorialized that Starr's "new McCarthyism . . . replaces the fear of communism with the terror of sexuality."

Of course, what one heard less often on this side of the water was that *Le Monde*, as blatantly pro-Arab and anti-Israeli as most French institutions, also none-too-subtly suggested Monica Lewinsky was a Zionist agent out to undermine the Palestinian-friendly President.

All of which leads us back to the clamor that we start looking to these people for direction, moral and otherwise. The novelist William Styron, who with former Minister of Culture Jack Lang helped launch a Paris-based, star-studded petition in support of Clinton, summed up the attitude as well as anyone. Writing in sorrow and deep frustration and ersatz understanding, in—where else?—yes!, *The New Yorker*, he opined, "For years, I've been attempting to convince my friends in France that Americans are quite as broadminded as the French. What the French don't possess is the equivalent of the American South, where a strain of Protestant fundamentalism is so maniacal that one of its archetypal zealots, Kenneth Starr, has been able to nearly dismantle the Presidency because of a gawky and fumbling sexual dalliance. Absent, too, from the French scene are media with fangs bared to go to work on the Presidential throat."

This sort of intellectual sloppiness is worse than mere partisanship, it borders on ethical negligence. For what one ought not expect the French themselves to grasp, should, on some level, be obvious to every even marginally informed American: that it is precisely our "innocence," our refusal to take corruption in the public sphere as inevitable or routine, that has distinguished us as a people, in times of crisis lending us cohesion and moral purpose. And the contrast with the French in this regard is particularly laughable, for where our civic culture has routinely in times of trial given rise to figures of towering character, theirs has invariably produced midgets. Our revolution brought forth Washington and Jefferson and led to a governmental model for all mankind. Theirs produced Marat and Robespierre and an unprecedented reign of irrationality and violence. While Lincoln was fighting a Civil War to make the United States live up to the promise of its founding document, French Emperor Napoleon III took advantage of our distraction to forcibly install his puppet Emperor Maximilian over the Mexicans (and then, when our

Civil War ended, with characteristic élan, hastily pulled his troops out, leaving his stooge to the tender mercies of a Mexican firing squad). Where we had FDR to rally us during the war, they turned to Pétain and Laval. And, today, where they have the smooth-talking and amoral Jacques Chirac, we have . . .

Well, okay, maybe we are starting to catch up with them.

But if we ever actually do, we should know that it is very much at our own peril. Just a few days after the pro-Clinton petition from Paris made news, there appeared another all-too-revealing story on the front page of the *New York Times.* Headlined FRANCE DETECTS IRAQI NERVE GAS, EXPERTS ASSERT, it revealed that the French had discovered that the Iraqis were arming their missiles with VX nerve gas, yet "had delayed releasing the final results because they did not want to undermine Iraq's push at the United Nations this week to lift economic sanctions." Nine months later, during the Kosovo campaign, it was reliably reported, as Britain's *Daily Telegraph* had it, that "Washington has started cutting Paris out of the loop on some operations because of the worry of information being handed either to the Serbs directly or indirectly through the Russians."

In the final analysis, *this* is the kind of maturity and sophistication the petition signers endorse: the corrosive amorality of a world-weary, old roué of a country which, in the end, invariably leads to calamity.

And if they say that's unfair, a wild overstatement, maybe they'll grasp the true meaning of the French abdication from responsibility if it's cast in terms they're able to understand: the French also sneered at us back in 1974, for driving Richard Nixon from power over a trifling matter like Watergate.

□

I picked up another life lesson during my time in Paris. As one might imagine, there are a fair number of interesting types to be encountered as a journalist in the City of Light—writers, filmmakers, politicians and activists of various kinds—but this one came from an unexpected source: a middle-aged French lawyer, the friend of a colleague, who happened into the office one day.

We'd gotten to shooting the breeze—his English put my okay French to shame—and at some point he mentioned that growing up in the Paris suburbs, he'd been the mid-fielder on a local junior championship soccer team. "Of course," he added amiably, "that was quite a while ago."

The reference had to do with more than just age. The guy had a cane and walked with great difficulty.

A little later it came out why. When he was sixteen, during the war, he and a group of high school friends got involved with the Resistance; not in any major way, he stressed, nothing *heroic,* just delivering messages at night on their bikes. In fact, he made it sound almost like a lark, the wartime equivalent of trying to get away with smoking behind the gym.

Except one of their number got caught and betrayed the rest of the group.

He recalled that when the Gestapo came, he was having dinner with his parents and sisters. Held in a Parisian police station that had been taken over by the Germans, over the next couple of weeks he was systematically tortured; his foot and ankle were smashed with a club and left untreated. When it was decided he had no information to impart, he was sent off to a work camp. It was only through the kindness of others that he managed to survive at all.

All in all it was a helluva story, the sort of firsthand history that I, as a young American, had never before heard. But what really stuck with me was an observation he made almost casually.

I'd asked if he was surprised the guy betrayed the group. No, he said, he wasn't really surprised by *anyone's* behavior during that desperate period. Not by those who showed character and courage, nor those who ended up actively supporting the Germans, nor by the majority who merely stayed quiet and kept their heads down. "Even the kids in my high school," he said, "I could have predicted beforehand how almost every one of them would act. It wasn't so different from how they'd always been before."

At the time it seemed a stunning thought: that by our routine behaviors and seemingly banal choices, we reveal what we're ultimately made of. But of course it is absolutely so. It is by the incidental tests, day by day and hour by hour, that we establish what we are about; and, indeed, how we will respond when most severely tested.

Years later, I heard very much the same thing from someone else in a position to know—a former Israeli agent named Peter Malkin, with whom I was writing a book on the capture of Adolf Eichmann. Peter, who'd lost much of his family, described how, face-to-face in a Buenos Aires safehouse with the man responsible for the killing machine, he kept pressing him for some kind of moral accounting: *How could he have done what he did and live with himself?* But in the end, Peter said, what was most chilling was that Eichmann didn't even seem to understand the question. He'd merely acted during the war as he had before—with perfect loyalty to his superiors and purposeful efficiency in pursuit of predetermined goals. Under other circumstances—had he, say, been a manufacturer of shoes—he would have been, said Peter, the best shoe manufacturer going, an esteemed member of the community. It's just that since circumstances were otherwise, so were the goals.

I'd like to imagine, as we all would, that under the same conditions

I'd act as that middle-aged French lawyer did when he was in high school; I honestly don't know. But I do think—and perhaps this is self-flattery—that wondering about it, and worrying, is at least a start.

The day Bill Clinton was acquitted by the Senate, Lincoln's one hundred eightieth birthday, his old Arkansas nemesis Paul Greenberg wrote a column in which he came up with a quote from the Great Emancipator I'd never heard before; one that should resonate with all of us who aspire to live our lives courageously and well. "If in the end," Greenberg quoted Lincoln, "when I come to lay down the reins of power, I have lost every other friend on earth, I shall at least have one friend left, and that friend shall be deep inside me."

❑

After running across that Lincoln quotation, I snatched up my handy *Bartlett's*. Therein are found almost four pages of things the great man said, many of them equally inspiring, most of them even less known. Who but Lincoln, with that wondrous mix of principle and whimsy, would have remarked, "Whenever I hear anyone arguing for slavery, I feel a strong impulse to see it tried on him personally"?

That is why I've never been able to understand those who say they hate history, especially our own. It is not just a great story, it is as rich in moral lessons as the combined works of Shakespeare.

Even the American Communists understood this—indeed, far better than most. When Earl Browder proclaimed "Communism is twentieth-century Americanism" he may have been wrong, but he meant it from the bottom of his soul. Party leaders and other leading lights quoted patriotic heroes in almost every speech. They named the brigades organized to fight fascism in Spain after Lincoln and Washington, and the Party school for Jefferson.

And the Party's idealistic and mainly young followers, my parents among them, emphatically agreed.

So I guess it is no coincidence that decades later, in turn, I was touched by that same sense of reverence for America's past.

Even now I recall the verse I produced in eighth grade when Mrs.

151

Grabel assigned us to compose a new version of Paul Revere's ride. (Why not? It was the first time I was ever asked to read something in front of the whole class.)

> *T'was an April night in '75,*
> *The crisp spring air was fresh and alive.*
> *Across the river were British troops*
> *to blow up munitions of colonial groups.*
> *It was well agreed by almost all*
> *that this could be the start of the English fall.*
> *Because my friend, the revolt depended*
> *on whether or not Concord was defended.*

And down to . . .

> *Who was this horseman, so free of fear*
> *T'was a Boston silversmith, Paul Revere.*

Indeed, during my college years, that was a part of the divide between most of us regular activists and the more intense radicals: We hated the war, but we didn't hate America itself. To the contrary, having been raised mainly in traditional households and educated in traditional schools, most of us grew up with immense respect both for our elders and for the American democratic tradition; in fact, that is precisely why we felt so betrayed by the miserably duplicitous bunch in Washington.

They, on the other hand, were often nihilistic and blindly destructive. Deeply alienated in their personal lives—many were products of disturbed family backgrounds—they lacked any sense of what made this country great and sustained it for more than two centuries.

The time I was probably proudest of at Pomona was the afternoon Jerry Rubin showed up at an antiwar rally. He began ranting about how it was the entire older generation that was the enemy, and that the only way to start turning things around would be to slip acid in the water supply. But instead of the wild cheering he was evidently used to, people mainly just stared at him, amazed at the unembarrassed idiocy of it all. Finally, snorting "You people are really fucked up," Rubin strode off the platform.

Funny, it felt like he was the one who didn't get it.

For even at that dark and bitter moment, we realized there remained something immensely ennobling in the American story. As the grandson of Eastern European immigrants, I felt it as strongly as my future wife up the coast in Berkeley, whose forebears had come on the *Mayflower*, and whose family included a Revolutionary hero and many involved in Abolitionist work and the Underground Railroad. Long before we even knew each other, it was our common inheritance: this wondrous American idea that here there truly are no limits and birth need not be destiny.

Nor was that merely grandiose theory. I was among the millions who'd seen it work close at hand, in my own family.

The stories were awe-inspiring, the heroes—Franklin, Washington, Jefferson, Lincoln—at once intensely human and larger than life. These people stood for great things, *achieved* great things, often against insuperable odds. The American Revolution. The Civil War. Manifest Destiny. The crusade for Civil Rights.

Yet it was very much a warts-and-all story. Unique among nations, grudgingly, haltingly, often accompanied by terrible pain and turmoil, Americans struggled to get it better and righter. At times, that made the tale immensely complex morally. Learning about the westward expansion, for instance, we could recognize the noble impulses behind it and still be shocked by the savage inhumanity toward the indigenous peoples; and, recognizing that the tribes were far from monolithic, could even understand that the savagery also cut both ways.

The key was that the animating idea of America's promise and essential decency was never held up to ridicule. That is what enabled us as a people to act nobly even in the face of self-evident contradictions: why we could honestly believe we were saving the world for democracy (as the World War I rallying cry had it), even as the Attorney General's office was strongarming it at home; and why, a generation later, we could justly pride ourselves on our colossal role in ridding the world of Nazism, even as the triumphant Army remained rigidly segregated and thousands of American citizens languished in internment camps back home.

Those things could happen for precisely the same reason such evils were finally recognized for what they were—because we never lost faith in the idea of America.

That is what many of us find so dispiriting in the way our collective past is so often regarded today. Not long ago I was talking to some guy at a Little League game and he started telling me how pleased he was about his kid's high school history department. "It's terrific," he said, "every one of those guys is a sixties lefty. My son gets the real deal—about the incredible racism in this country, and the power of the military-industrial complex, and our history of exploitation in the Third World. None of that rah-rah, jingoistic crap we got when we were kids."

I hardly knew the guy, so why get into it, right? But I'm thinking: *hey, jerk, you really think you're doing your kid a* favor *by teaching him to despise this country?*

But, in fact, for many today that is precisely what American history now seems to be: an endless saga of cruelty and injustice.

This is the beef many of us have against multicultural history, so much the vogue these days in academia. On first glance, the notion sounds so reasonable, so *fair.* Why shouldn't we tell the American story from multiple viewpoints? Why should the white European perspective be unquestioningly taken as valid?

Yet in claiming to correct the distortions and deletions of previous accounts, the multiculturalist agenda obsessively makes distortions and deletions of its own. How was it possible that in the guide of recommendations for National Standards for United States History, issued in 1994 for use by administrators and teachers, there could be six references to Harriet Tubman and not one to Robert E. Lee? They were *both* key to the story. Why has Christopher Columbus been reduced in so many classrooms to little more than a despoiler of the environment and a ravager of native peoples? Are we truly incapable of even trying to place events in their historic context?

In *The Weekly Standard,* David Brooks wrote harrowingly of the degree to which the multicultural approach has infected even the Smithsonian's National Museum of American History, for many of us a veritable shrine, the place where, as a seven-year-old on my family's first visit to Washington, I stared wonderingly at Lindbergh's flight suit and Lincoln's stovepipe hat. Today, reports Brooks after a recent visit, "this is a museum of multicultural grievance . . . Six times more space is devoted to the internment of and prejudice against Japanese Americans than to the entire rest of World War II. There is no mention of Eisenhower, Patton, Marshall, or MacArthur, leaders who weren't exactly incidental to American conduct of the war. Similarly, there is but one showcase devoted to World War I. And that showcase is devoted to the role of women in the war."

Even more troubling, there is the flat-out corruption of history. Wellesley's Mary Lefkowitz, a classical scholar of high standing and a political liberal, was so disturbed by the baseless claims being taught as history by Afro-centrists—that Socrates was black; that democracy, astronomy, and geometry originated in Africa; that Aristotle stole his ideas from Africans—that she wrote a carefully documented book to correct them (and—big surprise—ended up branded a reactionary for her trouble). Then there is the amazing case of Rigoberta Menchú, the celebrated Guatemalan "peasant activist" awarded the Nobel Peace Prize in 1992 after the publication of her heart-wrenching autobiography made her a symbol of the racist and colonialist exploitation of indigenous Central American peoples. When it turned out that large elements of her tale were complete fabrication—in fact, her brother did not die of malnutrition, he's alive and relatively prosperous; she herself was not illiterate, but a product of a prestigious Catholic boarding school—one would have expected deep embarrassment. Instead, the powerful multicultural wing of American academia were outraged, not at Menchú, but at the anthropologist who exposed her, arguing that though the particulars of the autobiography may be false, its political and social essence is accurate.

That may well be so, but it also speaks to the underlying problem of multiculturalism: it represents not an honest search for truth but the promotion of a political agenda. Facts, even inconvenient ones, are facts; the history we should learn should be the history that occurred.

It is, moreover, not incidentally, a highly destructive agenda. For in stressing our differences—even as we supposedly "celebrate" them—inevitably we are only further balkanized.

In its formation and development, American history was indeed made principally by white European males, and so be it. (No ax to grind there—my forebears were four thousand miles away getting chased by Cossacks.) But the larger truth is that, until recently, history wasn't seen as *belonging* to anyone. As Martin Luther King rightly is owned by all of us, so, too, are Washington and Lincoln; and, yes, even Jefferson Davis and Lee. It is a sprawling saga with infinite twists and turns, truly, as Hollywood promos used to boast, with something for everyone.

Indeed, there are wondrous angles that kids almost never hear about and would eat up—some even with legitimate multicultural themes. How many know about the Battle of New Orleans in 1815 when, with the city under British attack and facing imminent destruction, Andrew Jackson forged perhaps the most diverse coalition in the history of warfare: Americans, French, blacks, Spanish, Seminole Indians, Tennessee riflemen, Creoles, *pirates,* coming *together* to thrash the world's greatest military force.

Why isn't that taught?

Allowing the particulars of American history to fall by the wayside has served only to deepen cynicism; today it is everywhere smugly asserted that history was never inspiring, that America's leaders were always corrupt and small, that we're well to be done with the myths that used to say otherwise.

The response should be: that is a lie—no doubt self-serving for those who pass it on, but a colossal disservice to the whole.

That such an abuse of the record has quickly gained such currency itself shows why an understanding of the past is so vital. History is a truth detector. It helps us distinguish the gold from the dross in our own time.

Among those who've taken the fiercest beating in recent times is, of course, George Washington. High schools have removed his name from their portals, historical gossips have eagerly sought to link him with a comely neighbor. So every once in a while it's worth recalling what this titanic figure was really about. There are clues all over, if we only bother to look: what he did, what he said, what he wrote.

For now, let's just stick with his observation, from his first inaugural address in 1789, that "the foundation of our national policy will be laid in the pure and immutable principles of private morality."

Among Washington's quirkier heirs (though in some quarters the comparison will surely elicit horror) is New York's Rudy Giuliani. For on the matter of the link between good citizenship and private morality, no contemporary politician has been more forceful or explicit.

It is a theme Giuliani strikes all the time, reflexively, bringing it to bear on civic issues both minuscule and grand. "This is really something that people have to learn in society," he soberly instructs fellow New Yorkers, urging them to give holy hell to dog owners who fail to clean up after their pets. "The reason not to 'block the box,' " he lectures an angry caller complaining on his radio show about a crackdown on drivers who block intersections, "is a very, very important one for your development as a responsible human being. It means respecting the rights of other people, understanding that there are some things you would like to do, things that feel better to you, but in doing them you disrespect the rights of other people."

Then, of course, there was his famous brawl with the Brooklyn Museum of Art over its "Sensation" exhibit. In seeking to cut the museum's city funding for displaying works, including a Virgin Mary executed partly in the medium of elephant dung, profoundly offensive to large numbers of the citizens he represents, the mayor may indeed have overstepped his bounds; the First Amendment is no minor consideration. But he was also saying clearly some things that cried out to be said: both about the "sick stuff" that passes for daring among today's self-congratulatory cultural elite (though heaven forbid anyone should assault any of *their* icons) and the obligation of government *not* to uncritically subsidize it. Cynics may have dismissed it all as political, which to some degree it surely was. But no one who witnessed the passion with which he made his case could doubt that this was also a matter of deep conviction.

Yet for some of us even more memorable was his reaction four months earlier to a most unusual caller to his radio broadcast—the mother of an eighteen-year-old who'd been killed by police during a robbery. When the woman began bitterly denouncing the cops, Giuliani cut her off. "Maybe you should ask yourself some questions about the way he was brought up and the things that happened to him," he came back at her, noting the boy's long history of arrests. "Trying to displace the responsibility for the criminal acts of your son onto the police officers is really unfair."

Aimed as it was at a mother in mourning, such a response was nothing short of startling; and, of course, to Giuliani's critics, it offered yet more evidence of his rank insensitivity and contempt for those who hold differing views.

But I have little doubt most listeners found it as bracing as I did. For even in the wake of the unspeakable tragedies that have transformed schools across America into high-security zones, when the role of parents in shaping their kids has never been under closer scrutiny, such plain speech on the subject is almost never heard.

Why, when it comes to screwed-up kids, do we continually shy away from bedrock truths, focusing instead on insidious, impersonal forces like drugs, popular culture or the Internet?

Why, getting right down to it, do we keep giving a pass to parents who fail to give their kids enough love or time or structure or discipline?

Well, no, let's get real, we know why. Because more and more, inept and ineffectual parenting is less an aberration than the norm. Because in an era of never-enough-time and tube-as-baby-sitter, many have all but forgotten what it means to do it right. Because, for all the lip service paid lately to the ethic of personal responsibility, precious few (and even

fewer in the public arena) are willing to risk being seen as harsh, judgmental or mean-spirited.

And, absolutely, because the insidious, impersonal forces *are* such an
irresistibly fat target.

Beyond question, in an age when a teenager's tee shirt is more sexually explicit than the grossest vulgarian of a half century ago, it *is* harder
than ever to raise decent kids. A mere couple of generations back, it was
unthinkable that popular culture might routinely rob kids of the innocence that wise grown-ups knew to be the foundation of security. The
raciest music of my kid years might have been Jan and Dean conjuring
up "two girls for every boy," the sexiest sight on the tube Mary Tyler
Moore as Laura Petrie in those capri pants. These days, before kids even
reach school age, they are confronted with the near-pornographic at
every turn, on newsstands and in reports about the President, on terrific
shows like *Seinfeld* as well as on *Jerry Springer.*

There's no shielding them from it.

But it's our job to try, arming them with what they need to protect
themselves. For we're the ones from whom our kids take all their major
cues—and relinquishing that primary responsibility sends as clear a
message as any other.

That is why the indifference of many parents toward junk culture is
itself so undermining. In her book *What Our Mothers Didn't Tell Us,*
Danielle Crittenden imagines one of today's hip young urban moms
pushing her two-year-old up a city street in a stroller and confronting a
giant jeans ad of "a man having sex from behind with a woman he'd
pushed up against a brick wall. 'What's that lady doing, Mommy?' asks
the child. The hip mom doesn't miss a beat: 'Oh, just getting buggered
in an alleyway, dear. It's just one of the many sexual opportunities you'll
have when you're older, if you're lucky.'"

Indeed, we have moved so far, so fast, that today parents by the millions no longer expect (or even *want)* their children to retain their innocence. Innocence—say, still believing in Santa at eight—might
stigmatize a child as pitifully naive. One hears variations on the line
constantly, from the parents of twelve- and ten- and even eight-year-olds,
the all-purpose explanation for a cynicism and world-weariness that
ought to elicit horrified concern: it's "age appropriate."

Far more accurate, as sociologist David Elkind so memorably observed twenty years ago in his classic *The Hurried Child,* is that "children today know much more than they understand." For all their "pseudo sophistication," they "still feel and think like children."

It is no coincidence that what might be called the subversion of childhood was greatly accelerated when our generation assumed control of the culture. On TV, the authoritarian dads of yore, the Ozzies and Wards, were banished forever, replaced by a new breed of hipper parents. Suddenly, even shows supposedly designed for tiny kids started featuring wry grown-up asides and heavy doses of sarcasm and irony; which, confusing as they may have initially been, over time had an immense cumulative impact. And, natch, all at once sex was everywhere, even in the bubble-headed sitcoms during what was still called "family hour"; if not the heavy-duty kind found in the afternoon soaps, then in coy double entendres and little misunderstandings about what the grown-ups were up to.

Some years back, I did a piece for *TV Guide* on the creators of some of the most popular programs for children and found them most proud of what they took to be their shows' hipness and sophistication. "Kids are no longer naive," said Tom Miller, co-creator of *Full House,* explaining why a program top-rated nationally among two- to eleven-year-olds so often played compromising sexual situations for laughs. ". . . And if what you put on doesn't reflect that, they're gonna say 'Who are these people? They're geeks!' " Added Don Reo, creator of NBC's *Blossom,* of that show's relentless preoccupation with early teen sexuality: "My father and I had so little common ground that we had almost no basis for emotional connection. That isn't true now. We children of the 60's who now have children of our own are far less 'parental.' We can relate—because we have rock n' roll in common."

As much as anything else, relating and not being "parental" is presumed to mean never imposing our own standards and values on our own kids, even if those values happen to be superior. Such a view was neatly summed up by David Denby, *The New Yorker*'s film and cultural critic, who wrote that though he and his wife are appalled by many of the messages embedded in popular culture, they refuse "to stand over the children, guiding their progress all day long like missionaries leading savages to light. To assume control over their habits and attitudes, we would have to become bullies."

Watching the guy make virtues of hand-wringing and weak will, one is left wondering exactly what role parents like Denby and his wife *do* see for themselves in their children's moral upbringing. (But then, chances are they've taken comfort in the notion—advanced in the much-hyped *The Nurture Assumption* and celebrated in Denby's own magazine—that parents don't much matter, anyway, since today's kids take their cues from their peers.)

I'm by no means claiming to have all the answers. In our home, Priscilla and I went back and forth forever on the question of the kids and TV. After years of trying to monitor viewing and limit TV time to several hours per week per child—this last resulting in an ongoing debate with our son who counted minutes, constantly insisting he was owed eighteen here or forty-three there—we decided we would instead watch a select handful of shows each week together as a family. This seemed to make good sense; notwithstanding all the junk polluting the airwaves, between cable outlets like the History Channel and A&E and the smartest of networks' character-driven dramas and sitcoms, this is TV's true golden age. Yet what eventually became inescapable, sitting there with the kids, was that even these shows often contained elements that made us acutely uncomfortable. Over a year and a half of watching *Seinfeld* as a family, there must have been a dozen times when—with the talk turning back to masturbation or someone's sexual performance, or with Jerry about to bed yet another young woman—my wife and I would announce "Inappropriate," and the kids would know to get up and run from the room.

I have no doubt this little moral fire drill would have been regarded as silly by lots of people we know; almost all our kids' friends watched *Seinfeld,* most of them presumably without interruption. Frankly, we felt a little silly ourselves; but, more than that, we were annoyed that we felt we so often had to. Granted, times change, and the show is aimed at mature audiences, but then so was *The Dick Van Dyke Show* when my brothers and I were my kids' age, and my parents never had to worry about shooing us from the room.

Then, again, as we know, for vast numbers of kids today, across all income levels, the parents are no longer around.

In our own little upscale suburb, the nanny-mother ratio at the local park has gone in the past ten years from perhaps fifty-fifty to more like eighty-twenty; and while a lot of those tiny kids are really well dressed (two corporate salaries will do that) it hardly compensates for the fact that many of the nannies seem to interact with their charges hardly at all and some, indeed, speak almost no English. Then there is the woman I know at a nearby day care facility who matter-of-factly reports that some of her three- and four-year-olds don't even know how to use silverware—they've been raised on burgers and Chicken McNuggets.

It usually doesn't take long for the consequences to show themselves. When I coached Little League a few years back, like the other coaches I was soon aware of the kids who'd come of age without strong adult guidance; they were the ones who were angry, sarcastic, disruptive.

Often, they were the kids of the most aggressively careerist parents. My friend Kevin, a filmmaker with a background in psychology, tells of arriving a few years back to pick up his eight-year-old son Trevor from a birthday party and finding him in tears; another kid, a notorious weasel and sneak—the child of a pair of super-successful lawyers—had smashed him over the head with one of those plastic baseball bats. Like his father, Trevor is big, but he is also extremely gentle. Now Kevin took his hand and marched him to the other kid, who started frantically denying any wrongdoing.

"Don't even bother," Kevin cut him off, "I spoke to two grown-ups who saw you." He paused, staring the kid down. "I just want you to know," he said, "that if you ever touch Trevor again, he has my permission to hit you back as hard as he can and he *won't* get in trouble."

Kevin likes to think there was an important lesson learned that day—less by the other kid, who never bothered his son again, than by Trevor. Still, he worries a lot, as do I, about the world our kids will inherit: one likelier even more screwed up than our own, where those who in their formative years returned from school to empty homes and learned life's most vital lessons from daytime TV or strangers in health class will hold enormous sway.

This is why it is so disheartening to hear politicians signal their concern for children by pushing increased government spending for "affordable child care" and tax relief for working parents. One recent plan proposes up to $240 monthly in cash and tax incentives for workers who

carpool, use mass transit or bike to work, yet suggests a tax
stay-at-home moms of just $14.83 a month.

It's not that the politicians are insincere—just that they so obviously
fail to grasp what it is kids need *most*.

So let's keep it simple: it does not take a village to raise a child. It
takes loving, responsible, committed parents. Ideally, two of them, together for the duration.

Of course, the central idea of the book that bore Hillary's name—this notion that kids ought to be as much a community as a family responsibility—is hardly an original one. A staple of socialist thought for over a century, it has been a key policy goal of the movement with which Hillary Rodham has identified since the days she was exhorting her fellow Wellesley grads to seek after "more immediate, ecstatic and penetrating modes of living."

Feminism.

Fair warning: this is a subject on which I have a tendency to go a little crazy.

That is not because I fail to see the tremendous good the women's movement has done. As the father of both a daughter and a son, I am deeply grateful for a world in which her possibilities are as limitless as his. Who with a shred of decency *doesn't* support equal opportunity, and a level playing field, and equal pay for equal work? Not long ago, I happened to catch *The Paper Chase,* the fondly remembered 1973 flick set at Harvard Law School; and what was even more of an eye-opener than the insipid love story was the shocking absence of women in John Houseman's contracts class.

Yet that kind of equity was achieved quite a while ago now—there are more women law students today than men—and the movement that made

164

it happen, morally speaking, is long gone, replaced by an army of ideologues seeking to impose their own narrow, joyless version of how things ought to be on us all.

(See what I mean.)

I'm acutely aware that when the talk turns to today's feminism, or even when I happen to run across some new outrage in the morning paper, I'm apt to quickly tumble over the line into irrationality.

But what can I tell you? Over the years it has become ever more clear that feminism, for all the great good it achieved, has also been the root cause of much of the social dysfunction we now take as routine. It has reshaped our sense of children and their needs; redefined relations between the sexes; changed how schools, industry, the military and even sports do business; fundamentally altered the way we think, feel, behave.

Some of my progressive friends seem amused by the passion I bring to the subject. They tell me they're as put off by the excesses and myriad hypocrisies of the feminist crazies as I am; the difference is, they know they're harmless. "Those people are such old news," as a close woman friend puts it. "By now everyone understands feminists are just another interest group pushing an agenda. No one takes them nearly as seriously as they take themselves."

"These things are always cyclical," adds a male friend of mine mildly. "Feminism became a force because there were real injustices to be addressed, and maybe the pendulum swung too far. But now it's swinging back."

I say the real difference is my friends are willfully naive, refusing to face either the tremendous power feminism continues to wield throughout society or the maliciousness of its agenda. And, sorry, guys, but for my money those things *should* generate some heat.

The question is what happened?

How did a movement with which so many of us began as true believers turn us into implacable foes?

It's a tough one to sum up—we're talking thirty-plus years of social history, from Vietnam to the Internet, Nixon to Clinton. But for convenience's sake, one need look no further than the career of America's leading feminist.

For no one so vividly represents the ways feminism altered course over those years—or, at pivotal junctures, failed to—as Gloria Steinem.

Back at the start, no one seemed to better sum up feminism's idealism and generosity of spirit. I remember meeting a smart but seriously overweight girl in Paris in the fall of 1971 who clued me in on how much Steinem meant to the women's movement. With her great looks and her mini-skirts and her aviator glasses, the girl said, Steinem reassured her that "the issues are real. The movement's not just for lesbians, or women like me who feel left out."

Hugely touching as this was, it came as a genuine surprise. As a right-thinking young man just a year or so out of college, I'd never for a moment thought the movement *needed* any justifying. Everyone with half a brain supported it; only total morons spouted that idiocy about ugly girls and lesbians.

As for Steinem . . . well, yeah, I guess I could see the girl's point. But for me she was so much more than the sum total of her looks. Five or six months before, I'd heard her speak at my journalism school, and, boy, did she ever seem smart; talking in that oddly uninflected monotone about making "the personal political," but doing it with such ease and self-effacing humor! Jeez—no offense to the girl in Paris—but if I could get my confidence level up a bit, this was the model for the sort of person I'd want as a girlfriend—maybe even, someday, a wife.

It was about a year later, relocated to Richmond, that I actually met Steinem. A few weeks before the '72 presidential election, the doomed McGovern campaign, unwilling to spend more than eight or ten bucks in a state where the day after the election people like me would be able to see their votes in the paper, dispatched a bunch of mainly minor pro-McGovern notables to travel around Virginia for a day by bus. On assignment, I boarded the bus, dubbed *The Grassroots Grasshopper*, with a photographer for our little paper to ride from Richmond to Williamsburg.

The photographer was key: the piece was to include lots of shots of the quasi-celebs doing their thing. This was also a source of some concern since, in the first couple of months of the paper's existence, this photographer had sometimes failed to deliver quality work.

Anyway, after interviewing Liz Carpenter, former press secretary to

Lady Bird Johnson, and fellow-Texan and blacklist survivor John Henry Faulk, I sidled over to Steinem in the back. She was as pleasant as expected, seeming genuinely pleased when I complimented her on her speech back in Richmond's Monroe Park. "Well," she said, "I've stopped being so nervous. I learned that I wasn't going to die. I had to learn, because I have to do things like this."

Then we started talking about the campaign and her role in it. But after a couple of minutes I became distracted: the photographer was sitting nearby, gazing at the passing scenery. In fact, since we'd boarded the bus, she hadn't taken more than a handful of shots.

For, that was the thing, it was a woman.

"Sally," I finally couldn't help myself, sounding as pleasant as I could manage, "maybe you can get some of this."

No big fan of mine to start with—we'd had a run-in over a previous assignment—Sally shot me a look of pure hatred, and ever so slowly got to her feet. Steinem caught the tension—I actually saw her eyes widen—and I could sense her thinking: *what an asshole!* And though she didn't say anything, whatever rapport we'd established was shot.

And, truly, in my annoyance and confusion, I was for the first time struck by a thought of my own: *this isn't* right. *The movement is about* equality. *Are we supposed to hold her to a lower standard because she's a woman?*

In fact, Sally's work this time proved so shoddy it was barely usable. Two weeks later, when she abruptly quit, she left me and the several others who had complained about her work (one of whom was a woman) souvenirs of shredded photos and a note charging us with sexism.

Steinem, of course, was soon on to grander things—notably serving as founding editor of *Ms.* magazine. In this role she was much celebrated, and by none more so than those in my circle of young, ambitious journalists. When called upon, we could all speak fluent feminism, and saw the magazine as the prime vehicle for the realization of feminism's primary goals, legal equity and full access to education and the professions. And if already it was involved with the far more dubious proposition that gender differences are meaningless and superficial—that men and women have not only the same capabilities but the same innate drives—in the spirit of the time, it was easy to agree.

Besides, let's get real, this notion that, sexually speaking, women were as voracious and indiscriminate as we were served men like me remarkably well. Never mind that to anyone with a functioning brain it was complete hooey—that era's version of the big lie; suddenly getting laid was also a *political* act! And—talk about the best of both worlds!—if a woman assumed sex should imply commitment—hey, what was wrong with *her?*

People like Steinem never cast it in those terms, of course, but in my circle even the densest men learned to play the game.

What never occurred to us, good liberals that we were, was that the magazine we so admired was itself off base, stifling debate on a range of contentious issues by imposing a narrow, authoritarian vision of right-thinking feminism. Steinem's "glib anti-intellectualism," says Camille Paglia—a truly original thinker, at the time barred from the fray—"ruined *Ms.* magazine, which should have been a forum for diverse feminist voices but instead silenced and ostracized all opposition."

That was the essence of the problem right there: not just that feminism was grounded in theory rather than actual human experience, but that its leadership from the start adamantly refused to engage in the freewheeling give-and-take that might have redeemed it. On the subject of male sexuality, for example—staying with one of the most pernicious and insistent instances of feminist folly—as women by the millions made it clear they preferred commitment over the blissfully-horny-as-thou model (and AIDS panic put the final nail in its coffin), movement theorists vigorously propagated an entirely new version of the male ideal.

That the New Man was a wholly imaginary being was perfectly apparent to most at the time, but so what? The feminists were as sincere as they were determined—why *shouldn't* men be as sensitive, communicative, empathetic as women?

"We're halfway there," Steinem proclaimed to the graduating class at Smith College, her alma mater. "We've begun to raise our daughters more like sons—so now women are whole people. But fewer of us have the courage to raise our sons more like daughters. Yet until men raise children as much as women do—and are raised to raise children, whether or not they become fathers—they will have a far harder time developing in themselves those human qualities that are wrongly called 'feminine' . . ."

Thus it was that such an idea, appealing on the face of it, also dovetailed with an ideological need: the problem of children. Though relatively few in the feminist leadership had any of their own (the model of success being achievement *outside* the home) and even fewer seemed to have any actual interest in what they were about, it was impossible to ignore that most women in the real world cared about their children immensely—more, in fact, than anything else. Even so, the thinking went—betraying the lack of understanding of the complementary role fathers play in their kids' lives—it just wasn't fair that women, more than men, should be *burdened* with most of the traditional child-rearing tasks!

Not incidentally, plenty of men in the media were happy to go along. "Until now," feminist poster boy Alan Alda wrote in *Ms.*, "it has been thought that the level of testosterone in men is normal simply because they have it. But if you consider how abnormal their *behavior* is, then you are led to the hypothesis that almost all men are suffering from *testosterone poisoning* . . ."

In point of fact, with the possible exception of Steinem herself (who, though she usually dated well-heeled society types, listed the likes of Swedish Prime Minister Olof Palme and Bella Abzug's husband Martin in *Ms.* among "Ten Men I Admire as Truly Liberated"), it was hard to find a woman who actually *wanted* to spend her life with such a man, a being that can best be described as basically a woman with a penis. Alda's own immensely popular Hawkeye Pierce on *M.A.S.H.* was himself an old-fashioned, wise-cracking womanizer, as was TV's other stud of the era, Ted Danson's Sam Malone on *Cheers*.

Yet the incessant feminist pounding away on what women are supposed to look for—make that *demand*—took its toll, adding immeasurably to the slag heap of misunderstanding between the sexes. If the movement had long featured a strong undercurrent of antagonism toward men—the conviction that, inherently selfish and jealous of societal privilege, they'd never accord women full understanding or respect—by the early nineties that sense of grievance had moved front and center. Susan

Faludi's *Backlash: The Undeclared War Against American Women* offered the sort of palaver heretofore heard almost exclusively in college women's studies classes. But now, proclaiming as it did a sort of unified field theory of female misery—a vast patriarchal conspiracy involving consumerism, male doctors, male social scientists, male politicians, consciously or not, almost *everyone,* to put women back in their place—it proved hugely influential.

As a friend of mine balefully observed at the time, the weighty Faludi tome, coming on the heels of the Hill-Thomas hearings, became an updated version of the frying pan: all at once routine squabbles about the remote turned into screaming matches about male power and arrogance.

Hill-Thomas was of course the most dramatic cultural turning point of all, the event that famously galvanized women in the conviction that men just "don't get it." Yet simultaneously, for many fair-minded souls, it fully revealed for the first time the brazenness of the feminist double standard.

For Thomas was indeed, as he melodramatically proclaimed, a victim of a "high-tech lynching." It is one thing to savage a genuine sexual predator; had Thomas been one of those bosses who wield power as a club over women in their employ, he would have had no case. But it takes a rare fanaticism and capacity for self-justification to destroy a man over an unsubstantiated claim of locker room talk.

Steinem was, of course, among those leading the charge. As she afterward put it to Hill personally, from the speaker's platform of the "Women Tell the Truth" conference in New York, she had succeeded in "corralling our anger." Steinem added that she looked to the day when Anita Hill herself might sit on the Supreme Court.

Not that by then there was any longer even the pretense of either even-handedness or allegiance to the movement's early goal of mutual respect among women. In fact, the ideological litmus tests applied to women above all. When Steinem was asked by candidate Bill Clinton early in the 1992 campaign for her assessment of Jeane Kirkpatrick, rumored at the time to be Ross Perot's choice for vice president, she replied with dismissive contempt: "She looks like a man, and thinks like one, too." Two years after that, campaigning for the male opponent of Texas Republican Senate candidate Kay Bailey Hutchinson, Steinem repeatedly derided one-time cheerleader Hutchinson as a "female impersonator."

It was as if it was no longer necessary to give so much as a passing glance to consistency or credibility: there had simply been too many strange twists along the feminist road, too many willful interpretations of fact to match the agenda's ever-changing needs. A few years back, ABC News' John Stossel—that rarity in TV news, an original thinker—did a special the title of which said it all: "Boys and Girls Are Different." Steinem was one of three leading feminists arguing otherwise and, frankly, it was almost painful to watch. Asked at one point by a highly skeptical Stossel whether it was really prudent for fire departments to lower their strength standards to accommodate women—meaning that it's now within regulations in some municipalities to drag someone down the stairs of a burning building rather than carry them—America's preeminent feminist actually replied that, well, "there's less smoke close to the ground."

Still, even some of Steinem's friends were startled two months into Sexgate, following Kathleen Willey's tale of an Oval Office sexual assault on *60 Minutes*, by Steinem's blanket defense of Bill Clinton on the *Times* op-ed page. While allowing she was inclined to accept Willey's claims and, for that matter, those of Paula Jones, she dismissed them as inconsequential. After all, she explained, he was just being a *guy*. All that mattered—the late night comics dubbed it the "one free grope" rule—is that in the end "President Clinton took 'no' for an answer."

As it happens, Steinem's defense of Clinton occurred not long after my second personal exchange with her, this time secondhand, all those years after the first. It had to do with an *Esquire* piece I'd done on the role played by the women's magazines in the ongoing gender war, its point being that women should at long last accept, and even appreciate, the way men really are. When it appeared, *Esquire*'s PR person managed to get someone at the *New York Times* to write about it and there— surprise—was Steinem answering back. "Ms. Steinem rejected Mr. Stein's portrayal of maleness. 'He has such a negative view of men, assuming they are animalistic and destructive and can only be kept in check by personal repression and legal rules,' " she said, a truly strange interpretation of what I'd actually written. " 'His opinion of men is far more negative than mine.' "

Uhhh, I don't think so.

Listen, I'm trying hard not to go over the top here. At least by feminist standards, Gloria Steinem has usually been a model of civility and restraint, and for that she merits respect in kind. Her place in history is assured—and, knowing who writes history, a lofty place it will surely be.

In fact, it's being written already. The most definitive Steinem biography to date is by Carolyn Heilbron, herself a leading feminist. Supporters also write virtually all the articles about her in respected academic publications. Just recently, I happened to catch a documentary about her on Lifetime, the women's channel, that likewise gave every passing event in her life precisely the spin she'd want.

So I was taken aback when, toward the end of the program, asked why she'd never married or had kids, Steinem didn't even skip a beat: "I've been a parent to my own mother," she replied, referring to the severely mentally ill woman for whom Gloria had to care from the age of ten. "So a powerful reason why people get married, which is to have children, was less powerful for me, to say the least."

It was not only an unspeakably sad admission but, more to the point, a devastatingly revealing one: that Steinem regards the extraordinary, life-affirming experience of nurturing and raising a child as comparable to the burden of having to tend for an angry and delusional old woman.

But what's even more astonishing is that for three decades someone who believes such a thing has been held up as a model for all women.

◻

Looking back on the monumental changes of the last thirty or so years brought on by feminism, what seems strangest of all is how much slipped by virtually without debate.

Back in the early seventies, when opponents of the Equal Rights Amendment used to argue its passage would result in coed bathrooms and women in combat, ERA supporters like me would *sneer.* The change was absurd, these reactionary lunatics would say anything!

So, how'd it happen that today the sneering is reserved for those so backward they'd dare even question the propriety of those things? That on many campuses today, single-sex dorms have ceased to exist? That in today's military, traditional types get cashiered out for making an issue of the staggering number of pregnancies aboard Naval vessels or of gutting standards to placate gender equity enforcers?

Well, no, I think we have a pretty good idea what happened. There were people sounding warnings all along; flip through back issues of *Commentary* and it's all there. But at those places where it mattered most, their views were almost never accorded a full or respectful hearing. At the networks and the *New York Times,* at prestigious universities and within the halls of major foundations, the feminist viewpoint was simply presumed the right one, a basic part of everyone's belief system;

which is to say, those who challenged it were not just mistaken, but wrong. *Morally.*

By definition, to many, they were *bigots.*

Thus it was that the blacklist Camille Paglia describes at the upper echelons of feminism carried over to every part of the opinion-making culture. "People say, 'Oh, you gain so much by criticizing feminists,'" says Christina Hoff Sommers, another "anti-feminist feminist" and the author of *Who Stole Feminism?* "Are they crazy? The path to academic success is to *totally* go along with feminist dogma. I've seen women from obscure colleges, community colleges in Maine, go right to the Ivy League, while Paglia, one of the most brilliant, original thinkers in this country, was basically stuck teaching at a museum school in Philadelphia."

This is by no means to suggest that the majority of the changes in our lives and daily behavior wrought by the women's movement are negative; innumerable kids are clearly well served by coed dorms, many guys in offices had been getting away with monstrous behavior for years. The problem is, in the absence of free and open debate, the most sweeping social transformation in history occurred in a vacuum, with virtually no consideration of potential repercussions.

That is not how we're supposed to do things in this country—our republic was born in a riot of fierce argument over contending philosophies and those debates have served us admirably ever since.

Of course, it is the nature of silence that most of us never missed the conversation, any more than many realized the degree to which radicals had hijacked the movement. "Those in the sensible middle are always at a disadvantage," notes Sommers, "because most of us just want to go about our lives. We don't really understand extremism. But extremism generates fanaticism, and fanatics get a lot done."

I only became aware of how hard it was to publicly stake out an antifeminist position when I tried to do so myself. It was soon after the appearance of *Backlash* and it struck me that the time might be ripe for a book taking on feminists of the Faludi ilk. There were, after all, plenty of people out there whose life experience had nothing to do with the grim vision the Faludi feminists were peddling, and presumably some of these bought books.

My initial title was *Pandora's Box*, a nice fit I thought for something about good intentions gone terribly wrong. But I was out to make a case, not offend; and when my agent at the time noted the double entendre would make it even more difficult for her to sell, I readily ditched it.

In fact, I hastened to reassure potential editors on the very first page of the proposal for the book that it would be "moderate in tone and the opposite of mean-spirited." And, yes, though its aim was to look into "a broad range of beliefs and assumptions central to the contemporary feminist movement," one thing "it will not question—indeed, will aggressively defend—is the right of every woman to chart her own course. Its beef is with a mindset that, in crucial ways, has victimized us all."

Since my days as a novice peddling the Communist proposal I had never had trouble selling a book, but this one brought only one modest offer—and that from an old friend, and for far too little to make it feasible. I recently found some of the rejection letters buried away in a filing cabinet, and they're pretty interesting. The ones from women ran from dismissive to outright nasty. But it was the ones from men that are even more telling. "Mr. Stein has entered a mine field here," wrote one, "and I don't feel like stepping along behind him right now." "Over here," observed another, of his large and influential publishing house, "as you can imagine, the heat is all on the other side of the argument." "I agree with Harry in much of what he says," chimed in a third. "However, I don't have the stomach for the fight, to be truthful."

We're talking, remember, *publishing*, where even the janitors claim to be defenders of the First Amendment.

Yet in the course of putting together the proposal for the book, I came upon something else: a sense of what a rich and lively debate on feminism might have looked like. For in trying to pick up some perspective, I spent several weeks in assorted libraries, rummaging through old periodicals, exploring the era that gave birth to the movement.

My preconceptions fell like dominoes—starting with the understanding that, right up until the passage of the Nineteenth Amendment, a majority of American women as well as men actually opposed votes for women; indeed, the leader of the "anti" forces was Frances Cleveland, much admired widow of a popular President, the Jackie Kennedy of her day. And, further countering the latter-day depiction of antisuffrage types as a mob of moron Neanderthals hooting along the sidelines at the March of Progress, their number included some of the most formidable intellects of the day, arguing their position with a confidence and passion fully equal to their opponents'. The legendary muckraking journalist Ida Tarbell, who singlehandedly brought John D. Rockefeller's Standard Oil to heel, counted herself against the suffragists. So did the young Eleanor Roosevelt.

For the debate was not merely about the matter of the vote, but the character of the feminist revolution itself and the fundamental changes in human behavior and the structure of society it was even then championing.

Indeed, it remains of such interest precisely because those people so clearly anticipated many of the issues we are struggling with today.

The *Readers' Guide to Periodical Literature* for the years 1912–13, the height of suffragist ferment, revealed literally hundreds of articles pro and con; after a time, plowing through them, one begins virtually to see the debate through contemporary eyes.

The mainstream, moderate suffragist position is pretty much as expected—arguing, as reasonable people do today, for simple fairness. At the time, being born female meant not just that the larger world was all but beyond reach but, often, that one had to struggle for respect even within one's own family. "Brains are still unfashionable for women to wear," as Dorothy Dix put it tartly in *Good Housekeeping*, "and it has always been proof of women's superiority that the more intelligent a man is, the more women admire him, while the bigger fool a woman is, the more men run after her."

But the most vocal radical feminists of our great-grandparents' time were nearly as vicious as those of today, and in some of the same ways. Here, for instance, is I. H. Gilmore, a regular contributor to *Harper's*, expressing her contempt for the average housewife. "The picture which, in imagination, I always draw of her is a slim, weak, pale, bowed, weary figure—meek, humorless, inarticulate, standing timidly on the threshold of life, peering through the open door but not daring to enter. And as she stands she kisses the chains which bind her wrists and ankles."

Then, again, shades of the Mommy Wars, women on the other side of the divide answered back with some seriously nasty digs of their own. "With the era of Woman-Emancipation," wrote the philosopher-ethicist Ellen Key in *The Atlantic,* comes "a deep transformation in the view of life, during which all values [are] estimated anew, even the value of motherliness. And now women themselves borrow their argument from science when they try to prove that motherliness is only an attribute woman shares with the female animal . . . Motherliness has diminished to such a degree that women use their intelligence in trying to prove not only that day-nurseries, kindergartens and schools are necessary helps in case of need, but that they are *better* than the too devoted and confining motherliness of the home, where the child is developed into a family-egoist, not into a social modern human being! . . . When they say the women of today want to be 'freed' from the inferior duties of mother and housewife in order to devote themselves to higher callings as self-supporting and independent members of society, how much more will that be the case with the women of the future! . . . Has our race ever been afflicted by a more dangerous disease than the one which at present rages among women: the sick yearning to be 'freed' from the most essential attribute of their sex?"

Yet that is only the start of the astonishing clarity with which some foresaw today's furious cultural battles. On those dry pages and seldom viewed microfilms are found warnings that feminism would undermine marriage and make divorce increasingly the norm, and would so dramatically blur distinctions between the sexes that even the military would eventually not be immune to its effects.

Some argued men would adjust well to the coming changes, others that legions of ball-busting females would surely provoke a vast increase in male anger and violence. "As woman claims her new and perilous privileges," editorialized the very *New York Times* in 1912 (arguing *against* suffrage), "man will develop into a dominating brute."

It is worth noting that none of the direst consequences predicted by the alarmists on both sides came to pass. At least in part, that surely has to do with the vigor of the debate itself. As we embarked on what was finally seen as a noble social experiment, there was widespread awareness of the dangerous turns it might take, and the radicals were effectively isolated.

In our own time, in contrast, it was the more conservative and traditionalist voices that were muted, and feminist ideologues who were increasingly allowed to pass as mainstream. Though in fact the actual number of hard-core feminists has always been small—at its height, the National Organization for Women counted fewer than half the members (250,000) than there were female subscribers to *Playboy* (600,000)—the media's assumption that they speak for the mass of women has repeatedly enabled them to cow politicians and policy makers.

This was never more so than in the emotion-fueled aftermath of Hill-Thomas, with male pols (and journalists) on the defensive and more eager than ever to establish their nonsexist *bona fides*.

That season, the feminist rhetoric was even angrier than usual, and it went to the very heart of the matter: *it is not just that certain men are monsters, there's something in the very* nature *of male sexuality that is aberrant*.

According to feminist super-lawyer Catherine MacKinnon at the time, fully "47 percent of women are victims of rape or attempted rape at least once in their lives"—adding that that figure is almost surely low.

What's key is that MacKinnon made this observation not at some feminist conference but on ABC, in the panel discussion following a network special entitled "Men, Sex and Rape"—and that she was being hired at the time to design sex harassment statutes for municipalities around the country.

MacKinnon naturally had the support of the other leading feminists on the broadcast, armed, as they often are, with incredible statistics of dubious origin. Faludi, for one, added, "we have to see rape on a continuum with sexual harassment that, what, 40, 50 percent of women in the workplace say they experience. I mean, these are problems that are not just coming from a few men. This is a culture-wide problem."

But most meaningful is how eager the show's host, Peter Jennings, was to agree. "To learn about rape," he solemnly intoned at the outset, "we must consider this: Men on the street do not see the other half of the population as a potential physical threat. Most women do.

"The modern view," he observed a bit later, "is that the miscommunication men describe—'She really meant yes'—is only an excuse to hide the obvious—forced sex originates in the minds of men."

And a bit after that, looking deeply troubled, he asked a sociology professor and "rape expert": "Given the overall relationship between men and women—men superior, women inferior, historically—is there a potential aggressor, is there a potential rapist in every man?"

Yes, agreed the expert solemnly, there is.

When essayist John Leo, the panel's voice for common sense, spoke up to challenge the statistics being so cavalierly tossed around, the feminist heavies seemed positively aghast. "That means you don't believe women," shot back MacKinnon.

The elections that fall—in what the media would dub the "year of the woman"—proved pivotal. Soon feminist tacticians were moving even more aggressively to turn gender theory into social legislation, criminalizing behaviors that previous generations had regarded as merely boorish and explicitly refusing to make the sorts of sensible distinctions that rational people have made through the ages.

Dissenting voices were few and mainly timid. "No doesn't always mean no," wrote Paglia, in what today registers as a clarion call to sanity, but in the spirit of the time was swept aside.

Within months of Bill Clinton's assuming the presidency, his Equal Employment Opportunity Commission issued stringent new regulations on sexual harassment in the workplace. Three months after that, the Supreme Court ruled that women no longer have to prove "psychological injury" to make a sexual harassment claim, but merely establish conduct that creates a "hostile or abusive work environment." Around the same time, the Senate overwhelmingly passed an amendment loosening the rules on admissibility of evidence in antiwomen sexual crimes.

Effective as Democrats were in harnessing "women's issues" for partisan purposes, Republicans were not much better. Indeed, even more clueless in this area than most, over the next few years they actually outpandered the Democrats. One especially odious civil liberties trashing Senate amendment, extending the evidence-gathering apparatus in gender cases, was sponsored by Bob Dole; in the 75–19 vote that followed, a mere two Republicans voted against.

Yet in retrospect, what's more telling than the politicians getting stampeded is how unprepared were the rest of us, after years of silence on the particulars of the feminist agenda, to grasp where turning their program into law might lead.

For many, that only began to become clearer on May 6, 1994, with an Associated Press story datelined Little Rock: "A former Arkansas state employee sued President Clinton today, accusing him of making an unwanted sexual advance while he was Governor in 1991."

I'm sure by now you won't get me wrong: obviously, I found it hard to muster much sympathy for Clinton. After all, in addition to all the rest, he'd always been a feminist stalwart himself. Looking up the word "petard" in my trusty old *Webster's*, I am pleased to find listed among the meanings "a firecracker," from the French verb "to break wind."

In fact—talk about arrogance!—it was four months *after* Paula Jones lodged her charge that Clinton signed into law the Violence Against Women Act, harboring the clause on evidence-gathering in harassment cases that would lead directly to his impeachment.

Still, as the ACLU gang reminds us when going to bat for the KKK and other moral cretins, it's the most morally problematic cases that establish the principle. Clinton is definitely a creep and maybe a sociopath; before this thing was done he would commit perjury, obstruct justice and lie through his teeth to the American people. Many of us have little doubt that under other circumstances, or if he were almost anyone else, he'd have been brought up on any number of other charges, up to and including rape.

But, in this instance, he was ensnared by bad law, the kind that has too often been brought to bear against better individuals guilty of nothing at all.

No one this side of Charlie Manson questions that any animal who slips his date a dose of GHB and sexually assaults her oughta be locked up someplace where keys haven't been invented; hell, in the old days, before chivalry got identified as just another form of sexism (and lawyers got into the act), other guys would often take an s.o.b. who physically mistreated a woman into an alley for some impromptu sensitivity training.

Yet with amazing frequency what we're talking about these days is run-of-the-mill male behavior—flirting, teasing, kidding around, the sort of edgy interactions between the sexes that used to be seen by almost everyone as normal and even healthy.

I've only had one firsthand brush with a baseless charge, in the early nineties, but it was more than enough. It was directed at a friend I'll call Jack, a talented writer and editor I've known almost twenty years and, by the way, a solid liberal; which is to say, like Clinton, he'd much always assumed the sexual harassment agenda he supported could never be turned against people like *him*.

I was doing a stint as executive editor for the start-up of a glossy new men's magazine and as such had a hand in hiring Jack as managing editor. He in turn hired much of the rest of the staff, including a female assistant editor fresh out of journalism school. She seemed capable enough, and as friendly as everyone else around the place, and my friend thought nothing of going out with her a couple of times for lunch.

Though contentedly married and doggedly faithful, Jack's an upbeat guy who when comfortable can also be pretty quick with a one-liner or double entendre.

Big mistake. Caught in the act of being himself.

One afternoon, the young woman went to the head of the company, and reported Jack had been inappropriately suggestive. This set off a hush-hush crisis. The top guy knew full well the charge was ludicrous, but the timing couldn't have been worse; his chief concern was getting out the magazine. A public stink just as we were about to launch could've been disastrous.

So my friend was eased out.

It caught him totally by surprise; he was handed a line the "personality mix." When he asked me, and I told him the truth, he first refused to believe it. It made no sense, he hadn't done anything wrong. Things like this just didn't happen.

But, of course, they were happening all the time—and, all things considered, he got off pretty easy.

Around the same time I read about a case at Pomona College, my hitherto sleepy and sensible alma mater, involving a senior awaiting graduation who'd been charged with rape by a young woman he'd slept with *two and a half years* before. It seemed that in the fullness of time, the young woman, who did not even disagree with the young man on the essential facts—that they'd met at a party, gotten drunk and gone up to his room; even that she never actually voiced any objection when they had sex—now decided she'd been coerced.

Yet the school took her side, holding up the guy's graduation without so much as a hearing. And a concluding touch: after he'd gone to court and won the right to participate in the ceremony, a couple of fellow graduates unfurled a banner screaming THERE IS A RAPIST AMONG US.

As anyone who's paid attention knows, there have been innumerable such episodes on campuses around the country. Sometimes even sticking up for an accused can be dicey. *Civilization* magazine columnist Mary Karr writes of supporting a male colleague who'd been accused of sexual harassment at the college where they teach and suddenly finding, in a Kafkaesque turn, that vicious rumors were being spread about her. "Under normal circumstances, sexual harassment charges would've sent me reeling with laughter. But the atmosphere had banished all reason, painting everyone in the . . . department as an accomplice rapist."

This was the real sexual McCarthyism, and it reached everywhere. By the mid-nineties, each week seemed to bring a new headline of an alleged high-level transgression in government, the military, or a corporate suite. And those were just the high-profile cases; it's anyone's guess how many anonymous corporate managers accused of piggishness were led to ritual slaughter. Forced to pay through the nose to settle legal claims, businesses subsidized a new cottage industry of "equity specialists" and "gender rights counselors" that more and more resembled a protection racket.

A year or so before the Woody Allen--Mia Farrow standoff, I did a piece for *Playboy* on the astonishing rise in child sexual abuse charges against men involved in bitter custody battles—charges that, though almost never proved, had the effect of instantly ending the court fight and cutting them off from their children. Like Woody, the guys I spoke to were outraged by the charges and fighting them with everything they had—but, unlike him, they were not readily cleared. The stories—of presumed guilt and a systematic denial of due process by the legal authorities, of the lengths to which social workers would go to persuade tiny kids to endorse the charges—were beyond chilling, all the more so for their redundancy.

Christina Hoff Sommers' *Who Stole Feminism?* gave chapter and verse on the radicals' shameless cooking of statistics—from a massive overstatement of annual anorexia deaths to an equally imaginary increase in male violence on Super Bowl Sunday—so useful in achieving their policy ends, and on the irresponsibility of a compliant media that let them get away with it. Among the most shocking, she says, "one of the most vicious libels against men, was the phony claim that battering causes more birth defects than all other causes combined. By the time I read that statistic, I knew that damage inflicted by battering is relatively rare—and birth defects are not that rare. Battering causes more birth defects than Tay-Sachs, spinal bifida, Down's syndrome, alcohol *combined?* But it was put out all over the place, attributed to the March of Dimes. So I called the March of Dimes. They said, we've never seen this research before, it's not true, but the rumor is spinning out of control. Their office had been flooded with phone calls from governors, journalists, Senator Kennedy's office. That's the interesting thing—everyone wanted that report. Not only are they libeling men, but everybody wants it. There is a market for incendiary statistics that implicate men as monsters."

And though even now many insistently look the other way, all this, too, is a legacy of the feminist revolution.

My friends, for their part, acknowledge the excesses. But they choose to think we're past the worst of it.

Would that it were so.

Absolutely, Sexgate opened a lot of eyes. In its wake, a greater number of people than ever before see the women's movement as more partisan than principled, and have a clearer idea of the joyless world its leaders would create. Even entrenched ideologues like Mary Daley—the women's studies prof fired by Boston College for refusing to let men into her classes—can no longer automatically count on a sympathetic press.

For that matter, the tolerance-of-idiocy quotient is down in general. Just yesterday I spotted a newspaper article that would have been impossible five years ago, belittling as absurd the firing for sexual harassment of a postal worker in upstate New York who'd sent flowers to a coworker.

Too, more than a few books have appeared, from mainstream houses and to respectful notice, taking on some of feminism's most cherished truths. "Girls are not silenced or ignored in the classroom," writes Cathy Young in *Ceasefire! Why Women and Men Must Join Forces to Achieve True Equality.* "Medicine has not neglected women's health. Abuse by men is not the leading cause of injury to American women . . . Gender disparities in pay and job status are not merely a consequence of sex discrimination. The Eighties were not a 'backlash decade' but a time of steady progress for women . . ."

Hey, even this one got published.

Yet that's all trees and we're dealing with a deep, dark forest.

No question, the *word* "feminist" is in disrepute. Even a *Time* magazine survey notes that women, especially younger ones, are uncomfortable with the label.

But if the good guys have belatedly made up ground in the semantic battle, the larger realities are unchanged. The laws remain on the books, and the gender equity business continues to boom. For all the hits women's groups took on hypocrisy, few—least of all, Clinton himself— hold them accountable for creating the mess in the first place.

Like the Viet Cong, radical feminists are indefatigable, highly motivated, have good P.R. and fight dirty, and there is no reason to believe there has been even the slightest pause in their war of attrition.

Easily overlooked in the news glut the very day the Clinton trial began in the Senate, there appeared on the *New York Times* editorial page a chilling letter. It was from Marie Wilson, president of the Ms. Foundation for Women, seizing this moment to press the next item on the sisterhood's agenda: seeing to it that sexual harassment laws are extended to cover *elementary* schools.

□

On the other hand, why wouldn't the feminists go after boys? Knowing what they grow into, it's a natural progression—getting at the *root* of the problem.

But we're getting ahead of ourselves. For, naturally enough, their initial focus was on girls. They were the ones, so it was said, in crisis. Born into a culture stacked against them—one where, for all the sisterhood's best efforts, engineers are still overwhelmingly male and Barbie sells like hotcakes—they desperately needed enhanced training in self-reliance and self-esteem. Thus, the Ms. Foundation created Take Our Daughters to Work Day. And a group of feminist academics called the American Association of University Women brought forth a report asserting that in early adolescence girls "lose their voice," shunted aside by boys (abetted by inadvertently sexist teachers) who dominate aggressive classroom discussions. The theory was quickly accepted as common wisdom and in due course led to congressional passage of the Gender Equity in Education Act, mandating, among other things, federal money for gender equity specialists to sensitize teachers to girls' needs.

It's only recently—through the efforts of Christina Sommers and others—that word has gotten out that we appear to have been focusing on the wrong crisis in American childhood. For by almost every measure, it is boys (and especially minority boys) who are truly hurting. Boys are far likelier than girls to have learning disabilities, to fail in school, to commit crimes and be incarcerated; they are four times as likely to be diagnosed as emotionally disturbed and seven times as likely to kill themselves.

And now, belatedly, the feminists have also turned their gaze on boys. They claim to *empathize*. They want to remake boys' behavior and their emotional lives so at long last they, too, can be whole.

It is a prospect that should make the blood of parents everywhere run cold.

It is not that we parents of boys are necessarily under any illusions. We know what pains they can be. That they're often unruly, disorganized, blind to reason. That at an age when girls are focused on school, they're likely to be far more passionate about fart jokes or movies featuring ear-shattering explosions.

The difference is that we love them, deeply and without qualification. And we know the quality of their hearts and minds as well as we do those of their sisters.

For years, they didn't even bother pretending to *like* them.

A pertinent story.

When my son Charlie was in fourth grade, his teacher inadvertently scheduled "Authors' Day"—the morning the kids were to show off their literary skills for parents—on "Take Our Daughters to Work Day." Thus it was that about half the girls were missing.

All in all, this turned out to be not that bad a thing for the boys—or their parents.

The first kid the teacher asked to read was a tiny little girl, who dazzled us with a remarkable essay on the lives of Australian aborigines. She was followed by another girl who, with the calm assurance of a young Emma Thompson, read a tale entitled "A Grandfather's Imaginings," about lessons learned, forgotten and relearned over the course of a long life.

Then came the first boy. His story was called "The Battle of Planet Brain Gook" and it involved not only brain matter and interplanetary warfare, but professional wrestling. This was followed by my son's opus—"Stupid Dogs." Proud as I remain of what a lit critic might call the story's "energy" and "daring logical leaps," I couldn't help noticing it was only four sentences long.

As his sister, three years older, afterward observed with disgust, "I left behind the best reputation for writing in the whole fourth grade and he just frittered it away."

Then, again, he should not be singled out. For so it went for the better part of an hour: most of the boys making like Bart Simpson, and most of the girls on hand making like Lisa.

"How'd you like 'Stupid Dogs'?" my son asked me afterward.

"Very much. It seemed a little short, though."

"Yeah, I know. It didn't turn out as good as I wanted. I couldn't think of anything else to say." He paused. "The girls were better, didn't you think?"

"Not better, darling," I lied. "Different. Anyway, don't worry, it all evens out eventually."

"Really?" He was incredulous. "Even in *handwriting?*"

At the time I was far from sure and so, it seemed, were some of the other parents of boys I chatted with afterward.

I think that was the first day I ever heard the word "Ritalin."

Of course, soon the subject, and the arguments pro and con, would be impossible to avoid. Today it's estimated that nearly four million kids are on the stuff—and at least three times more boys than girls.

This says more than a little about how we as a society regard our children, and especially our boys. For while even the drug's critics acknowledge it can be useful in controlling severely disruptive behavior, no one questions that it is now being prescribed to cure problems that prior generations never even knew were there. Indeed, "symptoms" like chronic fidgeting, ignoring instructions, even calling out answers were regarded (though perhaps with pained indulgence) as normal. It was just the way some boys acted, until they outgrew it.

Yet in this feminized age, notes one alarmed California psychologist, the goal seems to be ridding the average classroom of "high energy and fierce independence." Adds Emory University anthropologist Peter Konnor, "There is now an attempt to pathologize what was once considered the normal range of boy behaviors ... Tom Sawyer and Huckleberry Finn surely would have been diagnosed with both conduct disorder and ADHD." "The old saying 'boys will be boys' " sums up a mother from New Orleans in a letter to *The Wall Street Journal,* "has evolved into 'boys will be medicated.' "

And boys get the message. Oblivious as they often are—part of their charm—they have a pretty good idea where they stand. How could they not? They're reminded constantly—by popular culture, by impatient teachers, even by slogans on apparel.

As one of the ubiquitous "girl power" tee shirts favored by suburban seven-year-olds has it:

> *Jack and Jill went up the hill*
> *Jack fell down and broke his crown.*
> *Jill picked up his pail, filled it,*
> *and kicked Jack's ass down the hill.*

Most every little boy growing up in contemporary America knows full well that if *he* showed up at school wearing such a put-down about girls, he'd be summarily marched to the principal's office for a lecture on sexism and sensitivity.

Pick up a contemporary book aimed at preteen boys these days and the role reversals start on page one. Boys are not allowed to do anything truly noble or heroic anymore unless, observed David Frum in *The Weekly Standard,* they "have girls with them, doing everything they do—indeed, doing it better." How do fictional boys strut their stuff in today's publishing universe? "Here is a publisher's blurb for a book about a boy who courageously 'defies teasing to remain enrolled in ballet class.' Here's another about 'Lame teenager Shem' who 'finds manhood in the Michigan wilderness with the help of an old Indian woman.' And a third: 'Doing volunteer work at Santa Barbara's Sidewalk's End, a day-care facility for children of the homeless, Ben witnesses an instance of physical abuse and—for the best of reasons—decides to take matters into his own hands.' "

Meanwhile, needless to say, old-fashioned interplay with the opposite sex in real life is ever more suspect. As it turned out, women's groups had no need to expand the definition of sexual harassment to cover the schools; the Supreme Court did it for them, with a 5–4 ruling in May 1999 holding schools themselves responsible for controlling adolescent behavior, including speech. Wrote Justice Anthony Kennedy, in a brilliant, disbelieving dissent: "The real world of school discipline is a rough-and-tumble place where students practice learned vulgarities, erupt with anger, tease and embarrass each other, share offensive notes, flirt, push and shove in the halls, grab and offend . . . It is a far different question, however, whether it is either proper or useful to label this immature, childish behavior gender discrimination . . ."

But putting even the youngest young men in their legal place is evidently just the start. Now feminist activists propose to lead boys to the light by altering the very way they see the world and their place in it.

There is, in this embrace, all the loving warmth one associates with the witch taking in Hansel and Gretel.

As enunciated by the likes of Susan Faludi and Harvard's Carol Gilligan, the very gender theoretician whose "girls-losing-their-voice" theory stigmatized boys' "aggressive" classroom behavior in the first place, the feminist position is that we must all now recognize young males are *also* victims of the patriarchy.

The root problem, notes Gilligan, reverently quoted in the *New York Times,* is that boys are raised "to conform to the norms of 'Real Manhood,' " which, natch, "can brutalize and scar them emotionally." They "find themselves in a struggle against a culture that says they have to be tough and independent, that they can't be too close to people."

And how do we get boys on track? Dumb question. Why, males must relearn the meaning of masculinity. "Just as women are now allowed to be more like men," as one "gender specialist" and Gilligan acolyte told the *San Francisco Chronicle,* "it's time men were allowed to be more like women."

"We want little boys to take on feelings," notes Merry-Murray Meade, a kindergarten teacher in the Boston area, in another approving *Times* article on the subject. "Boys were traditionally raised to be soldiers and every toy and cartoon dealt with not having feelings, and you could hurt people and nothing would happen."

Huh? Anyone else out there think boys have been raised to think they could hurt people and *nothing would happen?*

In fact, it's far closer to the truth that boys were traditionally raised to think of themselves as defenders of the weak and powerless. Look at the heroes in classic boy literature and movies and comic books—always incredibly honorable, generally self-effacing, models of courage, character and decency.

Ask any parent of an eight-year-old leaping from the couch in Superman pajamas: all that speaks in a profound way to the young male soul. Indeed, wonders the essayist David Gelernter, why should the toy weapons little boys so love always be sneeringly derided as "instruments of death"? Why not see them, as most kids do, as instruments of justice?

Which is also to say, when little boys play with guns (or, if that's forbidden, make guns of sticks or shoes or pencils or their fingers), this is not a bad thing, either.

The problem, of course, is the sisterhood's inability to acknowledge bedrock truth: boys can *never* be made into girls any more than the other way around.

And only the demented would want them to be.

In this regard as in others, reading the literature of an earlier and, in crucial ways, healthier America can be tremendously reassuring for parents. For kids, too. I'll never forget the night my son and I picked up *Penrod*, Booth Tarkington's near-forgotten 1915 masterpiece about a twelve-year-old boy and his circle, a copy of which I'd snared at a garage sale. Charlie was about ten at the time, and within a couple of pages we were both hooked. For Penrod Schofield was unlike any preadolescent we'd encountered in any modern kids' book. He wasn't troubled or sensitive or, for that matter, much interested in feelings of any kind. In the tradition of Tom and Huck and the Little Rascals, Penrod was rambunctious and always up to mayhem—and blithely unaware of the confusion and dismay he provoked among his elders.

Charlie was especially taken with a scene where Penrod's mind starts wandering during a math lesson, "following the operation a little while with his eyes but not with his mind; then, sinking deeper in his seat, limply abandoning the effort. His eyes remained open but saw nothing; the routine of the arithmetic lesson reached his ears in familiar, meaningless sounds but he heard nothing. And yet, he was profoundly occupied. He had drifted away from the painful land of facts, and floated now to the marvelous realness of a boy's daydreams . . ."

The daydream in question had Penrod literally floating from his seat and flying around the room—startling all his classmates with the feat, and especially a certain little girl. When his reverie is interrupted by the teacher's voice, sharply asking him a question, he reflexively snaps back at her with what at the time was appalling brazenness. "Can't you keep still for one minute?!"

At this, my son (who's had a couple of run-ins with teachers himself over the years) cracked up. "That's so great! How come they don't write books like that anymore?"

Good question. I wish there was a better answer.

It's four years later, and Charlie's only now begun to turn it around in school. There haven't been any complaints from teachers lately about homework not handed in; last semester there was only one grade under a B; suddenly he seems to have a real ear for French and has actually begun reading ancient history on his own. Even his handwriting has gotten pretty good.

It's been a long struggle, and we couldn't be prouder of him. One might say he's at last "found his voice," literally; for, in addition to the rest, he's speaking up more than ever in class.

And I'll tell you right now: if anyone ever dares make him feel like a bully for it, they'll have his parents (and a sister) to deal with.

What's less readily apparent than feminist hostility to boys—*that's* pretty clear—is the growing evidence that in vital ways the remade world has also ill-served many of those who are supposedly its greatest beneficiaries: younger women.

Beyond question, the fights for access to the professions and the boardrooms have been of incalculable importance. Women today can compete with men in almost every realm. They have freedom up the wazoo—economic, sexual, reproductive.

But then what?

For women do not live by bread alone or, more precisely, by what even bushels of it buys: homes, cars, Caribbean vacations.

Ultimately of even greater importance is what, in this post-revolutionary age, is harder to come by than ever before: romance, emotional sustenance, abiding commitment.

That is why the most important book for and about women since Betty Friedan got the whole business started may well be one by a twenty-three-year-old recent graduate of Williams College named Wendy Shalit. Entitled *A Return to Modesty: Discovering the Lost Virtue*, it vividly describes the social and sexual experiences of women like herself in the sheltered precincts of elite academia. These are seemingly hip and self-assured archetypes of modern, sexually liberated young women, and, yet, after years of meaningless sexual encounters, some are so worn down and alienated they actually cultivate eating disorders as a means of withdrawing from the social fray.

What they desperately seek, writes Shalit, is a world that makes emotional sense: one where men will be trustworthy and behave honorably, but, too, far more, one where young women will be free to trust their *own* instincts and move at their own pace. Her argument is that the demands of a sex-obsessed culture and an ethic that labels them prudes for the sin of reticence has, in the end, been less liberating than destructive. "The problem is that since the 1960's we have found it 'sexist' to expect girls to be morally good—no more eternal feminine, woman-on-a-pedestal business here," she writes in *The Wall Street Journal*. "So now the only womanly things left for them to be good at are putting on lipstick and being good—in bed."

To social conservatives, this all made uncommonly good sense. "The sexual counterrevolution is at hand," proclaimed *The Weekly Standard* in a cover story on the book. "And contrary to the darkest fears of some, it is being led not by Bible-thumping fundamentalists or prune-faced matrons with beehive hairdos. It's being led by young women looking for romance."

But most on the other side—for whom it is heresy that the women's movement or, for the matter, the sixties might have been a mixed blessing—were aghast. Shalit's "logic doesn't merely inform her thinking," wrote a feminist academic in an especially venomous put-down in the *New York Times Book Review*, "it envelopes her book like, well, a chastity belt."

Nothing new there. Repeatedly over the years, in large ways and small, the elites in the press and academia have gone out of their way to endorse the feminist version of reality. "The Higher Education Research Institute at UCLA recently reported a record-low support for casual sex among freshman college students: 39.6%," notes Shalit. "This is a striking fact. But an even more striking fact is buried deep in the institute's 170-page study—namely, that while 53.6% of male students still favor casual sex, only a low of 27.7% of female students do. Why did the researchers average the results? Because, one suspects, it is déclassé to notice an asymmetry between the romantic desires of men and women."

It is certainly true—witness that 27.7 percent figure—
hardly a one-size-fits-all proposition. Clearly, there are lᶠ
lighted with the existing social/sexual scene. Just recently ᵅ
sale, I ran across a young woman handing out buttons from a wickₑ.
basket.

"NO CONDOMS?" read one, "GET OUTTA MY HOUSE!"

"MEN," ordered another, angry black on sunny yellow,

"USE CONDOMS

OR BEAT IT"

I glanced at the person smiling at me from behind the table, maybe
nineteen and very pretty in a sundress. "Interesting . . ."

"Aren't they, though?"

"Do people actually wear these?"

"Not often." She laughed. "But it's useful to have 'em lying around,
just so guys'll know where you stand."

There is, needless to say, a fair amount of this going around; the sassy,
uninhibited woman is very much in vogue, and more power to her.

I wouldn't have minded a bit running into this one back in college
myself. . . .

Then, again, that's part of Shalit's point. Anyone with half a brain
knows this is far more a *male* ideal. "What's the definition of 'making
love'?" as a joke making the rounds of the Internet lately has it. "It's
something a woman does while a man's fucking her."

Crude, but more than a little true. And in promoting the ideologically
driven falsehood that the sexes are equally raunchy and undiscriminat-
ing, the movement is massively failing many for whom it purports to
speak.

Not that over the long term such an ethic serves men much better, encouraging as it does a kind of narcissism that sees sex as an end in itself. Once it was generally understood that it is precisely through
responsibility to others—to women, to children—that men earn their
moral keep in the world. Today many seem to feel no need to be responsible to anything larger than the state of their own pecs and abs.

If one were to begin an honest search for answers for what sometimes
seems an unbridgeable gulf between men and women of the *Ally
McBeal/Sex in the City* set, a good place to start might be the assumption

that this is what happens when society (a) absolves men of the need to be sexually responsible and (b) denigrates honor as an essential male trait.

This is something I think most women implicitly understand. In fact, on closer examination, sometimes even those who flash their own sexual bravura most aggressively are masking feelings far more complex. I happened to read an interview during the recent Sundance Film Festival with Grace Quek (alias Annabel Chong), a stunning twenty-six-year-old Singapore-born adult film star who was at the festival promoting a documentary on her claim to fame: a record for having sex with (count 'em!) 251 men in ten hours. A former USC undergraduate in gender studies, Quek described the experience to the reporter almost boastfully. "Growing up as a woman, I was taught that females are supposed to be passive. We like to be subdued, we like romantic things. But I think there is a certain segment of people out there, especially among younger generations, who prefer a more aggressive mode of sexuality."

And yet, farther on in the same piece it is revealed that in the documentary itself a distraught Quek is at one point shown "slicing the inside of her forearm over and over, sobbing about the 'numbness' of the world, and the 'need to feel something.' "

Shalit's voice is but the clearest of many that have been heard lately on the epidemic of romantic confusion in the culture brought on by the disconnection between sex and love. The search for answers has everything to do with why *The Rules*—the how-to on catching a guy the old-fashioned way—was such a spectacular best-seller; why Dr. Laura's litany of Shalt Nots draws by far the largest women's audience in radio; and, perhaps especially, why Calista Flockhart's flighty, neurotic McBeal, forever yearning for love and motherhood, has emerged as so potent a symbol for today's young women.

Time magazine was even moved to put Ally on the cover beneath the line "Is Feminism Dead?" "She's not a hard, strident feminist out of the 60's and 70's," *Time* quoted Ally's muse David E. Kelley on his creation. "She's all for women's rights, but she doesn't want to lead the charge at her own emotional expense." Which led *Time*'s writer, a feminist of the old school much upset by this sort of paleo-thinking, to bitterly lament: "Maybe if she lost her job and wound up a single mom, we could begin a movement again."

What such a mind-set refuses to grasp is that the craving for connection and intimacy is universal, and it is a profoundly healthy thing that even the hippest of the hip are no longer pretending to be immune. A talented young writer named Amy Sohn, until recently a columnist for the *New York Press*, turned her own romantic ups and downs—and her mounting wistfulness as she moved deeper into her twenties—into some of the best personal journalism of recent years. In one especially memorable piece she describes how, recently split from her latest boyfriend, she discovers that the one before him lied when he broke things off, not telling her he'd already impregnated an old girlfriend. And though she has plans to see yet another guy, "riding him til he cries," the column's pivotal scene has her alone in her apartment, watching a documentary on TV about the legendary caricaturist Al Hirschfeld. "They were showing a scene where he finished a drawing and he said, 'Come take a look at this, Dolly,' and his wife of many years came over and said, 'It needs more shading around the breast,' and he said, 'You think?' and they inspected it together and looked so peacefully unified and in love that I got choked up. The next 10 minutes were about the next 10 years of his career, and then suddenly he was talking about Dolly's death. 'My friends think I'm over it,' he said, 'but I'm not over it. I'm furious,' and they showed these old photos of young Dolly smiling and laughing and I started to sob. I wanted to know a love like that, a lifetime love that leaves you furious at God when they go. I wanted a Dolly."

There is nothing remarkable in this, of course. Lonely people have felt such longings since the beginning of time. Still, there is an especially sad quality to the plaint nowadays when it comes from such attractive and capable young women.

I don't know Amy Sohn, but I know a number of young women like her: smart, sassy, seemingly self-assured and serially alone. I was discussing one of these not long ago with a neighbor of mine, her uncle. "She intimidates young men," was the explanation he'd come up with, "I think she scares them away with her confidence."

Possibly there was something to this, but it was nonetheless quaint to see this loving and protective older man take it as the whole story; for I'd met some of the guys, and they had plenty of confidence also, and I got the impression hers was part of the *attraction*.

"I don't know," he said after a moment, "it's confusing. It just seems like they've thrown away all the rules."

Which pretty much nailed it.

Over the past few decades, we've heard ad infinitum about how poorly the old rules served women, and there's probably something to that. But we've heard far too little about how they served everyone well.

Observes Danielle Crittenden, one of feminism's most astute critics, urging young women to perhaps look back to the future: "The negative— we are no longer able to live entirely for ourselves, is also the positive: *We no longer have to live entirely for ourselves!*"

"Don't tell me!" exclaimed a friend of ours recently at a dinner party, her horror unfeigned; for she's one of those women for whom there is no other issue—and only one side to that. "Now you're against *abortion?!!!!!!*"

Well, no, not exactly. Given our history—mine, my wife's, ours together—that would be something like hypocrisy cubed.

But no longer were we pretending that it was a simple question, unworthy of intense soul searching. And—*more* blasphemy!—neither did we necessarily share her views on the definition of "humane" or the identities of the zealots.

Through my twenties, I never gave abortion's moral dimension a passing thought. I'm quite sure every woman I knew was pro-choice, and who was I to argue? In fact—let's not kid ourselves—who *wanted* to argue? When *Roe* v. *Wade* came along, greeted with jubilation by the young women in our midst, we guys recognized it as nearly as much a blessing for us.

Only recently out of college, at that point I'd experienced no actual pregnancies of my own, but the close calls had been more than bad enough. I'll never forget the fall evening in my junior year when my distraught girlfriend, maybe a week overdue, went off on this jag about how we had to go down to Tijuana, where she had the name of some guy who'd take care of it; never mind her, I could already see *myself* lying murdered in some godforsaken Mexican alleyway.

Why, these modern kids today can't even imagine the relief we felt back in them days after a serious false alarm.

So legal abortion was, figuratively speaking, a lifesaver; and it seemed very few were doing much thinking about the literal part. If it is imprecise to assert, as some pro-lifers do, that lots of people started viewing abortion as just another form of birth control—certainly among those I knew that was never remotely true—it was a damn useful safety net.

I must report that eventually I was party to three abortions. The first two were with a longtime girlfriend with whom I lived for four years in my mid-twenties. Just starting her career, certain she wasn't ready for children and not much surer over the long run she wanted me, for her the decision seemed a no-brainer; and though the experiences were trying, she appeared to bear up pretty well.

The third was with Priscilla, a year or so after we met. Although we'd already tentatively talked marriage, kids seemed a long, long ways off, so again abortion appeared the obvious course. After all, she'd already had one before herself.

So I was stunned when, afterward, she seemed shaken to her very core. Unwilling as she was to talk about it, I didn't begin to know how to comfort her. *What was the big deal?*

Only much later would she come entirely clean: it was the realization she had destroyed not a tissue mass, but a child she'd already started to love.

That is why, when she got pregnant again some months later, it was clear we were not going to proceed the same way again. Either we'd get married and raise this child or we would split—in which case, quite possibly, she'd have the baby anyway.

It was a terrifying dilemma; at times I felt I had a shotgun to my head. It was also the best thing that ever happened to me.

Not that the experience changed her view, let alone mine, that legal abortion was both necessary and right. When we moved from the city to the suburbs, there was a clinic in the adjacent town that was picketed every Saturday morning by pro-life activists. Priscilla used to get outraged when we had to stop at a light mere yards away and they held their gruesome photos of aborted fetuses close to the window. "You people are *disturbed!*" she'd yell at them, trying to cover the kids' eyes, and as we drove off she'd mutter about the self-righteous jerks who loved children, all right—as long as they *were* unborn!

I couldn't agree more. Didn't these people know what they were suggesting? Could they honestly believe outlawing abortion would make the world a better place? Didn't they remember the days of coat hangers and backroom butchers?

Actually, I didn't remember those days all that clearly, either—I was a kid and those things weren't much talked about. But I do recall reading, with horrified fascination, a story in our local paper about a young woman from the nearby College of New Rochelle—a Catholic institution—whose body had been found stuffed in a drainage pipe, and gathering from my parents' conversation that she'd died in a botched abortion. And I remember that the story was pretty upsetting to my mother.

Later my mother told me that back in the thirties, as a very young woman, she'd had an abortion herself. Evidently in her crowd the procedure was not all that uncommon, so in theory it wasn't supposed to be a big deal. Yet for my mother, as for my wife forty-five years later, it was. Still, in her case there was a major difference: at least partly, the horror had to do with the illicit aspect of the experience: the professional but creepy abortionist, the makeshift operating room, the sense of doing something shameful.

If there'd been the slightest question, her account made me fully understand why even the remote possibility of a return to that era gives so many women the willies.

In the grand scheme of things, I still count myself as pro-choice.

Yet over time that feeling of utter certitude has been tempered by others far more complex. Partly that came from the growing realization that the blind self-righteousness cuts both ways. But far more, it had to do with actually getting to know some committed pro-lifers and finding them both personally gracious and deeply thoughtful—about as far as humanly possible in fact, from the caricature so useful to the other side.

"One of the things pro-choice people do to comfort themselves is re-assure themselves that opposition to abortion is based on hatred of women," notes writer Cynthia Gorney, the author of *Articles of Faith: A Frontline History of the Abortion Wars*, who, pro-choice herself, likewise gained a deep respect for pro-life activists in researching her book. ". . . It's comforting to people to ignore the amount of genuine compassion for what are seen by some as defenseless people."

In fact, given the tremendous reserves of decency and selflessness so many bring to the fight against abortion, the depiction of the average pro-lifer as a wild-eyed ideologue who is not-so-secretly pleased by the killing of abortion providers is an especially revolting slander. How's this for a neutral and fair-minded question, the centerpiece of a recent *Glamour* magazine poll: "Should anti-abortion activists be allowed to advocate murder?"

"When that doctor was shot outside Buffalo, everyone I know was appalled," observes my good friend Larry, today as passionately opposed to abortion as he once was to the war. "Pro-life leaders condemned it immediately as a sickening and heinous crime, and they kept saying that over and over. But day after day, there it was in the press: we were all guilty by association! There's no understanding that most people arrive at this position from a great *respect* for life."

Indeed, while Catholics and other believers obviously provide the movement's core, many pro-lifers are not especially religious at all. "My position," as veteran civil libertarian and *Village Voice* columnist Nat Hentoff, perhaps the best-known leftist in the anti-abortion camp, puts it, "is that if you're truly in favor of life—against capital punishment and nuclear war—you've also got to start asking questions about abortion which just cannot be resolved."

And, true enough, the basic case for keeping abortion legal, persuasive as most people I know find it, is at heart more pragmatic than moral. A matter of facing the reality that, whether the procedure is legally sanctioned or not, women are going to seek abortions. In the unimaginable event the clock were turned back, those with money would find ways to have them anyway—and, as before, some of those without would die trying.

Then, too, the tragic fact is that there are far, far too many unwanted children already, and far too many cruel and inept parents. Knowing as we do how many such kids grow up rage-filled and conscienceless, to keep adding to that total seems like madness.

Yet the very bloodlessness of such a calculation is itself reasonably part of the pro-life argument. For while pro-lifers abhor above all the systematic taking of innocent life, they also make much of what the prevalence of such a procedure does to the rest of us.

And it's hard to argue: if abortion were strictly an abstract moral argument, the pro-life side would win hands down. Of *course* an abortion snuffs out a life; to deny it is to play the chilling modern game of using words to obscure rather than enlighten. *Is a fetus really a person? Doesn't it become one only once it is viable outside the womb?* When questions like that start getting asked, it invariably says a great deal about the person doing the asking. We now know beyond all doubt that infants respond strongly to stimuli before birth—to music, their mother's voices and, yes, to pain.

It is hardly for nothing that, addressing a woman who's just discovered she's pregnant, medical personnel know to refer to "the fetus," yet instantly switch to "the baby" on learning that it is wanted.

Anyone who thinks such moral sleight-of-hand hasn't taken a toll on the national psyche is in deep denial. Had the taking of human life not become so routine and seemingly stripped of consequence, surely there'd have been no Dr. Kevorkian, let alone a TV network ready to tape him in action before thirty million witnesses for sweeps week.

"All I want is for it to go away," a pregnant New Jersey teen named Amy Grossberg wrote her boyfriend accomplice, in just one of the celebrated recent episodes of soul-deadened middle-class kids murdering their inconvenient offspring. "As soon as everything gets better, I'll be my sweet, normal self. We'll be able to *uh uuh* lots."

Once almost everyone in this culture—religious and not, and inconsistent as we may have been in the application of the principle—accepted as an abstraction that a human life was valuable beyond measure. Today many will argue it is of no more intrinsic worth than that of a cat or hamster or fly. Linda Blair actually gets taken seriously railing against poor Christopher Reeve's campaign for increased research on nerve regeneration on the grounds it requires animal testing. According to *Men in Black* director Barry Sonnenfeld, the animal rights police had the run of his set, making sure the civil rights of the cockroaches used in a couple of key scenes were not being violated. "In each shot, we had to tell them how many roaches we were using. So, if we had eighty roaches coming out of a Dumpster, they would actually count—'We're missing three, guys!'—and we'd be shooting at $10,000 an hour, looking for three roaches."

Surely the most dramatic test of the redrawn limits of our humanity has been the fight over partial-birth abortion. The position of the pro-choice side has from the start been adamant: "intact dilation and evacuation," as they call it, is extremely rare and used almost exclusively in cases where the mother's life is at risk; the attacks on it are aimed at chipping away at abortion law with the ultimate goal of ending all abortions.

Of course, there is much truth to the second part of this argument. Still the reason the partial-birth debate has been so devastating to the pro-choice cause is that for the first time its leaders—heretofore portrayed by a sympathetic press as sensible and moderate, as opposed to the crazed zealots on the other side—have themselves been revealed as the rigid ideologues they are.

For what the public learned along the way is that partial-birth abortion is literally inches this side of infanticide; and, as a few honorable reporters readily established, it is *not* all that rare and in most cases *not* performed to save the mother's life. "[I]n New Jersey alone," revealed reporter Ruth Padawer, herself pro-choice, in a stinging exposé in the *Bergen Record*, "at least 1,500 partial birth abortions are performed each year—three times the supposed national rate. Moreover, doctors say only a 'minuscule amount' are for medical reasons."

Yet, horrific as the procedure is now widely recognized to be, from the pro-abortion side there has been not the merest suggestion of give. "You either believe a woman has the right to decide whether to continue or terminate her pregnancy or you don't," writes Alexander Sanger, the President of Planned Parenthood. "You either believe abortion should be legal, safe and available or you don't . . . There really is no middle ground."

In brief, over recent years there's been a growing recognition that *both* sides are as convinced of their own rectitude as John Brown at Harpers Ferry. *Both* sides indulge in combustible rhetoric and wildly exaggerated claims. *Both* sides will do and say anything to win this religious war to the death.

The only difference is the definition of sacred: human life or the woman's right to choose.

The partial-birth controversy has helped produce a consensus even among those generally supportive of abortion that the procedure should be subject to effective limits. Among women generally, 70 percent now favor increased restrictions on legal abortion. Parental notification laws elicit particular support—for sensible people know full well, often from personal experience, how ill-equipped a fifteen-year-old is to make a life-altering choice.

All this is encouraging. There are a lot more of us in the middle than absolutists of either stripe, and *our* interest is in a society that neither disrespects its citizens' needs nor makes moral decisions indifferent to the consequences.

For me, the surprise has been how much I've come to respect the pro-life side—but I'll never count myself among them. Even now, I can summon up the feeling of helplessness and foreboding that came with those long-ago unwanted pregnancies; and when I helped end them, I forever forfeited the right to condemn anyone else's choice.

And, call it selfish, but I don't want my kids ever to have to make the even more gruesome decision faced by their grandmother.

Still, as a particularly wise bumper sticker has it, "If you're still the same person you were twenty years ago . . . you've wasted twenty years."

For there have been plenty of times over the years I've also wondered who those lost children would have been. The oldest would be twenty-six now, the youngest, the one with Priscilla, almost twenty.

And I fervently hope my kids never have to go through *that,* either.

❑

I know, I know, I've spent an inordinate number of pages ripping feminism. So—for at least a moment—let's talk about something good and important it has done.

Feminism has brought to the fore a growing number of smart, truly independent-minded women to challenge the herd thinking the movement otherwise so vigorously promotes.

(Who says I can't hand out compliments?)

The women who've taken on the feminist worldview are a hugely diverse group. They often disagree with one another on the particulars. But what the best of them have in common is vastly more important: an intellectual rigor that has made them keenly aware of what may be feminism's most damaging legacy of all—the ascendancy in American life of emotion over reason.

Listen to NYU literature professor Carol Iannone on why she finally dropped from the movement: "Feminism is a series of self-indulgent contradictions and anyone following it for a while is going to have her thought coarsened. Women are the same as men, women are different from men, according to the ideological need. Women are strong and capable. And yet have been the slaves and victims of men throughout history. Women are angry, rebellious, even murderous in patriarchy, but also superior to men because loving and tender . . ."

Christina Hoff Sommers, as a professor of philosophy similarly trained in rigorous and precise thought, stumbled into her wrangle with organized feminism over its misuse of statistics in total innocence, after reading the claim of 150,000 annual anorexia deaths (the vast majority young women) in a news magazine. This terrible tragedy was said to be a result of the sexism permeating American life; or as best-selling feminist Naomi Wolf had it at the time (years before she turned up on Al Gore's payroll dispensing advice on how to be an "Alpha" male), this "vast number of emaciated bodies starved not by nature but by men . . ."

"I don't carry numbers around in my head," notes Sommers, "but I recalled from driver's ed that something like fifty thousand people die a year in car accidents. And I thought, 'Gee, *three times* more anorexia deaths? If that's true, at places like Wellesley College, they'd have to have ambulances permanently on call."

When she called the American Anorexia and Bulimia Association, its exasperated president volunteered they were being misquoted. There were 150,000 to 200,000 anorexia *sufferers,* but only 100 annual *fatalities.* The number of deaths was being overstated by a factor of 1,500!

The reality was the facts often seem not to matter much to those most avidly embracing the feminist worldview. And, as the movement's assumptions have come to permeate American life—through everything from revised college curricula and the rise in influence of teachers raised on sixties dogma to afternoon talk shows and the women's magazines—that increasingly holds true also in ordinary life.

Indeed, looking into it, Sommers found the preposterous anorexia figure was everywhere; having migrated from the feminist texts, it was being repeated by everyone from Katie Couric to Ann Landers.

The power of emotion is of course an old story. What is new in our time, notes British journalist Jenny McCarthy in a neat paraphrase of Descartes, is the degree to which emotion has become linked in so many minds to higher morality: "I feel, therefore I am right."

This was something else anticipated in the early suffrage debate. I remember being surprised, as I wandered through the archives with my late-twentieth-century sensibility, at how often the argument was made both by men and women that democracy was a fragile thing—and that its exercise was a serious and demanding business.

I first ran across it in a letter to the *Times* dated February 3, 1873, in regard to a legal case involving pioneer suffragist Susan B. Anthony. Signed simply "A Woman," it argued that well intentioned as Miss Anthony's efforts were, most women simply didn't care enough about politics and world affairs to undertake "the duties which are incumbent upon voters; for if we are made voters, we are in honor bound to fulfill to the utmost all the duties attached to the so-called 'privilege.' "

It shows how far we've traveled that it now rings as almost absurdly quaint, this notion that exercising the franchise should demand something approaching a cool head and a real grasp of the issues. Yet back then it was an article of faith that republican government was dependent for its very survival on an ethical and aware electorate.

Four decades after A Woman's letter appeared in the *Times*, that understanding still remained at the heart of the suffrage debate. Teddy Roosevelt had grappled with the issue for years, under intense pressure from both sides, when in 1912, as an ex-President in the midst of an attempted comeback, he at last, very tentatively, endorsed votes for women. But it was with the passionate admonition that if ordinary women failed to "live lives of duty, not only our democracy but our civilization itself will perish."

In fact, for the most adamant opponents of feminism, the dangers of "the feminizing of the culture," as one E. Barnes termed it in *The Atlantic*, went beyond the threat to good government to the character of daily life. "During these past few years," he wrote of a trend he already saw as deeply alarming, "hundreds of journals have sprung up devoted to women's special interests. They are almost all of them showy, fragmentary, personal, concrete and emotional. It is difficult to find one that represents general or abstract interests."

What he meant by "women's special interests" were those that he, and to his mind all sensible souls, assumed to be trivial: fashion, cooking, romance, the movies, what then passed for gossip, plus that era's version of the New Age, spiritualism and the occult—most of which, until a few decades before, had existed only at the margins of the culture, easy to ignore. Now, thanks to technology and booming demand, they were everywhere, redefining cultural norms. "These are the qualities of children's minds," he lamented, "and of underdeveloped minds everywhere."

Those were serious fighting words even then; today they are easy to read as frankly contemptible. Indeed, the record shows that, far from degrading the culture, the twentieth century's respect for the everyday concerns of ordinary people—the popular entertainments, fashions, shifting tastes; yes, even the interest in the lives of the celebrated—has in many ways been a healthy thing. A people's history is not all statesmanship and earth-shaking events, but the sum total of innumerable concerns, great and small, and the values played out daily in private life. Not just how people relate to what they read on the front page, but to one another, to their children, to their friends. We are not automatons, but highly complex beings, or should be.

As even old E. Barnes would have probably acknowledged, the great movements of history are themselves largely emotionally driven. The faltering rebellion against England might well have collapsed had it not been for Thomas Paine's stirring call to courage in *The Crisis;* on meeting *Uncle Tom's Cabin* author Harriet Beecher Stowe, Lincoln himself called her "the little lady who started the big war." I've always loathed the term "bleeding heart," now as much as when I might have been more reasonably accused of being one; what the hell *else* is a heart supposed to do? To be unmoved by the pain of others is to be functionally dead.

Yet, looking around today, it is increasingly clear that those from the past so readily dismissed as backward also had some things right. For coming as they did from an infinitely more serious and disciplined world, they were contemptuous of lazy minds that made easy assumptions without firm proof; they demanded rigor and accountability not just of themselves but in the culture at large. It is hardly for nothing that, back then, the American system of public education ranked as the very best on earth.

Obviously, in the years between then and now, many elements have contributed to the erosion of standards. But far from the least, especially over the last several decades, has indeed been what amounts to a systematic attack on the primacy of facts and logic over emotions and feelings.

In education, this has been most readily apparent in the "self-esteem movement." Astonishing as it sometimes seems to those of us who went to school as recently as the fifties and early sixties, in classrooms across

America today what children know is routinely less important than how they feel about themselves.

Worse, far from resisting the trend, liberal opinion makers enthusiastically embraced it—and none more so than the feminist leadership. Gloria Steinem's own 1992 bestseller *Revolution from Within,* packed full of trendy stuff about finding one's inner child and "reparenting" techniques, was originally titled the *Bedside Book of Self-Esteem.* Her hope, she explained at the time, was to help people "find a link between inward exploring and outward revolution."

This dovetailed perfectly with what academic feminist icon Carol Gilligan described as "women's modes of knowing," the idea being that what we've traditionally thought of as "logic" and "consistency" are themselves "male constructs," by definition linear, rigid and patriarchal. In contrast, women's awareness—more rooted in subjective experience—enables them to bring far greater innate sensitivity to the workings of the world.

In fact, there's some truth to it: women do tend to have a more intuitive and empathetic style than men and there *are* occasions when it is a useful counterbalance to decision making based solely on cold analysis of facts and data.

But, more generally, as they've trickled down to daily life, the results of such an approach are all too evident. Forty years ago, women may have daily competed on *Queen for a Day* to tell the most pathetic tale of personal woe in exchange for a few household items, but the show was also a national joke; Sid Caesar's parody of it remains a classic. These days, the sob story is a staple not just in the daytime but on prime-time newsmagazines, and there is no embarrassment attached to it at all—to the contrary, sometimes there is a real sense of nobility. I've been on Oprah's show twice; the second time, Oprah induced a fellow guest, an HIV-positive gay man (who'd been swathed in shadows), to come out on the air. The audience wept and cheered.

Which, of course, is run-of-the-mill TV these days. In a culture that systematically rewards feeling and, even more so, pain—the one-eyed man is . . . just another victim.

Such a mentality is by no means uniquely the province of women, of course—we're far beyond that. But to ignore feminism's pivotal role in the undermining of intellectual rigor is to be indifferent to the facts. For its march through the culture has increasingly allowed its own debased standard to pass as routine, so that today even the most amazing logical leaps and brazen inconsistencies scarcely give us pause. "Equalize biological opposites by denying their differences," as Harvard professor Ruth R. Wisse says, getting to the very root of it, "and lying becomes a universal principle."

Brought to bear on the workings of our representative democracy, such an ethic is nothing less than a prescription for disaster. At its most extreme, it has led radical feminists like Catharine MacKinnon to demand the suspension of traditional rules of evidence in women's rights cases, with the views of "the reasonable woman" accorded special weight; at its most benign, it enables an attractive chief executive to lie under oath and find cover in the debased cry "everyone does it."

Indeed, our political system has already been compromised in precisely some of the ways the early critics feared. More and more elections are decided not on serious consideration of the issues but on outright appeals to emotion, or spin, or the candidates' looks. It is hardly for nothing that historians speculate that Washington, and certainly Lincoln, would be unelectable today.

This is surely something we should be worrying about at least as much as those at the dawn of the century who only lay awake imagining it.

My guess is that if Teddy Roosevelt, who so struggled with the suffrage issue, returned to see what the century has wrought, some things would please him, including the number of women in high office and the likelihood that one will soon ascend to the presidency. Even more surely, however, this figure of legendary character and self-discipline—who once insisted on delivering a speech after being seriously wounded by an assassin—would be appalled by our flight from self-discipline and eager embrace of victimhood.

Where the antisuffragists had it all wrong was in attacking an entire gender. It doesn't work that way: foolishness, irresolution and ignorance are individual, not group, traits. Maggie Thatcher and (yes, Gloria) Jeane

Kirkpatrick are among the most impressive political figures of the age. Even some of those with whom I most violently disagree, like NOW's steely Patricia Ireland, can never be accused of being uninformed or otherwise lacking in civic competence.

Rather, in this respect as in others, it's Ireland's *cause* that has done the damage, by doing its considerable bit to foster a society in which individuals believe they can be good citizens without any obligation to be informed.

This hit home with special force one evening when I got into a political back-and-forth with a close family friend, a woman in her late thirties. Now, I happen to live for this sort of thing, and the more someone disagrees with me the better. Only this person, bright as she is, and attuned as she is to others' needs, rarely reads the front page of the newspaper or watches the news. Which is to say, like so many others, she follows things by osmosis, via conversation around the office, or what she picks up on the radio between songs, or from Jay Leno's jokes.

At one point during our tiff, this friend actually started laughing. "What fun can it be fighting with me, we both know I don't know anything about this stuff."

Still—this is what made it so exasperating—she damn well knows what she *feels*, which in this case, as the bumper sticker has it, is that "Mean People Suck."

Please, again, don't get me wrong, I like this person a lot. She never cheats anyone, is extremely generous, is wonderful with kids. We'd unhesitatingly trust her with ours.

But, forgive me, I know this comes off as terribly harsh and judgmental: I just have trouble trusting her with our country.

❏

ALL VICTIMS, ALL THE TIME

The following is a listing of all the movies shown during a single week—
January 3–9, 1999—on Lifetime, "the network for women," as described
in the *New York Times* TV supplement.

Abandoned and Deceived (1995) Lori Loughlin, Gordon Clapp.
Woman with two young sons fights back when ex-spouse stops paying
child support. (2 hrs.) Fri 9 PM

Because Mommy Works (1994) Anne Archer, John Heard. To retain
custody of her child, LA nurse fights her ex-husband and his new
wife. (2 hrs.) Sat 6 PM

Betrayed: A Story of Three Women (1995) Meredith Baxter, Swoosie
Kurtz. Lawyer's wife learns he's romancing daughter of her best
friend. (1³/₄ hrs.) Sun 6:30 PM

Change of Heart (1998) Jean Smart, John Terry. A woman is shocked
by her unfaithful husband's choice of romantic partners. (1³/₄ hrs.)
Sun 3 PM

Cries Unheard: The Donna Yanklich Story (1994) Jaclyn Smith, Brad
Johnson. An imprisoned Colorado woman must tell her teenage son
why she hired two men to kill his father. (2 hrs.) Thu 9 PM

A Cry for Help: The Tracey Thurman Story (1989) Nancy McKeon, Dale Mickiff. Fact-based drama of abused wife who later sues police for lack of protection. Fine McKeon (2 hrs.) Wed 9 PM

Eye of the Stalker: A Moment of Truth Movie (1995) Joanna Cassidy, Jere Burns. Wily legal consultant obsessed with judge's daughter. (1¾ hrs.) Sun 8:15 PM

Her Final Fury: Betty Broderick, the Last Chapter (1992) Meredith Baxter, Judith Ivey. Socialite on trial for killing ex-spouse and his bride. (2 hrs.) Sat 4 PM

In the Company of Darkness (1983) Helen Hunt, Jeff Fahey. Undercover policewoman with colleague lover lures out serial killer. (2 hrs.) Mon 9 PM

The Silence of the Lambs (1991) Jodie Foster, Anthony Hopkins. Brilliant cannibalistic psychic helps trap serial killer. (2½ hrs.) Sat 11 PM

Sin and Redemption (1994) Richard Grieco, Cynthia Gibb. Pregnant minister's daughter learns something shocking about the man she has married. (1¾ hrs.) Sun 4:45 PM

Trick of the Eye (1994) Ellen Burstyn, Meg Tilly. Artist unveils truth behind her mural. (2 hrs.) Mon 1 PM

When No One Would Listen (1992) Michele Lee, James Farentino. Murderous marriage. Two viewpoints. (2 hrs.) Sat 9 PM

A Woman Scorned: The Betty Broderick Story (1992) Meredith Baxter, Stephen Collins. San Diego woman accused of murder after spouse bolts for younger woman. (2 hrs.) Sat 2 PM

❏

Alas, far from decrying the legitimization of ignorance and feelings-over-thought, lots of pols today seem to *depend* on it. Apparently, given their enthusiasm for such things as the Motor Voter Law and M-TV's "Rock the Vote" campaign, if they could get away with it they'd come out for registering potted plants.

This is not how the Founding Fathers intended it. Believing a highly informed electorate was essential to the nation's safety and well-being, they explicitly limited the franchise to those, by virtue of education and the responsibilities they bore in daily life, who appeared most likely to exercise it conscientiously. At the time that meant male property holders.

Obviously, such a standard no longer makes sense.

But the underlying principle remains as valid as ever.

We're talking—why not?—a voting test.

Well, no, I know why not—the very idea rubs people the wrong way. *Isn't that what they used in the South to keep blacks from voting?*

Actually, no. What they did in the Jim Crow South was devise impossible "tests" explicitly to exclude blacks, coming up with questions that would've stumped the world's most distinguished historians and political scientists: a potential voter might be told to recite entire articles of the Mississippi state constitution verbatim; and if he somehow got that right, he'd be shown a huge jar of jelly beans and asked exactly how many were inside.

What we have below is the opposite of that: a rigorously *fair* test designed not to mock democracy but protect it. In seeking to establish the rudimentary understanding of current affairs and our country's history and government so essential to citizenship, it discriminates not on the basis of race, creed, gender or sexual orientation. Just ignorance.

Think of it as a sort of driving test to promote *civic* safety.

1. What is the name of the intern President Clinton angrily described as "that woman"?
   Hey, why not throw 'em a bone? Even the lowliest moron deserves a little pity.
2. What are the three branches of government?
   The winnowing begins.
3. Name both United States senators from your state and the representative from your district to Congress.
4. How many justices sit on the United States Supreme Court? Name three.
5. Which President declared "We have nothing to fear but fear itself?" What were the circumstances?
6. Which amendment to the Constitution protects freedom of speech and assembly?
7. Name the leaders of Britain, France, Germany, Italy and the Soviet Union in 1942.
8. What was the make and color of the vehicle O.J. was driving during his attempted "escape"?
   Make that two bones.
9. What was "Manifest Destiny"?
   Upping the ante.
10. Who proposed "Making the world safe for democracy"?
    Special Bonus Question: It has been said that Peggy Arnold, Benedict Arnold's unscrupulous young wife, who persuaded him to commit treason, was a model for today's feminists. Explain.
    Hey, what can I tell you—look who they got to write the test.

Probably some who've taken the time to take this test are offended right about now.

Good. That is as it should be. They have only themselves to blame.

See, that's one of the things I get to do these days: not apologize except when I really think I'm wrong. It's one of the perks of being a social conservative—no on *expects* you to be compulsively sensitive.

You even get to tell *jokes* at other people's expense.

This is no small matter. Humorously speaking, America is at a crossroads just now. On the one hand, it's almost impossible to shock anymore with mere words; thoughts and language that a generation ago landed Lenny Bruce in the slammer are today the stuff of your average cable comedy special.

On the other hand, as far as political progressives are concerned, whole vast subject areas are untouchable: anything that might be seen as offensive or demeaning to women, gays, blacks or any other minority, with the notable exception of Catholics.

Needless to say, this can make the job of trying to be amusing a minefield. In Al Franken's last book, he included something where the central character, President Al Franken, comes down with Chronic Fatigue Syndrome and is unable to function. Within days of publication, he was being barraged by e-mail from enraged CFS sufferers, who'd somehow summoned up the energy to demand he apologize for making actual *jokes* at their expense.

What did Franken do?

Yep, *apologized*. Over the net.

He tried to make it a funny apology, to be sure, but every morsel of crow got eaten.

In contrast, there was the reaction of my friend Denis Boyles, after *he* inadvertently insulted another highly sensitive interest group in his column in *Men's Health* magazine: bikers. Denis' blizzard of e-mails was prompted by his response to a woman asking how to get her fiancé to give up his motorcycle: "no matter where your beau thinks he's going, he's probably going to the hospital or to hell."

Some of the motorcyclists who wrote him were mad, said Denis, but mostly they were hurt. They felt misunderstood, abused, belittled.

Did *he* apologize?

Are you kidding? In the very next edition of his column he *mocked* them. "I suddenly realized I was facing a crowd of politically correct, overly sensitive *bikers* . . ." he wrote. "Not long ago, if bikers had a beef, they'd ride their Harleys into your office, lodge their complaints in person, and leave the empties on your desk. What have we come to?"

Which, by the way, on balance has got to be a lot riskier than it would have been to tell off a mob of Chronic Fatigue Syndrome sufferers.

Denis is one of those free spirits who, unrestrained by the heavy hand of p.c. (and in order to maintain his sanity), will sometimes offend the terminally self-serious just for the sheer, rip-roaring fun of it. Given the range of fat targets out there (by which I don't *necessarily* mean fat people), it is sometimes pretty hard to resist.

In fact, that's one of the things that tends to make conservative publications a better read these days than those on the other side of the political spectrum—they're often a *lot* funnier. *Heterodoxy*'s parodies of lugubrious and heavy-handed p.c.-speak are especially choice. Here, for instance, are some ersatz math questions they ran under the heading: "Problems from the Socio-Math Classes in San Francisco Schools."

- The City and County of San Francisco decide to destroy 50 rats infesting downtown. If 9,800 animal rights activists hold a candle-light vigil, how many people did each dead rat empower?
- A red sock, a yellow sock, a blue sock, and a white sock are tossed randomly in a drawer. What is the likelihood that the first two socks drawn will be socks of color?
- Todd begins walking down Market Street with 12 $1 bills in his wallet. If he always gives panhandlers a single buck, how many legs did he have to step over if he has $3 left when he reaches the other end and met only one double-amputee?

The fact is, if you have any ooomph or spirit, one of the tough things about being left of center these days is having to watch your back; a lighthearted remark made in the wrong place and you've crossed the line. If you're lucky, you're just momentarily embarrassed. If not, it can be full Clinton mode: backtrack, fudge, deny, deny, deny.

Like Ted Turner had to, for instance, when he got a *liiiiittle* too free with his Catholic bashing before a delighted pro-choice gathering, and made fun of not only the Pope but the entire country of Poland.

Or like Tom Brokaw, who made a remark on a recent return to the *Today* show about envying the homeless for how late they got to sleep. "Tom is the most sensitive guy in the world," the show's executive producer rushed to reassure us. "The last people he'd want to insult would be those who aren't as fortunate."

Then there was the brouhaha set off around the same time by a cover story in silly/hip *New York* magazine about a group of young women publicists at the top of their profession. One of the women, whose outfit represents a lot of rap singers, was quoted as saying "They used to have black publicists doing this. But they needed two big-mouthed Jewish girls to tell it to these guys straight . . ."

When the piece appeared, twenty black publicists signed a letter of protest, and the young woman got death threats. She then denied saying it.

Now, I don't know this person—I don't know for sure that she said it. But it sure sounds like something people half-jokingly say; in lots of years of reporting, I've heard people say far worse.

And why not? So she was bragging a little. Having been on the receiving end of a phone line with mouths like hers, I, for one, have no doubt that it was so; ball busters make terrific flacks.

The amazing thing is that in those circles—that is, *media* circles— even so obvious a truth is all but unspeakable.

Lots of older people don't get this. Even if they dearly want to be sensitive, age and experience have left them unable to readily strike all the necessary poses. For instance, my own father-in-law Moe Turner of Monterey, California, a political liberal without a mean bone in his bony eighty-year-old body, tells jokes all the time that would deeply offend people all over New York's Upper West Side. Ethnic jokes. Jokes about women with enormous breasts. Jokes about gays. It's something he started doing during his Arkansas boyhood in the Depression, and continued in the Navy while helping whip the Nazis, and he's not about to stop now.

Moe's a scientist who spent a lot of years working for the government, and I've mentioned that if he were still on the job, telling such jokes could get him in big trouble. He knows that's so—after all, he reads the papers—but I don't think he can get himself to completely believe it. Couldn't be—not for a *joke*. He knows people are stupid, but they're not complete idiots.

Look, I don't mean to be callous. No one ought to go around casually offending others; that is simple courtesy. But what's been going on is something else entirely. By the millions, we've blithely surrendered the freedom to be ourselves.

Yes, obviously, sometimes people inadvertently do say truly stupid and offensive things. But even then, context matters.

There were, for instance, the unforgettable cases of longtime Dodger General Manager Al Campanis who, in a live broadcast, stumblingly told Ted Koppel that blacks lacked "the necessities" to be successful field managers; and Jimmy "the Greek" Snyder, the CBS football analyst who was recorded in a Washington restaurant rambling on drunkenly about how selective breeding by slave masters had genetically equipped blacks to be great linebackers and running backs. Both were decent men who'd come of age in a time of wholly different standards and sensitivities, both were deeply regretful; yet each paid with his job and dropped from view, to die in disgrace, all they'd otherwise accomplished an afterthought.

Was *that* right? Is *this* what all our vaunted sensitivity adds up to? Nothing in the history of either suggested that racism had ever played the slightest role in his professional or private life. To the contrary, the Greek's comments, idiotic as they were, were intended to be complimentary; and Campanis not only ran the most racially open organization in the game but, according to Tommy Lasorda, "did more for black players, more for Latin players, than anyone." In fact, Campanis was on *Nightline* that fateful night to celebrate the life of his old friend and roommate Jackie Robinson.

Around the same time there arose the cases of Andy Rooney and Jimmy Breslin. Rooney first offended gay sensibilities with a remark on a TV broadcast reviewing the events of the year 1989 to the effect that, along with smoking and alcohol abuse, "homosexual unions" were among the chief "self-induced" causes of deaths among Americans; then compounded the offense some months later by allegedly saying in an interview with a gay publication that blacks "have watered down their genes because the less intelligent ones are the ones that have the most children." Columnist Breslin, as feisty in the newsroom as in print, got into it with a young female Korean-American colleague at the liberal daily *Newsday* who'd sent an e-mail attacking a lighthearted Breslin column where he complained that his wife, newly elected to the City Council, no longer had time to lay out his clothes. To be precise, he called the woman a "slant-eyed cunt" and a "yellow cur," then turned up on Howard Stern's radio show to kid around about the whole thing.

By any standard, these guys gave Campanis and Snyder a serious run for their money in the insensitivity sweepstakes. But they were also a lot better connected media-wise, and had more ostentatiously progressive credentials, and so generated lots more support. Both got off with a suspension—Breslin's was but two weeks—and by now the embarrassing episodes are all but forgotten; as, indeed, Ted Turner (in glaring contrast with his bellicose employee, John Rocker) was allowed to skate and the young woman publicist also easily survived her brush with the p.c. cops.

I was always a fan of both Rooney and Breslin, and it's hard to begrudge them the choices they made. But I also can't help but feel that, particularly in Rooney's case, it was an opportunity lost. After all, he was already seventy-one at the time of his infraction. His popularity afforded him the protection to make a principled stand. How much did he have to lose?

What if instead of meekly accepting his suspension he'd shown up on some other network, sitting behind the familiar cluttered desk, and started going on in that way of his, saying what so cried out to be said?

Have you ever noticed how much harder it is to speak your mind these days than it used to be?

I got in some trouble recently for saying some things that some people didn't like. That's their right. I might not like some things they say, either. But I didn't say these things to be mean or cruel or nasty. I said them 'cause they made sense to me at the time. Maybe they were wrong. Maybe they were even stupid. But they reflected the way I was raised and what I know of the world. And lots of us who fought on foreign soil to help protect the First Amendment figure that ought to give me the right to say them. . . .

Ah, well. . . . Here's hoping he at least gets to enjoy a good joke once in a while, far from the office.

Once, amazing as it seems today, the place where those who thought unpopular thoughts were surest to find refuge were the nation's colleges and universities.

Until a generation ago, higher education's mission was crystal clear, unchanged since the founding of Harvard in 1636: to preserve and defend the essential truths of the past while providing a safe haven for open debate on the wrenching questions each new generation must face in an evolving world. Here as nowhere else in society, Voltaire's immortal maxim, "I disapprove of what you say, but I will defend to the death your right to say it," was honored as living creed.

Thus it was that during the anti-Communist rampages of the fifties, the great institutions of higher learning stood up to mad-dog congressmen baying for the heads of leftist intellectuals when almost no one else would. Senator McCarthy's methods, declared Harvard President Nathan Pusey when Tail Gunner Joe was after one of his physics profs in 1953, are "against all the principles of our country."

That was then.

At colleges and universities today, the accumulated wisdom of the past not only often goes undefended, it's likely to be held in even greater contempt than elsewhere in the culture. Indeed, the widespread embrace of politically correct orthodoxy as absolute truth has bred a climate where the suppression of independent thought is taken as a positive virtue.

This is why, of all the culture war's ongoing battles, none has so engaged the passions of social conservatives as the assault on free thought on the nation's campuses. Sitting before me is a file of newspaper and magazine clippings on the subject more than two inches thick. Next to that is a pile of books, six of them, giving chapter and verse on the repression of ideas and speech at school after school after school.

It is so numbing a litany that one hardly knows where to begin. With the "speech codes" designed to mute talk deemed insensitive, or history reading lists offering only a single, narrow point of view? With the proliferation of politicized women's, multicultural and gender studies departments, or the denigration in more familiar ones like English and art history of Western values and dead white males? With the many campus publications that have been trashed for expressing a conservative point of view, or the administrators who've routinely backed those doing the trashing?

In one volume alone, *The Shadow University,* University of Pennsylvania history professor Alan Kors and civil rights attorney Harvey Silverglate record episodes of p.c. run amuck at no fewer than 150 institutions of higher learning.

Yet the obvious truth is that most people have scarcely noticed; or to the extent they have, they shrug it off as just more of the familiar campus same-old, affecting no more than a handful of malcontents. A college education is held in as high regard as ever, the elite institutions still regarded with something approaching awe.

So let's be blunt. The long-term consequences of what is afoot on the nation's campuses go far, far beyond the passing ideological battles of today. The real question is: when diversity of thought is in jeopardy at our top universities, where is it safe? For those who've tracked this stuff even reasonably closely, the conclusion reached by Kors and Silverglate seems incontrovertible: "Universities have become the enemy of a free society, and it is time for the citizens of that society to recognize this scandal of enormous proportions and hold these institutions to account."

In his perceptive memoir *Coming Apart,* the liberal thinker and essayist Roger Rosenblatt identifies what may be the precise moment when

American higher education lost its way: the Harvard student uprising in the spring of 1969. Rosenblatt was a junior lecturer in English at Harvard at the time, and was deeply embroiled in those events, serving on the faculty committee that tried to make peace between the radical students and the university. But in the end, the preeminent institution in American higher education, the one that, as during the McCarthy era, all others looked to for inspiration and guidance, simply caved.

The gentlemanly Rosenblatt reserves special scorn for the faculty's role in the debacle, terming it "morally careless. There were certain critical moments in those two months when professors had the opportunity to instruct their students usefully merely by voting the right way or saying the right things—things in which they supposedly believed. Yet, for the most part, they offered no opposition to what they disagreed with, as if to tell the students: 'If you want it, take it.' Liberalism rolled over on its back like a turtle awaiting the end."

Reading Rosenblatt's account of the chaos in Cambridge that spring—the kids taking over the administration building and issuing their nonnegotiable demands, the cops smashing heads as they dragged them out, the strike and endless rallies that followed—I thought back on my Harvard friend's breathless phone calls all those years ago. What most ex-radicals still cannot see is that in trashing the university they weren't noble or heroic, but childish and narcissistic—that, for all of their professions of building something new and better, they were mainly interested in tearing down.

Yet Rosenblatt is right to assign less blame to the students than to the putative grown-ups. College kids will always agitate for social change; it is the nature of the beast, and sometimes—witness the civil rights movement—a highly admirable thing. Yet, until then, their elders could be counted on to provide limits, protecting the institution itself and its larger mission.

No more. For during the turmoil of the late sixties, the grown-ups were paralyzed—or worse, aped the kids—thus abdicating the responsibility to help them grow into moral maturity.

And now that our generation has taken over the administrations and faculty lounges the old-fashioned way, through the front door, they've gone a long way toward finishing what they started.

One never likes to generalize. There are, after all, many thousands of individuals currently teaching and setting policy at the nation's institutions of higher learning, and—on the face of it, at least—it would seem loony to make sweeping claims about so large and diverse a group. But let's look at what would appear a representative sample: the liberal arts faculty at the University of Colorado's Boulder campus, the largest in the state. In 1998, a reporter for the *Denver Rocky Mountain News*, checking voter records in Boulder County, found that among the 190 faculty with party affiliation, Democrats outnumbered Republicans 184 to 6, a ratio of 31-to-1; this in a state where in the general population Republicans outnumber Democrats. In other words, as the paper's managing editor Vincent Carroll observed, students at the school "find themselves in an environment in which liberal professors don't merely dominate the faculty, they essentially *are* the faculty . . . One has to wonder about the self-correcting ability of an academic culture so in-bred that it reflects only half of the political spectrum. What arguments will be overlooked? What lines of inquiry ignored? Even the Apostles included one dissenter, and they were only 12."

Naturally enough, academics tend to get exercised when accused of being anything other than open-minded and fair. When in late 1998 student protesters at Columbia besieged a long-scheduled conservative conference—fittingly enough, it was on freedom of thought—the school's president responded by forcing the gathering off campus and into a nearby park. When questioned about this by the press, he heatedly defended himself by claiming organizers had failed to arrange sufficient security. Though this was provably false, at his own institution the president's actions earned him overwhelming approval. "It was a typical day on the modern campus," as *U.S. News & World Report* columnist John Leo, who spoke at the conference, later noted dryly. "The signals all came from the top—it's okay to shut down speakers if you don't like what they have to say."

One would hope such a state of affairs would be of concern even to intellectuals on the other side. But, no, with a few notable exceptions (the ever-reliable Nat Hentoff and, surprisingly, the *Times'* Anthony Lewis), these have almost all remained silent. Several years back, New

York's Town Hall hosted a massive pro-First Amendment rally, attended by a vast array of ostentatiously concerned celebs, from Paul Newman, Robin Williams and Alec Baldwin to Walter Cronkite, Carl Bernstein and Phil Donahue. There were speeches decrying book censorship and the blacklist; speeches were made in support of the NEA; rapper Chuck D. of Public Enemy even read Allen Ginsberg's "Howl." Yet there was not word one about the ongoing assault on open expression on the nation's campuses.

This is not to say that if the boot heel were on the other foot, the right would necessarily be any better. It's hard to recall many on the right being publicly troubled by crackdowns on student protests back in the sixties, let alone the witch hunts of the fifties.

Still, if only by default, today it is conservatives who are fighting the good fight on campus after campus, standard bearers for free speech and academic freedom against an often oppressive majority and hostile administration. In a truly bizarre turn of events, *they* have become the revolutionaries.

And it is they who are paying the price.

It is *hard* being conservative on most campuses today. The stories of students running afoul of the heavy hand of p.c.-speech codes are legion. To even enumerate the Orwellian particulars of such codes is a Herculean task: *Heterodoxy* recently ran eight thousand words on the subject, broken down by region, and still barely scratched the surface. "In New England," begins the lengthy section on that college-rich region, " 'harassment' has included, within recent times, jokes and ways of telling stories 'experienced by others as harassing' (Bowdoin College); 'verbal behavior' that produces 'feelings of impotence,' 'anger,' or 'disenfranchisement,' whether 'intentional or unintentional' (Brown University); speech that causes loss of 'self-esteem (or a vague sense of danger' (Colby College); or even 'inappropriately directed laughter,' 'inconsiderate jokes' and 'stereotyping' (University of Connecticut). The student code at the University of Vermont demands that its students not only not offend each other, but that they appreciate each other: 'Each of us must assume responsibility for becoming educated about racism, sexism, ageism, homophobia/heterosexism and other forms of oppression so that we may respond to other community members in an understanding and appreciative manner.' " And on and on and on.

Campus codes of conduct can get so over-the-top that even the most innocuous behavior risks crossing the line. "In some cases," noted the draft report of Columbia's Committee for the Promotion of Mutual Understanding and Civility, "unintentional offenses arise, paradoxically, from good intentions: the gesture or comment directed at a person with a disability, intended as friendly or helpful but considered by that person to be patronizing or intrusive; the gesture made in deference to gender or age (stepping aside to let women out of an elevator first, giving a seat to a person of a 'certain age' on the subway) that offends the object of the deference."

Now, I can't say if anyone has actually ever been prosecuted in the course of Columbia's campaign to stamp out offensive deference. But in recent years some prosecutions have been very nearly as bizarre. Generally such an episode draws widespread attention only when there is some newsworthy hook; for instance, when an Israeli student at the University of Pennsylvania was brought up on racism charges some years back for yelling the Hebrew pejorative "water buffalo" at some black students who disturbed his late-night studying; or when Ivan Boesky's son got suspended from Sarah Lawrence for "inappropriate laughter," which a gay student took to be mocking.

More generally, such conflicts pass unremarked upon outside the campus in question, and sometimes cause little stir even there. Intensely sensitive about negative publicity, and aware that a succession of courts have backed students in such cases (though those rulings apply only to public and not private institutions), most administrators make a policy of handling them quietly. Most often they are adjudicated in campus equivalents of star chambers. Generally, transgressors are sentenced not to expulsion but to reeducation or counseling.

Just as revealing is how little outrage is aroused when it is the rights and sensitivities of conservative students that get stomped on. According to the Washington-based Student Press Law Center, there were more than a hundred episodes in 1997 alone, involving schools from Maine to California, of theft or destruction of campus publications for running articles that angered racial or gender activists. On other campuses, conservative publications of long standing have been defunded by student governments under pressure from campus activists.

Yet in these cases, the official response tends to run from tepid to nonexistent. In one of the most telling of all such cases, the dean of students at Dartmouth ruled that the students who'd persistently destroyed copies of the conservative *Dartmouth Review* had not violated the student conduct code on the grounds the paper was "litter."

Standing up to this sort of thing often demands the kind of guts most of us only pretended to have back in the sixties. When the administration at Nashville's Vanderbilt University insisted the campus chapter of the Young Americans for Freedom conform to school policy by having prospective members identify themselves on the application form by race, culture and gender, the YAF-ers, citing their opposition to affirmative action, went to the mat. They ended up decertified as a campus organization and denied access to university facilities.

Still, trying as it can be to be a conservative student, it is immeasurably harder to be a conservative faculty member—or, perhaps more to the point, to get hired as one.

In part—seeking out the most charitable explanation—that has to do with the radically altered character of today's college curriculum. Conservatives tend to be traditionalists, and this is an age when the academic heat is all on the other side, especially in the liberal arts. According to a survey of seventy top universities conducted by the National Alumni Forum, in 1997 a mere twenty-three were still requiring even *English majors* to take as many as one course in Shakespeare.

And then we get to *how* the Bard is often taught these days—in ways those of generations past would find odd, to say the least. For it reflects the prevailing view that, in the words of critic Hilton Kramer, "what was once thought of as high culture is really only a mask for one or another form of political privilege and control." In the current climate, the quickest way to make a name for oneself is by bringing a "post-structuralist" or "gender-based" perspective to even the most traditional subject matter. Thus, for instance, it is now routinely taught that Shakespeare composed his immortal love sonnets for a man. In his recent book on Shakespeare, Harold Bloom quotes a retired Georgetown professor describing an ex-colleague who, teaching *Romeo and Juliet*, "tells the students that Juliet and her nurse are having a lesbian affair." Indeed, at Arizona State, theater professor Jared Sakren infuriated campus feminists—and was eventually fired—for teaching Shakespeare, Aeschylus, Chekov and other "works from a sexist European canon" the old-fashioned way, while ignoring such works as *Betty the Yeti*, a feminist, environmental work by one Jon Klein.

Even *The New Yorker* magazine has lately expressed alarm at some of what's passing for education these days, noting "porn studies" is available at many schools, including Columbia, Northwestern and NYU, with adult stars turning up as guest lecturers and professors doing "field research" in X-rated video stores. But, then, why not? "The academization of popular culture—in which movies, comics, detective fiction, rock, and now rap lyrics are seen as worthy of scholarly interpretation for the insights they yield—has shown itself able to absorb just about any cultural artifact, no matter how transient or bizarre."

When a friend of mine, an art historian with a specialty in eighteenth-century France, was seeking a job not long ago in the Ivy League, he half-jokingly suggested he might have to invent a homosexual relationship between the sculptor Houdon and his famous friend Voltaire to get by.

He probably should have; he didn't get the job.

Seemingly, as long as the politics are right, almost anything can pass as legitimate scholarship these days. Not long ago Professor James Pennell of Auburn University actually got some serious notice in academic circles for having proposed the "total integration" of sports, by which he meant equal numbers of men and women on every team—football included.

Still, as profound and meaningful are the differences in academic approach between traditionalists and trendies, they are just part of the reason conservatives are scarce on today's campus. Merely *being* conservative is itself often a professional death warrant. "Republican faculty members operate on a 'don't ask, don't tell basis,' " notes an associate professor of psychology at Cal Poly in San Luis Obisbo named Laura A. Freiberg, of her own awful experience. "Outed" when her husband ran for local political office as a Republican, she writes in *The Wall Street Journal,* she soon found herself replaced as department head and a "colleague told me 'We would never have hired you if we knew you were a Republican.'" And since then ". . . I have been turned down four times for promotion from associate to full professor, in spite of having some of the highest student evaluations on campus. . . ."

At least she already *had* a job. Michael Savage, a well-regarded conservative talk show host in San Francisco, tells of applying for the job of dean at Berkeley's School of Journalism, where he received his own Ph.D., and not even being invited for an interview. The job was given to someone with less impressive academic, but more acceptable political credentials.

In this bleak landscape, one sometimes does find cause for hope. At this school or that, the response to an episode of overt censorship or other ham-handed p.c. act is actually principled. Such was the case when the *Northwestern Chronicle,* a conservative publication on the Evanston, Illinois, campus, was forced to cease publication in 1998 after being "de-recognized" by the university's Associated Student Government. In response, thirty faculty members from the school's renowned journalism school shot off a letter to the university president. "As journalism editors," it read, "we believe deeply in the freedom of the press and the tolerance of divergent opinions. Regardless of how we viewed the editorial content of the *Chronicle,* it provided an alternative voice on our campus." The paper was eventually re-funded.

That's a nice story. It ought to make aspiring journalism students, whatever their political leanings, want to run to the place.

But my favorite story of resistance to prevailing campus values involves not highly regarded profs but a bunch of students I've never before had particular use for: frat types.

A few years back, administrators at the University of California's Riverside campus came down in the usual draconian way on a fraternity called Phi Kappa Sigma, suspending the organization for three years and ordering members to take a course in sensitivity. Their sin? They'd used a tee shirt showing a sleepy Mexican in a sombrero to promote a South-of-the-Border bash. Never mind that half of the frat's members were themselves chicano. The tee shirt had elicited complaints of racism from some other Hispanics on campus, and that was more than enough for the administration.

Only, the frat boys, bless 'em, refused to play dead. Seeking help from a group called the Individual Rights Foundation, which defends college kids who run afoul of speech codes, they brought legal action against the school. The eventual settlement was, as it turned out, exactly the one you'd want: not only were the charges against the fraternity dropped, but the two administrators responsible for going after them were held personally liable.

They were ordered to take sensitivity training—in the First Amendment.

□

How far have academic standards fallen over the course of the last century? Let's put it this way: the following are some sample questions from an 1885 examination for admission to Jersey City *High School.*

Algebra

1. Define a polynomial. Make a literal trinomial.
2. Write a homogeneous quadrinomial of the third degree. Express the cube root of $10ax$ in two ways.
3. Find the sum and difference of $3x - 4ay + 7cd - 4xy + 16$ and $10ay - 3x - 8xy + 7cd - 13$.

Geography

1. Name four principal ranges of mountains in Asia, three in Europe and three in Africa.
2. Name the states on the west bank of the Mississippi, and the capital of each.

U.S. History

1. What event do you connect with 1565, 1607, 1620, 1664, 1775?

2. What caused the Mexican War? What was the result? What American general commanded at the capture of the City of Mexico?

Grammar

1. Write a sentence containing a noun used as an attribute, a verb in the perfect tense potential mood, and a proper adjective.
2. Write the declension of (a) bird, (b) man, (c) fly, (d) fox, (e) it.
3. Make three sentences, using the plural of sheep (a) in the nominative case, (b) in the possessive, (c) in the objective.

ANSWERS

Algebra

1. Polynomial: Algebraic expression with terms designated by the use of plus or minus signs. Literal trinomial: $x+y+z$.

2. $2-x^3-2x^2+3x+5; \sqrt[3]{10ax}$.

3. Sum: $6ay+14cd-12xy+3$.

   Difference: $6x-14ay+4xy+29$.

Geography

1. Himalayas, Urals, Hindu Kush and Khangal; Alps, Carpathians and Pyrenees; Atlas, Drakenberg and Ethiopian Highlands.

2. Louisiana (Baton Rouge); Arkansas (Little Rock); Missouri (Jefferson City); Iowa (Des Moines); and Minnesota (St. Paul).

U.S. History

1. 1565—Pedro Menéndez de Aviles founded St. Augustine, Florida. 1607—Jamestown settled. 1620—103 Pilgrims landed at Plymouth Rock. 1664—British seized New Netherland from the Dutch. 1775—Battles of Lexington and Concord.

2. Manifest destiny, diplomatic blundering and instability of American government; California, New Mexico and Arizona became part of U.S. and Texas border was established at the Rio Grande; Zachary Taylor.

Grammar

1. My expertise tells me that I am going to fail this English test, since I'm guessing a lot.

2. (a) bird, birds; (b) man, men; (c) fly, flies; (d) fox, foxes; (e) it, its.

3. (a) The sheep are in the meadow. (b) The sheep's wool was carded. (c) We sheared all the sheep.

This college stuff is upsetting enough when seen at a distance; just reading about some kid getting slammed for running afoul of a campus speech code elicits the same visceral outrage I felt as a kid watching Bull Connor's snarling police dogs on our old black-and-white TV.

But the real trouble starts when it gets personal. My daughter recently started her senior year of high school, which means she's in the middle of the business of choosing a place to actually spend four years.

For parents like me, this is what's known as having to put your money where your morals are.

Politics aside, a lot of grown-ups in my circle are every bit as intense and obsessive about the college decision as their kids; at social gatherings, it's *the* topic of conversation. But the key assumptions—like, for instance, that going to the Ivy League gets your kid a terrific education—never vary.

We, on the other hand, worry about the *kind* of education she would get.

It's hard to know how to play it. Obviously, we want the best for our child. We want her to go to someplace that'll both excite her and give her a leg up in life. We understand how people tend to react when they hear someone went to a prestige school and certainly have no interest in burdening her with what my forebears would have called our own *mishegas* (nuttiness).

More than that, her mother and I know full well we can lose perspective about these things, and more than once over the years I've learned the hard way that what feels like a stand on principle can end up looking remarkably like self-destructiveness.

The fact is, our daughter doesn't care nearly as much about this ideological stuff as we do—she would far sooner pick up a five-year-old copy of *Gourmet* than any political journal. Plenty strong-willed, she'd probably do fine just about anywhere with a decent enough English department, focusing on her work and ignoring the p.c. silliness—which, in fact, is exactly what the vast majority of college kids do.

Then, again, nonpartisan as she is, Sadie has always had a keen nose for injustice and an impulse to defend the underdog—which, given who most often gets in trouble on today's campus, could end up being a problem. Indeed, as a high school sophomore, she was moved to write a letter to the school paper about the pressures to conform *there.* "How often have we all heard teachers make flip comments which subtly (or not) illustrate that teacher's political views?" she asked. "Everyone always laughs, confident of mutual agreement. I used to laugh, too. Lately, I have been thinking about what it must be like for those students who do not agree, who feel oppressed or even ashamed to admit their different views and so perhaps hold back in discussions of controversial issues . . ."

She got a lot of compliments on that letter, some from teachers. What she didn't tell them was that it was prompted by an experience of her younger brother, a free thinker and born wiseacre, who'd gotten into trouble for arguing with a teacher about his right to use the word "oriental" instead of "Asian."

Which is to say, while *he's* the one who'd be more apt to one day run afoul of some college p.c. enforcer, in her own quiet way Sadie has never been a go-along-to-get-along type, either. Nor, when it comes to it, is she interested in winding up at a school where people hesitate to speak their minds. Aside from all the rest, it's *boring.*

Like everyone else looking for direction, we started with a couple of those pricey college guides. They were of little help. For all the reams of information they impart about average SAT scores, financial aid and campus social life, they didn't begin to answer *our* questions. How serious—i.e., traditional—an education was our child going to get? And how much p.c. nonsense was she going to have to put up with along the way?

Not that what her mother and I thought would be the determining factor in our daughter's view. Though she was perfectly pleased to have the family along for the ride as she looked over various schools, she made clear the final decision would be hers alone.

At this point, we've seen maybe twenty-five colleges up close and personal.

While interesting, the campus tours—conducted by a student and generally preceded by an "information session" with a rep from the admissions office—don't really impart that much vital information, either. Basically, your reaction to the place has to do with the personalities of these two people and the look of the buildings.

The course catalogs are somewhat more revealing. The first place we visited was Williams College, and flipping open the catalog to the History Department while waiting for the tour to start, I perused the first course listing: HIST 101, America in the 1960's. ". . . The Viet Cong would prove that the war for their homeland would cost more lives than the nation was willing to sacrifice," it read in part. "Campuses across the land would be racked with student revolt. The Black Panthers and Brown Berets would arm themselves to protect their ghettos and barrios from police brutality. Cities across the country would be engulfed in the flames of popular uprising against economic, political and cultural oppression. In the words of the poet Linda Mendoza, 'the violent poetry of the times (was) written in the blood of youth . . .' "

In the words of some of the guys I play softball with, "Gimme a fuckin' break!"

Then, again—the danger of snap judgment by catalog—this was only one of many courses listed even in that department, and as I continued perusing, some of the others looked great. Perhaps "the violent poetry of the times" guy was one lonely ex-SDSer in a department of bona fide scholars.

I soon decided that the best way to use catalogs was to focus on how the multicult stuff got described. For instance, Pennsylvania's prestigious Swarthmore, like most schools, had lots of course offerings in Women's Studies. But since they were at least presented in a fairly neutral way, one could nurture the hope that class discussions might involve some actual honest back and forth and not just heavy doses of dogma. In contrast, The Women's Center at nearby Haverford is tremulously described in the catalog as the place where "events are provided to help alleviate the myths and judgments made about each other based on gender." Together with the school's Office of Multicultural Affairs, which works at "increasing the community's understanding of and sensitivity to people of color," this seemed to bode far less well for Haverford's potential as a hotbed of intellectual inquiry.

Still, when it came down to getting a real fix on a school, the catalogs were of little more use than the peeks I'd sneak at campus bulletin boards during the tours, or the school newspapers I'd pick up at every stop to read afterward in the motel.

Priscilla, for her part, exasperated Sadie a few times by asking our tour guides about some free-speech violation she'd heard about at the place, but the pleasant and upbeat kids usually just looked confused.

For our daughter, too, it was all pretty much guesswork.

By the end of our Southern swing—William and Mary, U. Va., Duke, Emory, Vanderbilt, along with lots of barbecue and ballgames in Durham and Atlanta—Sadie was as confused as ever.

In fact, the one who seemed to have gotten the most out of the grueling process was her younger brother, who, somewhere along the line, had gotten it into his head that *he* was going to Dartmouth, a decision he became even more confident about once he'd actually seen the place and gotten himself a Dartmouth cap and other paraphernalia.

My wife and I immediately tried to make use of this, repeatedly reminding our up-and-down scholar (in typically light-handed parental fashion) that Dartmouth's a terrific school, and he was really going to have to bear down to make it in.

"Yeah, yeah, yeah," he'd say, "no problem. I'm set—don't you envy me, Sadie?"

In fact, in her uncertainty, she sort of did.

Clearly, what the world needed was a different kind of college catalog, one for those with concerns like ours. I even mentioned this over lunch one day to a book editor who more or less shares my feelings about the drift of the culture, suggesting his company undertake the job. But since his kid's only eight, I couldn't get him interested.

And then, magically, just a short time later, precisely such a volume appeared. Entitled *Choosing the Right College: The Whole Truth About America's 100 Top Schools,* it was produced by the seriously scholarly folks at the conservative Intercollegiate Studies Institute, complete with an introduction by the estimable Bill Bennett.

Actually, the Bennett introduction is probably unfortunate, since its presence makes the book seem more partisan than it really is. In fact, the catalog assesses each school on an extremely straightforward basis, seeking to convey how serious the institution is about traditional scholarship (as opposed to the hipper, less-demanding version) and whether it offers an atmosphere conducive to the old liberal ideal of free and open inquiry.

In brief, for us it was a godsend, its lengthy and meticulously researched entries confirming our impressions of certain schools we'd seen, giving us new insight into others. Though brutal to certain "hot" schools—Bowdoin, in Maine, comes off as an intellectual gulag and Brown as someplace where every silly academic fad finds a happy home—it can be just as generous when it finds rigor and real respect for learning. For instance, tiny St. John's College, with a Great Books curriculum grounded in the Western tradition, is lavishly praised for seminars that run by just two rules: "all opinions must be heard and explored, and every opinion must be supported by an argument."

And—surprise—Priscilla's alma mater, Berkeley, comes off exceptionally well. Though acknowledging the place will be forever stuck with its reputation for radicalism, the authors maintain Berkeley has reclaimed its place as "one of the most prestigious universities in the world. Some even say it may be the best university in the world. At the very least, UC–Berkeley offers an exciting atmosphere and many excellent teachers and departments."

Which is to say, the book is highly persuasive. And Sadie leafed through it constantly as she began deciding on her final choices.

Among the schools to which it devotes particular attention is one our daughter had been considering since a visit to her school on College Day by its director of admissions: the University of Chicago.

A dramatic figure by usual admissions-type standards, somewhat older than most, he had the ironic humor and rather melancholic air of an Irish poet. Where the others talked up their schools by discussing the strengths of this or that department or the percentage of students they sent to top graduate schools, he began his presentation this way: "At the University of Chicago, we see our mission as saving Western civilization."

I swear, I actually saw a couple of mothers swoon.

A few months later, Sadie visited the campus and liked what she saw.

And now, here was this book, with its loving characterization of Chicago's tradition as "a scholar's university, a place where faculty and students alike needn't fear ridicule for their unabashed love of books and bookishness." There were pages full of descriptions of wonderful courses and brilliant professors and a student body that comes "prepared to work very, very hard."

Not that the account was uniformly positive. In an attempt to broaden its mainstream appeal, it said, Chicago has lately started to ask less of its students; indeed, has even watered down its vaunted "core curriculum." "There is a widespread notion in higher education today (more prevalent at other places than Chicago) that to demand too much of students is somehow to stifle them, as if a serious education was like watching too much television. If the administration at Chicago has its way, it will turn what is now one of the great treasures of American higher education into just another big, rich, research university."

I happened to reread this one of the weekends Sadie was working on her applications. Wandering into her room, I asked if that bothered her.

She looked up. "A little—though I actually *like* they're trying to make Chicago a little more fun." She smiled. "Despite what people think, I'm *not* a grind."

"Good. 'Cause I was sorry to read it."

She hesitated, then surprised me. "Want to read my answer to the question on why I'm applying?"

"Sure."

She hit a couple of computer keys and stood up, letting me take her place before the computer. Her answer was brief, just a couple of paragraphs. It described how, the first time she met the admissions director back on College Day, she was part of a group of kids to whom he showed an application from the previous year that had greatly impressed him— he thought the applicant's essay revealed a take on life that was mature, original and profound. Sadie recalled that she'd disagreed, finding the kid's essay fraudulent and pretentious. But what impressed her, the reason she was now giving for applying, was that she'd felt completely free to say that—far from being annoyed or defensive, he treated her contrarian view with understanding and respect.

"You think that sounds okay? I don't want to come across as arrogant. But that essay he liked really was awful, Papa."

"I think it's terrific, that's probably the best reason there is for considering the place."

But a few months later, soon after she'd been accepted, an even better one turned up, at least for my money. In an event unprecedented in modern American higher education, the kind of thing that gives even pessimists like me hope, the president of the school, so roughly taken to task by our trusty catalog, resigned: forced out, the reports made clear, by a remarkable coalition of faculty, alumni, trustees and, yes, students upset by what they saw as policies that risked lowering standards.

□

By the way, there was a postscript to those parental admonitions to Charlie about needing to bear down if he's serious about making it to Dartmouth. A short time later, the kids presented us with the following two documents.

October 12 2001

Dear dartmoth,

    Hello it's me agenn! I wrote you afore. I like it. I have to tell you I d'ont write good. But I write fast. In my other leters I told you that I was a congressunal page. You are probly wondering how was I a congress page. Well I tell you. my father is president of the united states. You are probly wundering why does he like dartmouth. Well i tell you. The Dartmouth colour is green the team is called Gren too. I play soccor this fall, I m good at the sport all times. I want to parlay-fransay at the dartmouth can this be arrangd for Me.I tell you earliet that I like donut. This is very specal kuality to know. You mite be thinking He's too goode to be true. Dont worry I am here and 100 percant reel! I look foward to atending your good institootion.I have no doubts you will luv me.

                                          Youre fred,
                                          Charlie Stein

The Daily Dartmouth

Hanover, Sept. 10th, 2002—

Yesterday, a man posing as a Dartmouth freshman was apprehended after three weeks of successful subterfuge. Charles Stein, 18, was turned in by his "roommates," Jim Roo and Beau Lockhart, who had begun to suspect the deception the first day of Freshman Orientation. "He wasn't listed as one of our roommates, and he didn't seem to be enrolled in any of his classes," says Roo. "It got weird—we decided he had to go."

Stein, who attended school in the New York area, was rejected by Dartmouth in December of last year. However, he appears to have arrived the first day of Freshman Orientation and proceeded to conduct himself like a Dartmouth student by attending classes, assigning himself a room and attending soccer tryouts. "He seemed to have a lot of school spirit," says Lisa Blum, a student in Stein's French class. "He wore Dartmouth sweatshirts and stuff every day."

Stein's professors noticed something strange almost immediately. Says Doreen Gray, who was Stein's professor of Philosophy, "At first, I thought [his not being on the attendance list] was just an oversight; these things happen. But then I started talking to his other professors, and it turned out he actually wasn't registered." The fact that all the classes Stein chose to attend had less than twenty students drew more attention to his presence.

Apparently attending Dartmouth had been an obsession with Stein since he was a young boy. "He was obsessed with [Dartmouth]," says his sister Sadie, 21. "He told everyone he was going there from the time he was 14 and first admired the school colors. I thought he was riding for a fall, since he failed all his classes junior and senior year. But when [the rejection] came, it just didn't seem to register with him."

A source in the admissions office reveals that they rejected Stein not because of his poor grades but because of his claims to be student body president, a congressional page and an award-winning "fluter" (sic).

When questioned, Stein merely replied, "I like donut" (sic).

Stein, who apparently applied to no other colleges, was asked to vacate the premises yesterday evening. His future plans are undisclosed.

One curious aspect of the college experience was that as the process moved along, one occasionally heard an unexpected thing: grumbling from some of the other parents about affirmative action.

They may have been liberal, but they damn well wanted what was best for their kids—which in this case meant getting into a top school. And, in this regard at least, this once, pale skin color was the opposite of advantageous. Every one of these schools has a space on the application for race or national origin. When you visit Harvard, they actually have a special sign-up sheet at the front desk in the admissions office— for minorities only.

The kids are as aware of it as the parents. One of Sadie's friends, an upper-middle-class black girl, listened one day over lunch to the others obsessing over college and teased, "I'm not worried, I'll get in anywhere I want—I'm black."

This was apparently accepted with far better cheer than the similar boast of another girl who, though otherwise white in every respect, got to fill in "Hispanic" because her psychiatrist father was born in Argentina.

Then there's the case of another black friend, lower middle class this time, who as copresident of the grade and a gifted math student earned a full scholarship to one of the most prestigious schools in the country.

Yet the pity is that from here on in, for the rest of her life, as she makes her way to a top graduate or medical school and then into the wider world, lots of people will always presume it wasn't her hard work that did it for her, but a racial quota.

Supporters of racial preferences will tell you at great length that this is hardly the greatest curse that can come with being born black in America. And of course that's true. We don't need the familiar litany of statistics—on black poverty, crime and out-of-wedlock births, on the number of young black men behind bars versus the number in top management—to remind us of that. Sure, it's easy to tune out another *New York Times* editorialist tut-tutting about cabbies who bypass black men—right, asshole, *you* try ditching your cushy job for a hack license and let's see how quick *you'll* pick up a South Bronx–bound fare at 2 A.M. Still, who can deny the cumulative impact of a lifetime of such small humiliations? Just the other day my daughter was saying how the friend bound for the top college, one of the sweetest, shyest kids I know, found herself being trailed around our local drugstore by a suspicious employee.

For most of us, such things are beyond conception. Hell, I can count on one hand the times in my life I've been slighted for being Jewish— once in Florida, twice in France—and every time I was ready to go berserk.

So it is completely understandable why this legacy of ingrained racism would, for many, make the case for affirmative action emotionally compelling.

All it takes is a willingness to suspend a commitment to genuine equality.

I remember with absolute clarity the day I first found myself arguing against affirmative action. It was a summer morning in the early eighties and I was already well into rethinking things. I'd accompanied a friend to the East Hampton train station to pick up his wife and while waiting for the train, we got on the subject of race.

At first, I guess, I did it partly to be perverse—such things simply weren't heard then, not in that crowd—and he was so satisfyingly appalled, it egged me on even more. But as I talked it out, the case was so obvious and straightforward I was amazed I could ever have believed otherwise. *Did we truly believe in judging people as individuals or was that just talk? Were the things we'd found so moving when Dr. King said them as eternal as they seemed, or just a matter of passing ideological fashion? How could we pretend to be for equality of opportunity if we were for penalizing* anyone *on the basis of skin color?*

How, indeed?

The answer I eventually came to was pretty unsettling. People like me had simply never had to foot the bill for our beliefs.

It was a young man named Steven Bakke who first touched off the affirmative action debate back in 1978 by suing the California state university system for turning down his medical school application while accepting minorities with lesser qualifications. Without following the case closely, I took it for granted Bakke was a racist. After all, in those days everyone was either part of the problem or the solution and he'd obviously tossed in his lot with the forces of reaction. If he'd been interested in the solution, he'd have seen it as his *duty* to accept that minorities deserved special treatment and take his lumps.

From this distance, the sheer chutzpah it took to think that way seems stunning, but what can I tell you? Maybe if I'd known Bakke personally . . .

As it was, blue-collar kids like him ended up paying the freight for affirmative action—while lots of people protected from the worst of it by money and social privilege got to take the moral high road. Ron Unz, author of the California initiative limiting bilingual education, recently ran a piece in *The Wall Street Journal* noting that while racial preferences have indeed succeeded in evening things out for blacks and Hispanics at places like Harvard, certain groups of white ethnics are today so wildly *under*represented that the only way to equitably remedy the situation without upsetting the affirmative action applecart would be to start handing *them* a hefty share of the spots now awarded strictly on merit— which would mean disadvantaging Asians and Jews who, on that basis, are vastly overrepresented.

A Harvard grad himself, Unz acknowledged that such a system "would be controversial to say the least."

The Unz proposal is characteristic of the turn the debate on preferences has taken in recent years as affirmative action proponents have been pressed ever harder to explain how justice can be born of injustice.

Theirs is not an enviable dilemma—on some level, many surely realize there *is* no good answer. That defensiveness has much to do with why this most vital national conversation has escalated—or, more accurately, plunged—to new levels. For over and over it has been the pro-preferences side that's been moved to the most shameless extremes of vituperation and distortion. It was they, during the bitter 1996 fight over California's anti-affirmative action Proposition 209, who invited David Duke to the state to speak on behalf of the measure, then tried to cast Proposition 209 supporters as being in league with the KKK; as two years later it was they who argued that Washington State's I-200 was really intended to deny women equal pay for equal work.

That both measures nonetheless won overwhelmingly at the polls was the best repudiation of such tactics. For the near-identical language in both measures was so straightforward, so obviously aimed at *prohibiting* discrimination, it was impossible to misconstrue.

Affirmative action proponents have repeatedly been reduced to playing the same kind of moral shell game in a range of court battles, feinting and dodging and bending the truth. In 1997, in the face of an expected ruling that preferences would be declared unconstitutional, civil rights groups actually paid $400,000 to the white teacher fired by the Piscataway, New Jersey, Board of Education in favor of a black teacher, so she would end her lawsuit before the Supreme Court could hear the case. In 1999, fearing a similar outcome, the NAACP and US Department of Education prevailed upon the Boston School Committee to let a ruling by a lower court invalidating race-based entrance policies at a prestigious Boston public high school go unchallenged in the higher courts.

Race was never a factor, testifies the former mayor of East Orange, New Jersey, straight-faced, explaining to a court why he appointed a black lieutenant as police chief over a white captain with many more years' service and a far higher score on the exam for chief. *He simply never considered other candidates.*

In Texas and Michigan, it took court decisions to unlock data proving that race was not, as claimed (and as mandated by the Bakke ruling), only one of many factors in determining acceptance at the state universities, but often the only one. In another notable case, involving Georgetown University's school of law, standardized test scores guarded like state secrets were brought to light only through the dogged efforts of a student with a part-time job in the registrar's office.

The numbers have always been a problem for preference activists for, alas, time and again they tell the same disheartening story: assessed strictly on academic performance, black kids have trouble competing. We now know that until the passage of Proposition 209, white and Asian applicants to Berkeley were being denied entrance in favor of black applicants with SAT scores three hundred points lower. Under affirmative action in some leading public law schools, *17.5* times more black applicants are admitted than would be the case if scholastic achievement alone were the standard.

And while proponents of preferences argue that this is precisely why affirmative action is essential—because to make such judgments on the basis of testing alone will always mitigate against those who come from poor schools in poor neighborhoods—as much as anything, the data suggests how badly preferences have failed black kids also. Of the 1,398 African-American kids who entered Berkeley between 1987 and 1990 under affirmative action, a staggering 42 percent left without a degree, a failure rate more or less replicated in colleges across the country.

Affirmative action defenders might try calculating the frustration and bitterness implicit in *those* numbers.

It is well that the debate has finally begun moving beyond name calling and feel-good simplicities toward a search for meaningful answers. There is no question more vital to our collective future: in the absence of favoritism, how do we move to create a more equitable society?

Since this is a subject long so seemingly resistant to solution, one almost hesitates to offer a response that sounds so simple: the old-fashioned way. Through the rigorous application of a single, merit-based standard.

Yes, obviously, the details are immensely complex. It is hard to exaggerate the degree to which poor minorities are disadvantaged by birth. They're likely to live in crime- and drug-infested neighborhoods, where children attend unsafe schools that don't teach, and—far worse—come of age understanding that many of their fellow citizens presume they're less capable and less bright.

And well-off whites are advantaged in equal measure, not just by access to educational and professional opportunities, but by a range of positive societal assumptions.

And yes, to a considerable extent, the achievement gap can indeed be addressed on a policy level. Even greater resources ought to be given over to early childhood education and tutoring programs. Further innovative measures of every kind should be taken to help ensure that minority kids *can* compete on an equal basis—starting with charter schools and vouchers.

Too, we should cast an equally jaundiced eye on what have rightly been termed affirmative action programs for whites—not least, public colleges' favoritism toward the children of alums. To his immense credit, Ward Connerly, the black businessman who headed the campaigns in California and Washington against preferences, has pushed for the abolition of those, too.

Still, the debilitating assumptions will be put to rest only with observable and generally acknowledged results involving performance.

Ours is a society that offers swifter, surer upward mobility than any in the entire history of the world—but only for those prepared for it. Which is to say, what must also change are attitudes about education within the black community itself, as well as the reflex common to many blacks and progressive whites alike, to find in racism an all-purpose excuse for passivity, hopelessness and failure.

In the end, it takes an appalling mix of cynicism and condescension to presume that the minorities are incapable of pulling even with whites *without* affirmative action. In Seattle, the schools commissioner—a black former Army general named John Stanford—certainly didn't think so. Setting out in 1995 to remake a failing system from bottom to top, he succeeded before his death in 1998 in dramatically raising standardized scores in math, reading and language at all grade levels, with black elementary school kids—those at the start of their educational lives— showing the most dramatic gains. He did it not with tired bromides about self-esteem but by insisting on high standards in both academics and behavior, including a zero-tolerance policy to remove chronic troublemakers from the system and linking principals' tenure to proof their kids were mastering the material.

Yet while John Stanford remains almost completely unknown, the entire country was treated to a weeks-long spectacle of Jesse Jackson raising hell in Decatur, Illinois, demanding the reinstatement in school of kids whose violently anti-social behavior precipitated a near-riot— daring to compare his Decatur crusade to Dr. King's legendary civil rights marches in Selma and Washington.

In fact, when it comes to making serious demands on minority kids and holding them to them, it's been a small band of black conservatives who have consistently dared to say what needs to be said. "We should cut the nonsense and abandon our culture of complaint," writes Gregory P. Kane of the *Baltimore Sun*. ". . . Where are these protesters when we need folks to speak out on what is truly a racial crisis: the alarming numbers of black children and teens who seriously believe a commitment to learning and academic achievement is a white thing?"

Essayist Thomas Sowell, decrying the "army of race hustlers, whose job it is to see that race relations don't get any better," points out that in 1899, under segregation, Washington, DC's, black Dunbar High School, led by a principal who was the first black graduate of Harvard, scored higher on standardized tests than two of the city's three all-white high schools.

When the overwhelmingly pro-affirmative action California press trumpeted initial post-Proposition 209 figures that showed a drastic drop in black enrollment at the state's top campuses, it took Ward Connerly to cut through the I-told-you-so crap. "I tell people, 'You don't like those numbers. Well, I don't like those numbers either.' But to solve the problem you have to deal with the problems in kindergarten through twelfth grade. Don't blame the university."

And, indeed, a mere two years later, after an aggressive recruitment program the number of minority students admitted was close to where it had been before. The difference was, these were kids equipped to succeed.

Not long ago on C-Span, I happened to catch the best known of all black conservatives, Clarence Thomas, addressing a school for troubled teens in Richmond, Virginia. "I'll tell you one of the most depressing things for me," he said. "It's when people say they have nothing to do on a Saturday afternoon. You go to the library and see how many people are there—then go to the mall and look at the contrast." He paused. "What you do with your Saturdays now will dictate what you do with your Saturdays twenty years from now."

Now, I know how much people hate this guy. Even now, you hear nasty references to him all the time. But I can't really figure out why. Are they listening with different ears than I am?

Looking around at where we've been and where we hope to be going, who could possibly argue with such a message?

Just kidding—I'm not that naive. I know full well why people hate Thomas, or at least the words they use when they say they do: He's an Uncle Tom, a stooge of the right, someone who, once he had it made, turned his back on his people.

The same things that get said about every black conservative.

Needless to say, plenty of public figures have taken vicious hits in recent years, ranging across the political spectrum. I certainly wouldn't have wanted to be in Bill Clinton's shoes lately, or Ken Starr's, or Newt Gingrich's. But none has been so routinely or viciously attacked solely on their *beliefs* as black conservatives. As Justice Thomas put it to an overwhelmingly hostile convention of black lawyers and judges in one of his rare public appearances, he had not "come to defend my views, but rather to assert my right to think for myself, to refuse to have my ideas assigned to me as though I was an intellectual slave because I'm black."

For me, that's what makes black conservatives the bravest of the brave: the indignities at the hands of ideological foes come not just as a matter of routine, but without fear of penalty, or rebuke, or even contradiction. Radio talk show hosts like Ken Hamblin in Denver and James Golden in Seattle daily endure the kinds of insults white colleagues never face over entire careers. In LA, a boycott aimed at getting Larry Elder off the air eventually failed, but not until it had such key advertisers as American Airlines, Ford and Sears running scared. On the political front, Gary Franks, the ex-congressman from Connecticut, was actually banned from the Congressional Black Caucus for the thought-crime of being insufficiently black.

Yet of all the black conservatives, Thomas naturally excepted, the one most regularly derided as a racial turncoat has been Ward Connerly, the masterful tactician in the fight to roll back affirmative action.

Like Thomas, Connerly has handled himself with remarkable seriousness of purpose, steadfastly refusing to be drawn into public brawling or bitterness. But on the issue that is his passion, he is never anything but to the point. "They've changed the course of American society so that we're not pursuing integration but separate but equal," he says of preference supporters. "We have diversity, but diversity without integration . . . is a modern, twenty-first century version of separate but equal." "I'm of African descent, Irish descent, French descent, Choctaw Indian descent. My race is the human race," he noted on another occasion, adding that his ex-daughter-in-law is half-Vietnamese. "What does that make my grandchildren? What box should they check?"

That Connerly so insistently remains focused on ideas rather than personalities is very much to his credit. But for some of us this only makes the character of the attacks on him all the more vile.

None of these was more noteworthy, at least in terms of impact, than Mike Wallace's 1998 Connerly profile on *60 Minutes*. Aired as Connerly was organizing the drive against affirmative action in Washington state, it was a virtual clinic on the dirty tricks of the trade. Here was Connerly shot in extreme close-up, forehead to chin, and thus made to look especially sinister. Here was the highly selective use of sources; notably a pair of bitter relatives caustically describing Connerly as being in the white man's pocket—yet not a word from any of the many other family members who respect and love him. Here, above all, was the interviewer himself, the viewer-surrogate, persistently skeptical, challenging, impatient, rude.

Toward the end of the piece, when Connerly notes that, in fact, overall his dealings with whites have *not* been negative, that his views on race have been largely shaped by positive experiences, Wallace literally erupts in scornful disbelief, accusing him of "looking at things through rose-colored glasses. I can see black folks all across the country looking at this and saying 'What world does this Connerly think he's living in?' "

Black folks?

Which ones would those be, Mike—you been talking to Ed Bradley or was it one of the help at the Martha's Vineyard place?

Sorry. That was a low blow. It's just that reflecting on the man's gall, I'm reminded of my own encounter with Wallace, and the extraordinary contrast between how he presents himself on TV and the real thing.

It was a long time ago, 1979, and I'd been assigned by the *New York Times Magazine* to do a piece on *60 Minutes*, at the time just a decade into its legendary run. As a relative kid and big *60 Minutes* fan, I went into my interview with Wallace awed, expecting to find the monumentally self-assured seeker of justice we'd come to know. Instead, now that he was in the unaccustomed role of interviewee, I found myself facing one of the most seemingly insecure men I'd ever met. The piece was to be a serious look at the show, so some of the questions I asked—say, about reporting techniques and how interviews were cut—were not of the *People* magazine, softball variety. But where the other correspondents then with the show, Morley Safer, Dan Rather and Harry Reasoner, sat through their sessions and were glad to be rid of me, Wallace seemed possessed by the notion I had it in for him, that the hunter had become the hunted. He kept calling me at home, trying to reexplain things he'd said and clarify false impressions, all the while making like we were *pals.*

Given Wallace's near-Clintonian fixation on his legacy, its anyone's guess how many have had the same treatment over the years. Wallace himself bragged, after hearing that an early draft of Michael Mann's *The Insider* had "me losing my moral compass" that he'd taken it up with Mann and "we'll see about that"; and, based on his ultimately sympathetic portrayal in the film, he seems to have gotten much of what he wanted.

You can bet Ward Connerly made no such effort to shape the content of Wallace's piece about him; he surely went in knowing full well what he was dealing with. Still, I do wonder how much got left on the cutting room floor.

For, indeed, though it was nowhere in the broadcast, Connerly's view on *black folks* and their historic role in this country are at the very center of his philosophy. "We who have lived the black experience have changed the American culture," as he wrote in a 1997 open letter to Colin Powell. "Perhaps the most significant contribution that we have made to America is the premium which our nation places on the civil rights of all Americans . . . *Equal treatment* under the law is one of those rights."

As we well know, when it comes to affirmative action, ardent progressives have no doubt they're on the right side. Though they understand the process of righting historical wrongs can be painful, they realize we've got to bite the bullet.

So here are a couple of ideas that've been floating around designed to make them feel even *better:*

- Every application to every college and university should include an easily checked box that reads: "As a proponent of racial preferences in college admissions, and in the interest of making this world a better place, I hereby agree and authorize that in the event I am admitted to (Harvard, Stanford, Yale, etc.), my place should be given instead to an individual of color."
  Note: The signatures of the parents are also mandatory.
- Since so many honchos at big corporations today are similarly pro–affirmative action, and have publicly bemoaned the absence of minorities in top management, January 1, 2001, shall be known as Fairness Day. On that day, the white male leader of every company the length and breadth of the land who has made clear his strong feelings on the issue—from Microsoft's Bill Gates to the *New York*

Times' Pinch Sulzberger—shall voluntarily step aside, along with his management team, to be replaced by minorities.

Suggested Fairness Day slogan: "Working alone we are powerless! Quitting together, we can change the world!"

Okay, make that several low blows.

Look, it's not like I don't understand white liberal guilt. I grew up rooting for sports teams for the sole reason they had more black players; for years I supported political candidates based entirely on skin color. And all that made me feel pretty damn good about myself.

That, after all, is the point.

Just recently, I had reason to recall just how seductive that feeling can be. My good friend Rich stopped by after a morning at a local synagogue for the High Holy Days and reported he'd been much moved by a story told by the rabbi. Apparently, the rabbi said he was in our town's supermarket late one night eight or ten years ago when an elderly woman started berating the black teenager at the checkout counter. The woman—identifying herself as a Daughter of the American Revolution—haughtily insisted on being checked out by a white person instead. At this point, so the story went, Bucky—the store's warmhearted middle-aged coot of a manager—politely informed the racist customer that the teen was the only checkout person on duty, it would be her or no one—to which the woman insisted on calling the police. Fine, agreed Bucky, and a few minutes later the cops appeared and readily backed Bucky up.

Only now did the monstrous old woman reluctantly agree to let

the girl check her out. But by this point the kid was so totally traumatized, she could barely function; and since this was before bar cod-
ing and items had to be individually rung up, she didn't think
she could handle it. So Bucky took her aside. "You've *got* to do your
job," he told her, *"that* is how you win." And positioning himself beside her, he slowly read off the price on each item, making sure she got
it right.

As my friend told it, a lot of people in the congregation were starting
to tear up. We know Bucky, he's a fixture in the town, so the scene was
easily imagined.

But the story had an even happier ending. Years later—only recently,
in fact—the girl, now a young woman, returned to the store. She is today
an assistant D.A. in Brooklyn and seemingly destined for even greater
things. And, said the rabbi, she told Bucky that that night was the turning point in her life. It taught her that she had within herself the resources to overcome all the ugliness and evil the world could throw at
her.

When my friend finished, the two of us sat there a long moment in our
dinette, silent. Like me, he has moved far from standard-issue liberalism, but for him, too, the old instincts die hard, and now they were upon
us again; critical facilities suspended, so caught up in the emotional
power of a great human story we were blind to the possibility of a more
complex picture.

"Wait a minute," I said suddenly. *"A member of the D.A.R.?* Shopping
at the supermarket in our little village at two A.M.?"

He looked up. "I know—that part struck me as a little fishy, too."

"I mean, that's a racist archetype out of the *thirties*—one of those old
biddies who wouldn't let Marian Anderson sing at Constitution Hall."

"Probably just some ordinary old lady." He smiled. "Or maybe a
refugee from a mental institution."

"And you know what? I'll bet half the people at the service don't even
like Bucky. They'd like to see him gone."

An exaggeration, perhaps, but not much of one; for all his helpfulness
and decency and compassion, Bucky does not run the tidiest supermarket you've ever seen, and many in the town's considerable yuppie element have griped about it for years.

In fact, the more we thought about it, the unlikelier the particulars of the story became—starting with the detail of the rabbi himself just standing there throughout, watching.

But, then, in a real sense, if he'd been the protagonist it would have compromised the story, or at least made it too blatantly self-aggrandizing. For though it was about Bucky and the girl and the reactionary old woman, it was also about the larger themes of hatred in the world and the redemptive power of decency; about how, even after all the years of struggle, so much more needs to be done; indeed, about how the good people must remain ever vigilant since bigotry continues to fester even in our own midst.

The bone I have to pick here is not, heaven knows, with anyone pushing decency and kindness. It's with those, white and black both, who in their eagerness to hold the moral upper hand, refuse to acknowledge how much better things are than they once were.

The fact is, in a country with any kind of functioning historical memory, it would be the past few decades' astonishing advances that would dominate our view of race relations. We've come so far so fast that someone materializing from the mid-sixties would find the revised racial landscape as disorienting as the news that mobsters and capitalist robber barons effectively run today's Russia.

Lately, for instance, we've heard complaints from NAACP president Kweisi Mfume about the lack of minorities with starring roles in prime-time TV series; and though this demonstrably has to do with nothing more sinister than a universe fragmented by cable and other bottom-line imperatives, embarrassed network programmers hurried to make amends, quickly shoehorning black characters into existing shows. No problem there—pressure politics are legitimately part of the way things get done. But the most honest reaction to the controversy was that of a black actor named Damon Standifer, who pointed out in the *L.A. Times* that it was "self appointed spokespeople for the black community" who are themselves "a big reason why the TV networks have shied away from using black actors in major roles. Time and again, TV shows that feature black leads are targeted for protests by these black activists. . . . Every type of 'black' show has been protested: If a show portrays wealthy black people, it's criticized for ignoring the plight of poor ones. If a show features poor black people [as in *South Central*] it's criticized for stereotyping black people as poor. . . ."

And yet, a generation ago even such a discussion would have been beyond imagination. In a time when black faces are as much a commonplace in newscasts and commercials as on city streets and whole networks are devoted to black programming, it is with a jolt one recalls that until 1968, when Diahann Carroll starred as *Julia*, pretty much the only black people who *ever* turned up on TV not singing or serving meals were *Amos 'n' Andy*.

And, indeed, back then blacks were just as invisible in business, civic affairs, academia and the higher echelons of the military. Remarkable to think, their numbers were limited even in music and sports.

Quite simply, this was a wholly segregated culture then, and the fact touched almost everyone. In forever changing that, the civil rights movement and the legislation it inspired simultaneously greatly spurred the growth of the black middle class; which, in turn, has exponentially increased the sort of casual interactions between the races that have inevitably inched us toward the ideal of a color-blind society. Back when I was a teenager, we did lots of singing about black and white together, but it is my kids who, without taking any particular notice of the fact, actually have close black friends. Back when I was in college, the interracial romance in *Guess Who's Coming to Dinner?* was considered daring; today it seems nearly as dated as *Birth of a Nation*.

Why isn't more made of all that? Why isn't a system with the moral determination to remake itself so dramatically more often celebrated instead of routinely condemned?

Of course, from the perspective of what passes today for black leadership, we have a pretty good idea why. "It used to be that civil rights leaders had freedom on their minds," observes Michael Myers, a black writer long deeply involved in the movement. "Nowadays, they have merely loot, economic blackmail, reparations, self-aggrandizement and racial paranoia on their agenda . . ."

Which is to say, for these there is no percentage in stressing the positive, because it is precisely the perception of an ongoing racial crisis fueled by white racism that keeps them in business. So what if this is a nation where Oprah Winfrey now regularly ranks as the most admired woman and Colin Powell was a consensus favorite for president? Over and over we are still told that racism remains as stubbornly pervasive as ever.

Thus it is that Mfume's colleague, NAACP chairman Julian Bond, feels free to declare, as he did at the group's 1998 convention, that "for those Americans whose skins are black or brown, their prospects are poorer and the gap is growing wider"—an observation so patently false that even the *New York Times* had to describe it as "wildly at odds with the research." Several months later, to commemorate Martin Luther King's birthday, Bond was back with more of the same: "Everywhere we look, we see clear racial fault lines that divide America now as much as in the past." To which Michael Myers could only ask: "Really? Where are the segregated hotels, bus depots, train stations and other public accommodations? Are taxis in D.C. still designated for 'colored' and 'white' riders?"

This is hardly to minimize the many injustices in our midst that remain. Civil rights leaders maintain—and who can argue?—that if Dr. King were around today, there'd still be plenty to keep him busy. But with rare exceptions, in moral terms, the issues today are far less straightforward. Yes, there are racist cops—and harrowing episodes of police brutality—but those are cases of individual behavior, not institutional policy. Not even Al Sharpton can find a department in which such an event will pass without dire consequences. Nor, for instance, in making the case against racial profiling by police, can activists cry "racism" and simply leave it at that—for what are they to do with figures (published in the very *New York Times*!) that show black males between the ages of fourteen and twenty-four make up 1.1 percent of the American population, yet commit more than 28 percent of the country's homicides?

The tragic truth is, King's death left a moral vacuum in black leadership that has never come close to being filled. When there is obvious injustice today, or sometimes only the perception of injustice, the first and loudest response is likely to come from a race hustler like Sharpton, ever ready to exploit tragedy and provoke greater divisiveness by ascribing the worst motives to his adversaries. Though such people like to claim King as their inspiration, what is often forgotten today is that even before his murder, Dr. King's vision of a color-blind society stressing individual responsibility was being mocked by younger black activists as Uncle Tomism.

No one can reasonably doubt that the sense of victimization encouraged by black leaders over the years has taken a heavy toll. It has so massively undermined black confidence in our civic institutions that one is no longer surprised when distrust spirals off into outright paranoia. AIDS is a government plot. So is the crack epidemic. Tawana Brawley was telling the truth. O.J. was innocent.

Never mind the facts. They too can be manufactured.

But the role of white progressives as—as the current terminology might put it—"enablers" cannot be underestimated. "[T]he glue that holds all liberal critics together is the conviction that white America is fundamentally racist and has to be continually restrained from its punitive racist impulses," as John O'Sullivan writes in the *National Review*. "Hence the trends in media coverage and political rhetoric ... White-on-black crimes must be highlighted to shame white America out of its racism; black-on-white crimes must be downplayed lest they encourage white America in its racism; and any broader social indicators—whether crime statistics or police tactics—must be judged by the test of whether they serve to encourage or restrain white racism."

Like so much else, this is at least partly a legacy of the sixties. Tom Wolfe nailed it for the ages in his legendary essay on Radical Chic that had Lenny Bernstein at the height of the "revolution," playing host to a thrillingly scary-looking band of Black Panthers and making all the right revolutionary noises himself.

Given the ridicule heaped upon Bernstein and his friends in the wake of that episode, and the fact that the Panthers turned out to be thugs, one would think some lessons might have been learned.

But, no, of course not. The condescending paternalism keeps on coming.

I remember reading, in the early days of what was not yet called gangsta rap, something on the *Times'* op-ed page by one of the new breed of recording artists insisting people like him shouldn't be made to learn about, for instance, the Founding Fathers, because that stuff was "white" history, for them it had no "relevance."

At the time, I didn't even bother getting upset—clearly no one could possibly take such a thing seriously.

Boy, was I dumb. Even serious academics were soon taking that contention to heart, avidly revising curricula for "relevance." And of course, the *Times* itself was writing about rap lyrics with the seriousness it accords Beethoven and Bach.

As, indeed, the same attitude is now evident in almost every sphere. Today we find public health "experts" like Nancy Krieger of the highly influential Harvard School of Public Health preaching, in a time when every teenager in America knows that avoiding HIV means avoiding risky behavior, that such restraint is impossible for women of color, since they are subject to "daily assaults of racial prejudice and the denial of dignity" by "white Europeans." Elaborate Krieger and her colleague Sally Zierler of Brown University in the 1997 *Annual Review of Public Health*, "Seeking sanctuary from racial hatred through sexual connection as a way to enhance self-esteem . . . may offer rewards so compelling that condom use becomes less of a priority."

In today's health establishment, this sort of thing is actually taken seriously. Surveying the wreckage of the public health sector wrought by such high-minded progressives, Monroe Lerner, emeritus professor of the Johns Hopkins School of Hygiene and Public Health, observes that the current assumption is certain people simply have "no impulse control, no sense of personal responsibility . . . The words *sin* and *deviance* have vanished from the vocabulary."

Those words long ago vanished from the vocabularies of progressive defenders of the welfare establishment. Never mind that the devastating damage inflicted on the black community by the welfare system is harrowingly evident: just three in ten black babies are born to married couples today (against nearly eight in ten in 1960), virtually a whole generation in the nation's inner cities being raised fatherless. Still, notes Myron Magnet of the Manhattan Institute, which studies urban problems, inner-city blacks keep getting from progressives "messages that will keep you poor forever . . . It's okay to have children out of wedlock

. . . Working for chump change is ridiculous and unmanly . . . You are a victim and can't accomplish anything unless we make things right for you." This despite the fact that former welfare recipients forced into the workforce by welfare reform, even those working very low-level jobs, assert overwhelmingly that the change has led to new self-respect and a sense of equal citizenship.

Even now a relentless rear guard action is waged to restore the old system in every morally disabling particular. In 1999, New Jersey passed a "family cap," restricting additional welfare payments to women who have additional children while on public assistance. "Financial wherewithal is a critical consideration for every working family in America when deciding about having another child," noted Governor Christie Whitman. ". . . Our welfare reform law doesn't restrict choices, it promotes responsibility."

But for National Organization for Women President Patricia Ireland, one of the measure's chief antagonists, that seems an alien concept. You can bet she knows all about "rights," though. In her view, the bill is "a violation of a fundamental human *right* recognized under our Constitution: The *right* to make our own decisions about procreation uncoerced by church or state. Just as the government must protect our *right* to birth control and abortion, it also must preserve our *right* to have and raise children, irrespective of our economic or social class."

Over the years, those who've challenged this sort of thinking have gotten used to seeing themselves branded racists. And when the matter at hand was trying to rework the federal mandate on the school lunch program or opposing census by sampling, not *just* racists, but akin to Arlo Guthrie's mother rapers and father rapers in *Alice's Restaurant:* they were trying to *starve children* and *take the vote from black folks.*

Quite simply, for many white progressives it's as if there should exist no fixed behavioral standards for their black fellow citizens; for, so the logic goes, blacks have been so damaged by history they are incapable of exercising the self-discipline, restraint, brains or even common sense they expect of themselves.

Never was this clearer than during the flap following the ousting of a white aide to the mayor of Washington, DC, after the aide's use of the word "niggardly" was taken the wrong way by black associates. What should have happened was . . . absolutely nothing. When the aides misunderstood the term, they should have been told to pick up a dictionary and straighten themselves out.

In fact, even some whites who make a point of their race consciousness agreed the mayor overreacted. After all, as I heard a guy intone on NPR, "niggardly" *is* a perfectly legitimate word, of *Scandinavian* origin actually—though naturally he himself would have been sensitive enough not to use it around African-Americans.

But the NPR guy had it completely backward: to assume that another person speaks his native language properly signals basic respect; to do otherwise is flat-out condescension, betraying the opposite assumption that black people need special consideration at every turn because, finally, they are NOT equal.

Indeed, as black academic Shelby Steele points out, it is precisely such low expectations that foster the notion "that black progress is contingent on interventions from on high . . ."

Unspoken, that idea is deeply ingrained in the mentality of modern liberalism. The racism of the right is both obvious and ugly; yet for that reason, decent souls at least know to call it what it is. The paternalism of the left is so damaging precisely because, confidently well-intentioned, it everywhere makes itself felt without apology.

But by promoting shibboleths about white oppression and the glories of multiculturalism, and embracing the most degraded and destructive elements of black culture, white progressives do the black community no favors. Taking this week's gangsta sensation as a behavioral model is a mistake for a child of any race; if acting "white" means studying hard and avoiding trouble, that's what grown-ups of all races and political persuasions should be pushing. "It is bad enough that the larger society believes that's the authentic way [black] people live their lives," notes Maya Angelou of the hip hop music and gangsta films spat out by today's pop culture. "But young men and young women take their lessons, too, from those caricatures and they begin to live that out. . . . It's not hip, it's not trendy, it's not heralded by the slick magazines. But for most of us, life is about the Ten Commandments and getting some grits on the table."

In the end, it is this that many white progressives cannot fully accept: that, as black columnist Bill Maxwell of the *St. Petersburg Times* has it, blacks "are often their own worst enemies, and . . . may not be noble victims after all."

"How long are we going to say, 'The white man treated me so bad?' " says a mother from Oakland, California, birthplace of Ebonics, to a researcher from the nonpartisan group Public Agenda. "We know what the situation has been; we know what it is. So now, 'What are you going to do about it?' "

She asks the question of herself, which is absolutely the right way to go about it.

But the rest of us should have an answer, too, and it is this: help out in every possible way, short of disadvantaging anyone else or gutting standards; refuse to trade in stereotypes, taking individuals as they come; above all, offer what we should demand for ourselves, understanding, honesty and respect.

□

All right, I'll admit it: there are times even I wonder if I've gone off the deep end.

Like, for instance, the day not long ago some junk mail showed up from a conservative book club. "If you, like us, are appalled at what the dominant culture has done to our country . . . our values . . . our children . . ." announced the copy on the envelope and—*damn RIGHT I am!*—in a nanosecond I was ripping it open.

The letter inside sent me crashing back to earth. Surely, then, it continued, you are "the kind of reader who would gobble up controversial books like *The Great Betrayal* by Patrick Buchanan . . . or *No More Wacos* by David B. Kopel and Paul H. Blackman . . ."

Me?

Well, sure, fine on Waco. But, sorry, Pat Buchanan lost me even before he came out against American entry into World War II.

The fact is, at this point I think of myself far more as the kind of reader who'd sooner gobble up a book called *No More Wackos*.

How'd I end up with *these* guys?

No, I have a pretty good idea. It's the part of winding up a social conservative you've just got to grin and bear. You may get to choose your enemies, but you have no say at all in who they'll accuse you as having as friends.

Frankly, in this part of the world—not merely the New York suburbs, down the road from the Clintons' new place, but almost anywhere in America itself—people like me can sometimes get to feeling pretty lonely. Just flipping on the TV can be enough to make clear how woefully out of step we are with the most visible elements of the culture: why isn't *everyone* upset about the craven media and the feminists, the race baiters and the teachers' unions, the endless double entendres on family sitcoms, the blather that passes for serious thought? "Clinton's the least of it!" as my friend Denis exclaimed at the height of Sexgate, "we have to bring down Geraldo!"

It was precisely this attitude—actually, the realization that no one was bringing down anything—that soon thereafter prompted longtime conservative activist Paul Weyrich to throw up his hands and declare the culture war lost. Those on the losing side, he declared, had to find ways of living in America without being of it, locating communities, even virtual ones, that would be islands in a sea of toxic values.

I don't think things are nearly that bad. In my experience, even many of those with whom I strongly disagree have a powerful innate understanding of right and wrong, decent and indecent; and the case is just as readily made that the yearning for moral nourishment is greater today than ever before. I'm surprised by how often these days someone I never would have expected pronounces himself disgusted by the crap his kids are force-fed in school, or by a nasty remark someone made when he had the temerity to express a maverick political view. Just last week a writer I know was telling me about his sojourn at one of those hip, foundation-supported literary retreats and, as an aside, mentioned the feminist "performance artist" who showed up one evening. She performed her entire act in a cage to symbolize female oppression and, said the guy, it was a complete insult to his intelligence. But at the end he politely applauded along with everyone else. It was only over subsequent days, when the subject came up with others, that he discovered they *all* felt that way. It's just every one of them, emperor's-new-clothes-like, had been afraid to respond honestly.

Back in 1946, for better or worse, Dr. Spock launched a revolution in this country with a book that began with what would become the most famous opening sentence in American publishing since *Moby Dick:* "You know more than you think you do."

And so we do in this regard also. It's just that our innate sense of right and wrong, just and unjust, good and evil, has been compromised by thirty years of values-neutral nonsense: from the media, certainly, but also from pols who debase language, religious leaders who refuse to lead and "experts" who hold forth on what were once matters of common sense and simple decency.

Just yesterday, my wife's quick trip to the supermarket took most of the afternoon. It turned out she'd run into an extremely nice woman we know whose marriage was in distress.

As Caroline told her over coffee, her husband was having an affair with a woman at work. A marriage counselor they'd seen had told him he shouldn't feel guilty, that people change and he was only meeting his needs. Now the husband was in counseling with their minister—who was saying pretty much the same thing. The result was, he'd declared he was willing to stay with her and their two children, but only on the condition he be allowed to continue seeing the other woman while they worked things out.

"Amazing, isn't it?" said Caroline, a truly good soul. "I've lost faith in my President, my husband, the psychological profession and my church—all in the space of a year."

Amazing, but given the state of what passes for moral wisdom out there, hardly surprising.

The message of today's therapeutic culture is especially corrosive: Nothing is ever fully one's own fault. The very range of exonerating rationales sanctioned by that culture is staggering, a vast litany of only recently discovered psychological conditions that make life an ethical adventure. Prior to the 1990s, who this side of the Marquis de Sade would have even *dared* claim "sex addiction" as an excuse for disgraceful conduct?

In the end, there is a terrible psychic price to be paid for those who allow themselves to be governed by such dishonesty: having to live within their own skins. For, figuratively, we *do* have crickets on our shoulders, and we ignore them at our peril. When we behave miserably, even if assured otherwise, we *know* "self-esteem" is the last thing we deserve to feel.

Such an understanding is fundamental to human well-being and more and more it is reasserting itself: that the old ways worked precisely *because* they were demanding and unforgiving; that, far from constricting, they provide the security for a full and contented life.

My point isn't to knock the psychology field. Obviously, there are plenty of insightful therapists out there, even some highly moral ones. This was never more evident than when Hillary Clinton sought to pass off her husband's miserable behavior as the result of long-ago "trauma and abuse" at the hands of squabbling relatives. Such an explanation, as one New Jersey–based psychologist flatly declared, was "a sham. At some point in your life you have to stop and say, 'I'm an adult and I'm responsible.' " "Despite what one might have heard from daytime television," concurred psychologist Alfred Lawrence, in a letter to *The Wall Street Journal*, "there is no empirical evidence to suggest that chronic philandering and predatory sexual behavior are logical or expectable sequels of childhood abuse."

Nor do I question for a moment that therapy does a great many people good. I was in therapy myself a couple of times, trying to get a handle on some seriously stupid behavior and, no question, the process forced me to think things through I'd otherwise have happily ignored.

But I also remember, early on in treatment the second time, an exchange with the therapist about something that had been troubling me. I was aware she was also seeing a journalist I knew slightly—someone widely reviled for his cutthroat behavior toward everyone he perceived as a rival—and, without naming names, I asked about the object of her work. If someone had rotten values, was it ever the goal to alter them? Absolutely not, she said, seemingly taken aback by the question, her concern was mental health, not morality—she saw her task as making people comfortable with whatever values they chose to embrace.

I was in my late twenties then, far less than fully formed, but I remember thinking that had to be wrong, that over the long term it couldn't even work. For in the absence of a decent belief system there *is* no lasting satisfaction. One *must* make serious demands on oneself, there *must* be a genuine sense of shame and remorse when one fails to meet them. Otherwise, how can there be self-respect?

That is to say, I guess I was fairly conservative before I even knew it.

The story of the last fifteen years has been finding out for sure. If, as we so often hear, politicians who've moved left have "grown in office," those of us moving the other way, following our gut instead of the crowd, like to feel we've grown in life.

Truly, I don't mean to come off as holier than anyone. It's not like there haven't been plenty of rough times along the way, or that my own marriage has been wholly untroubled.

In fact, shortly after Charlie was born, Priscilla and I went to see a counselor together. We were at a low ebb. Both sharp-tongued to start with, we were exhausted and worried about money, and our fights had taken on a particularly nasty edge.

Sure enough, once in her office, encouraged to let it all out, we ripped into each other anew, giving vent to a whole rash of previously unspoken complaints.

The therapist refereed this encounter the requisite fifty minutes, then sat back in her chair, looking troubled. Normally, she said, choosing her words carefully, she'd never say something like this: but in our case the hostility was simply too great, we were clearly a mismatch—she had to recommend we consider splitting.

Splitting?! What was she talking about?

Yeah, sure, all right, maybe if there were no kids. But we had two of them, one barely three, the other a newborn. And—though I'm not sure we'd yet articulated it in so many words—we *knew* we were going to stay together, that seemed the minimum we owed them. There was nothing noble-feeling in this, it was simply the way it was, like the fact we'd never knowingly destroy each other by having an affair. In fact, those things were the easy part, because they were so utterly within our control.

I'm not trying to sugarcoat our marriage—too many people who know us will read this. We've had plenty of vicious fights since then, too many of them, I'm ashamed to say, in front of the kids. At moments, we've actually hated each other. (Trust me, my wife can be pretty hateful.) But even then, there was no possibility of coming apart.

And it's a funny thing, the very process of working through the bad times has only made us stronger. For as time has passed, the differences seem less consequential and what we have in common, all we've shared, ever more vital. Soppy as it is to say this, we love each other more now than the day we married. And the kids know this, too.

I've heard the same sort of thing from couples who've been together far longer. They know that, though perseverance doesn't get the respect it once did, it's the key to everything.

As we left the therapist's office that afternoon, we were both pretty down, stunned by her observation. Only once we were back in the car did we turn to one another. And then, looking into each other's eyes, we cracked up. Then we embraced.

Obviously, we hadn't said enough about all we have in common.

Then, again, even if we had, I'm not sure the therapist would have understood. We were speaking different languages.

About the Author

❑

HARRY STEIN is a writer and journalist whose work has appeared in a number of publications in which he will likely never appear again, including *The New York Times Magazine, New York, Esquire* and *GQ*. Among his previous books are *Ethics (and Other Liabilities), One of the Guys, Eichmann in My Hands* (with Peter Malkin) and the novels *Hoopla, The Magic Bullet,* and *Infinity's Child.*